FANNIE LOU HAMER

FANNIE LOU HAMER

The Life of a Civil Rights Icon

Earnest N. Bracey

McFarland & Company, Inc., Publishers
Jefferson, North Carolina, and London

LIBRARY OF CONGRESS CATALOGUING-IN-PUBLICATION DATA

Bracey, Earnest N.
    Fannie Lou Hamer : the life of a civil rights icon /
Earnest N. Bracey.
      p.   cm.
    Includes bibliographical references and index.

    ISBN 978-0-7864-6030-4
    softcover : 55# alkaline paper ∞

    1. Hamer, Fannie Lou.   2. African American women civil
rights workers — Biography.   3. Civil rights workers — United
States — Biography.   4. African American women civil rights
workers — Mississippi — Biography.   5. Civil rights workers —
Mississippi — Biography.   6. Civil rights movements — United
States — History — 20th century.   7. Civil rights movements —
Mississippi — History — 20th century.   8. African Americans —
Civil rights — History — 20th century.   9. African Americans —
Civil rights — Mississippi — History — 20th century.   I. Title.
E185.97.H35B73   2011
323.092 — dc22 [B]   2011001465

BRITISH LIBRARY CATALOGUING DATA ARE AVAILABLE

Front cover © 2011 Shutterstock

Manufactured in the United States of America

*McFarland & Company, Inc., Publishers
  Box 611, Jefferson, North Carolina 28640
  www.mcfarlandpub.com*

To my sister,
Maggie Jean Bracey-Cole

Table of Contents

Acknowledgments

For six years this book has preoccupied my life. And it has been a difficult book to write. Occasionally, when I couldn't think of exactly what I wanted to communicate, I felt like giving up this important project. However, I struggled on because I considered what Fannie Lou Hamer might have thought about me if I had given up piecing together her remarkable life. At one point I was completely absorbed in writing this account of Hamer from my own perspective.

Although some readers might not totally agree with my specific interpretations of Fannie Lou Hamer, it is a most honest effort. I have tried to share with the reader my passionate interests, knowledge and understanding of this great black woman. The many aspects to her life let us know that Hamer lived a rich and varied life. I wanted to touch upon the indefinable sparkle that made up this cultural icon. Her many interviews were very revealing, and I quoted from them extensively in describing her hard life.

Although this portrait is solely my take on the life of Fannie Lou Hamer, I would like to make special mention of Dr. Leslie Burl McLemore, emeritus professor of political science at Jackson State University, and director of the Fannie Lou Hamer Institute. He has been my mentor, colleague and friend for many years. I have always been grateful for his tutelage, as I was once his political science student, more than thirty years ago.

Dr. McLemore's important doctoral dissertation on the Mississippi Freedom Democratic Party remains the definitive study of this important but now defunct political group. I appreciate the encouragement he has always given me. His infectious enthusiasm for Fannie Lou Hamer actually inspired me to write this book.

I want to also express my deep appreciation to Dr. Mary D. Coleman, former professor of political science and associate dean of liberal arts, Jackson State University, for hiring me to serve as the chairman of the Political Science Department, Jackson State University, for a short while. Again, I thank Dr. Coleman for her consideration and the privilege she gave me to serve my *alma mater*.

I am also grateful to Dr. Michelle D. Deardorff, who was a tremendous help to me when I was chair and professor of political science at Jackson State University in 2005-2006. Additionally, Dr. Deardorff was particularly supportive and helpful in sparking my interest in writing this portrait. She also made some useful suggestions to me about hard-to-find sources. Dr. Deardorff also provided me with a copy of the "Annual Report of the Fannie Lou Hamer Institute, 2005-2006."

Furthermore, I want to thank Professor Robert Partch, the College of Southern Nevada, for providing me with the map of Mississippi and two signs used during the segregation era in the state. In addition, I am grateful to the library staffs of Jackson State University, the University of Nevada, Las Vegas, and the College of Southern Nevada for helping me find several works and collected correspondence relating to Fannie Lou Hamer. They also provided me with newspaper clippings, copies of seminal interviews and even books for young adults about Hamer. I am indebted to them for putting up with my various quirks and almost impossible requests for historical documents and biographies about the civil rights movement, as well as identifying some related autobiographical materials.

Finally, I am grateful to my wife, Atsuko, who read every word of this manuscript, perhaps with some sadness. Although Atsuko was born in Japan, and English is her second language, she was still able to grasp the horrors and hardships black people like Fannie Lou Hamer must have endured in Mississippi, myself included. I love my wife's curiosity, wonder and inquisitiveness. Atsuko still makes me proud. She was my rock from the very beginning to the end of writing this book.

Any particular errors or inaccuracies in this portrait of Fannie Lou Hamer are my own.

Preface

In her 1971 lecture at Tougaloo College, Fannie Lou Hamer urged, "Stand up, black men, this nation needs you." She did not say, "Stand up, niggers."[1]
— Jabari Asim

I wrote this book about the great Fannie Lou Hamer not only because I was born and lived in the state of Mississippi during its terrible segregation years, but because I was also a child of the civil rights movement. This book began to germinate in my mind as a young man when I first heard Fannie Lou Hamer speak at a political rally in Jackson, Mississippi, the capital of the state, which was a very different world back then. Additionally, as a teenager, I had the unique opportunity to participate in mass demonstrations and marched against total "white rule" with the best civil rights activists in Mississippi. But I really decided to write this book when I served as the chairman of the Political Science Department at Jackson State University in Mississippi. It was during this time, 2005-2006, that I re-read the late Erik H. Erikson's famous book *Gandhi's Truth: On the Origins of Militant Nonviolence*. I thought a similar or political treatment of Fannie Lou Hamer's life should be told, in a general way, as I consider myself a political historian. Although Erikson was not a historian or expert on India,[2] he wrote this seminal and influential book on the psycho-history or historical psychology of Mahatma Gandhi's colorful life. Gandhi, of course, became "the leader of the first nationwide act of civil disobedience,"[3] in India, against the British Empire, which ended with them leaving that country. Fannie Lou Hamer also became a leading proponent of civil disobedience in Mississippi as a black civil rights activist. Therefore, Hamer's extraordinary story provides rare insight into the flaws and ugliness of Mississippi politics during the early part of the twentieth century. Blacks had suffered for years under the racist politics and policies of the state, and Hamer wanted to change this cowardly institution of white supremacy, as it was such an oppressive and repressive system.

To say the least, Fannie Lou Hamer was a towering figure in Mississippi

1

politics during the civil rights era. She was known as "the First Lady of Civil Rights" in 1972, a sobriquet bestowed upon her by the League of Black Women[4]; and it was a richly deserved appellation. Hamer was also an up-by-the-bootstraps type of black woman whose street smarts, as you will see in this book, carried her a long way. Although this book does not discuss Hamer's heroic life in excruciating detail, it does address her entire life in a political and generalized manner. While some might say that this is a one-sided portrait, this book attempts to give an unvarnished portrayal of Fannie Lou Hamer. Lauded for her efforts to improve and change the political climate in Mississippi, Fannie Lou Hamer's life story is more pertinent today than ever in understanding race relations in this country. It is also a story about the triumph of the individual over an uncompromising Jim Crow system.

This work will tell you how Fannie Lou Hamer met and dealt with the various challenges placed before her. She was a woman of energy and action. Her larger goal was to send a message to white political leaders in Mississippi — that black people would no longer be held back in any endeavor. In this respect, Fannie Lou Hamer was unwavering in her convictions and commitment to eradicate segregation. In fact, she rebelled against any form of segregation, including the infamous Separate-but-Equal doctrine. Hamer was an outspoken personality. She was also arguably one of our most consequential black leaders in the long and sad history of Mississippi. Later she became the standard bearer. And she had a great back story, with her unique experiences drawing attention to several fronts of the civil rights movement. This book is also an uncompromising look at the evilness that existed in Mississippi during the segregation period. Racism in the state, of course, was not a figment of someone's imagination. It will become clear why Hamer was so special in this work. Hence, to argue that Fannie Lou Hamer was only a minor figure in the civil rights movement is really not telling the whole story, as she left an indelible mark on the politics and history of civil rights in Mississippi.

Fannie Lou Hamer was a living, walking, philosophical masterpiece of a person. Hamer's appeal as an activist and civil rights leader was undeniable. Thus, she exposed the American public to the racial problems that existed throughout the United States, especially in Mississippi. She would eventually become a *cause célèbre*. To be sure, her insightful and unique voice was profound and penetrating, as she had such a unique and eloquent way with words. Hamer tirelessly provided sage advice to everyone, often having a profound affect on people. Her honest and open opinions and straight talk endeared her to most who met her. By the force of her personality, Hamer was able to captivate an audience, as she often said things with confidence and conviction. She also had a genuine concern for people, who were powerless. In the final analysis, she became a major driving force and an incredible spokesperson for the constitutional rights of blacks and other less fortunate people. If nothing else, Hamer suggested something quite significant and practical in terms of solving racial problems. Her magnetic personality and tired, serious eyes drew almost everyone's attention. Hamer was often described as outgoing, big-hearted and contagiously curious. But she set out to change *everything* political, championing the cause of freedom. She also tried to respond positively to any kind of situation that called for it — like fighting to protect the basic rights of people.

It was difficult for anyone to forget Hamer after hearing her speak. Even today her words continue to reverberate throughout the state of Mississippi and the South. Indeed, black people in Mississippi still care a great deal about Fannie Lou Hamer. In the end, many people told Hamer how much they appreciated what she tried to do for them. Also, many people today talk about Hamer in rapturous terms. Whites and blacks praised her for making them feel good about themselves — and proud. Fannie Lou Hamer was all about promoting racial and/or ethnic understanding, as well as strengthening the ideals of human rights and tolerance. Fighting poverty and human suffering were also a part of her political agenda. Noted for her forthrightness, Fannie Lou Hamer was emotionally vested in the civil rights movement; and she never shied away from a political challenge. Hamer, of course, came from strong, spiritual black parents — but from a struggling and relatively unremarkable background. Equally important, she was a down-to-earth person and never a prima donna. Nonetheless, Hamer's voice and sincerity never failed to impress. Not only was she an incredibly talented orator, Hamer was an influential personality, and a noble trailblazer — a black, über-woman. Her life exemplified the idea that if you wanted to make a difference in the world, especially regarding human rights, you only had to get directly involved.

Fannie Lou Hamer was a fearless, unstoppable force of nature. And her commanding presence, while she lived, made people love and trust her. Hamer had a knack for getting black people involved in the movement, while making untold sacrifices. As we shall see, Fannie Lou Hamer worked very hard to see that things would improve for poor people in Mississippi. However, her fear of being poor, and the brutality of white racists, remained with her for the rest of her life. It is definitely not an exaggeration to say that there was a white backlash against the modern-day civil rights movement, as blacks were still being discriminated against and discouraged from voting up until the Voting Rights Act of 1965. Some white Southerners today have short memories and would, perhaps, like to forget the terrible acts and deeds of white racists and segregationists of the past. And they would probably rather forget many of the harsh episodes detailed in this book. But I am not talking about ancient history, as some heinous acts of domestic terrorism, against mostly black people, happened only forty plus years ago. Fortunately, because of Fannie Lou Hamer and others like her, "Racially motivated violence has been drastically reduced. Many blacks have made economic, social, and political gains that their grandparents never would have thought possible. Yet America remains two societies, separate and unequal."[5]

In the final analysis, Hamer stood tall during a time and place of civil rights giants. Young black leaders today, especially in Mississippi, could stand to learn from Fannie Lou Hamer, who galvanized groups of people for racial and political change. Writing this book has given me a renewed appreciation for what Fannie Lou Hamer did for the people of Mississippi. This portrait tries to make the reader understand and empathize with the real Fannie Lou Hamer, a grand lady who was idealistic, compassionate and determined to do the right thing, like the great and illustrious Mahatma Gandhi.

It is unfortunate, but I was unable to get the necessary permission to use several photographs of Fannie Lou Hamer for this book. It was not for a lack of trying. The hours, days and months in trying to get the appropriate photographs and rights were a monumental effort, but with only the results presented in this book. It proved to be an impossible task, for unknown reasons regarding the Hamer estate; but this work, without specific photographs of Fannie Lou Hamer, speaks for itself.

Introduction

She was big and black, and not very fashionable. She made no attempt to be endearing — or even accommodating to the public's interest in her. Comporting herself with a reserve and dignity that demanded respect, she seemed to embody an ancient ideal of nobility.[1]

— Mary Beth Roger

The great Fannie Lou Hamer was one of the most noted and influential black activists during the civil rights movement of the late 1960s and 1970s in the United States, ranking alongside the famous Dr. Martin Luther King, Jr., and the formidable Rosa Parks. Indeed, shortly before she arrived on the scene, the civil rights movement in Mississippi was basically lethargic and floundering — to the point that some wanted to give up. Black people during this time, of course, especially in the segregated South, were victims of political and racial oppression, and always taken for granted. Consequently, their lack of self-confidence had to be brought to task.

Hamer, in this respect, personally convinced blacks to forget their fears and become politically engaged in Mississippi. It was an uphill battle. Hamer, of course, understood the significance of black political participation. But she was not some fire-breathing agitator. Hamer, a child of the Mississippi Delta, born October 6, 1917, in Ruleville, Mississippi, believed that she had an important responsibility to those black people living in the state of Mississippi, as she wanted to protect the rights and defend the black community. During her adult life, Hamer wanted to bring public awareness to an ever changing world in terms of race relations. She paved the way for other blacks, as she challenged the status quo of White Supremacy because Hamer understood the big racial picture.

Blacks everywhere in the United States turned to this daughter of poor black sharecroppers for suggestions, encouragement, advice, support, and leadership. What made Hamer unique among others, and among civil rights activists in particular, were her political insights, integrity, and honesty, as

5

well as her vision. She was also a great listener, absorbing everything she could as a lifetime student of the human condition. Particularly listening to black people during her activist years, provided her with a clearer understanding of their individual and specific needs. And often Hamer's caring heart and affection for people shone through. Indeed, as we shall see, she was capable of overwhelming acts of tenderness. And being a part of the civil rights movement changed the course of her adult life, as it profoundly affected her very existence.

Some might place her on an altar, or consider her a modern Joan of Arc, in that Hamer was willing to die for her beliefs. She certainly exuded an aura of invincibility. Rather than concentrating on herself, however, Fannie Lou Hamer focused on building a coalition of blacks and whites across the nation who would take the issues of voting rights for minorities, as well as stumping for equal and human rights, straight to the dominant group. In this respect, Hamer was fearless, as she paved the way for voting rights for blacks. In fact, "she became the most powerful voice in the voter registration movement in Mississippi."[2] However, Hamer didn't believe that the end always justified the means.

And as blacks in Mississippi became more involved in the Democratic Party at the city, county and state levels, white voters began to flock to the opposing Republican Party. As a black activist, Hamer was not shy about marching into a particular meeting and telling seasoned civil rights workers what she actually thought, reading many the "riot act," so to speak. Indeed, she would not even hesitate to scold black leaders when she thought their approaches were inflexible and terribly wrong. In this regard, Hamer had impeccable timing. And when Hamer had the opportunity to lead, she did so willingly. To put it another way, Hamer never attempted to assume leadership unilaterally in Mississippi (black) politics. But she was fiercely brave, in going toe-to-toe with white racists almost everywhere in the nation.

Although Hamer was later instilled with much hope and optimism for the future of black Americans, especially their ability to fully participate politically in our society after the cursed Jim Crow era, she also looked at things with an objective eye. In essence, Hamer never did anything against her better judgment. Hamer knew that for blacks to sit back and continue doing almost nothing about their plight just wouldn't do. Of course, white racists of the day had no intention of relenting or sharing their positions of power with blacks, never mind giving in to the civil rights movement. But change was inevitable.

Many whites, especially in Mississippi, felt that giving equal rights to the descendents of black African slaves was wrong, ridiculous, and unsupportable, as black people were thought of as inferior and sub-humans during the 1950s and '60s. According to the former executive director of the National Urban League, the late Whitney M. Young, Jr., "White people could not dare think of the Negro male as a man, simply because of white racism."[3] Indeed, as we shall see, the naked hatred of some evil, violent-minded whites in Mississippi was evident and palpable. Blacks suffered indignities and domestic terrorism from whites in the South at almost every turn. Many white Southerners during the 19th and 20th centuries believed that there wasn't anything inherently wrong with the Separate-but-Equal doctrine, which was essentially condoned by the Supreme Court and continued to segregate and polarize the nation. Fannie Lou Hamer wanted to know about the cold-hearted indifference of whites. She found it hard to believe that anyone could be so callous and hateful, or so insensitive to human beings. Unfortunately, the evil acts and deeds of some white Southerners during the height of the civil rights period had reached manic levels. Hamer also wanted whites to especially examine their conscious and false assumptions about black Americans. Some whites in Mississippi argued that Hamer was naïve and unsophisticated when it came to racial issues and the necessity to segregate ethnic groups, but she never concerned herself with such trivial criticisms. More importantly, "Hamer's nature made her see the advantages of help from anyone who offered it."[4] Hamer was also realistic about the prospect of whites willfully giving any rights to black Americans, since they had routinely been denied their constitutional rights for so long.

At the time it seemed almost incomprehensible that black people would be given parity and respect as humans. The lives of blacks were of no consequence for some whites, especially in the South; and many blacks in the civil rights movement thought that white resistance would prove too great to change things for black Americans. Hamer was not discouraged, however, because she had long preached that what whites were doing to black people in Mississippi and elsewhere was wrong, and eventually the entire nation would listen to her impassioned plea. Moreover, she was able to play on the conscience of whites everywhere. Yet, for a long time, white Americans, especially in the South, just couldn't get their minds around the idea that black people deserved equal rights. Of course, white Southerners didn't like Hamer and other blacks who broke the rules of white authority in Mississippi. But Hamer made her feelings clear:

> What I really feel is necessary is that the black people in this country will have to upset this apple cart. We can no longer ignore the fact that America is *not* the ... land of the free and the home of the brave.[5]

Hamer, of course, was determined to push things as far as she could with white America. And she didn't pull any punches. After all, Hamer wanted to do something positive about the terrible conditions, disenfranchisement, and deplorable situation of blacks in Mississippi and elsewhere in the United States, as she too was struggling with the very same issues and discriminatory policies. So her message to white America was unmistakably clear. Hamer offered bold words in remarkable speeches that essentially told the truth about racist America. With her faith, Hamer thought she could overcome almost anything. In point of fact, Hamer was magisterial, always keeping her resolution to change things socially and politically for blacks in Mississippi and throughout the United States, especially in regards to lawless racism and brutality by some ruthless whites. Equally important, Hamer had the courage of her convictions.

Hamer felt that she didn't have to apologize to anyone for her actions and activism. Hamer was stoic in the face of death threats and the unrelenting verbal and physical abuse from whites in Mississippi. Her personal victories showed us the triumph of her spirit and character. And Hamer's shrewd sense of duty and responsibility, as well as her easy manner, propelled her swiftly to the top of the civil rights hierarchy. She was a formidable presence to say the least, as she provided strength and stature that others could not match. To meet Fannie Lou Hamer in person was to understand immediately that she was brilliant and extraordinary, a complex figure to be reckoned with. Indeed, she exuded an almost supernatural aura of kindness, intelligence, wit and selflessness.

For some, the gregarious Hamer was a guiding light, a beacon of hope, a scion of moral courage, fortitude, and determination. There was certainly a regal air about this strong, savvy, and unapologetic black woman of the Delta South. Hamer commanded your attention. And you immediately noticed her inner self-confidence, despite her limited, sixth-grade education. This is to say, Hamer showed remarkable poise in front of sophisticated and educated people from all walks of life, even as she sometimes misused words in the English language when she spoke. Of course, Hamer didn't really care about what others thought about her, especially about her unadorned language and unappealing, high-pitched speaking voice. She just wanted to get her message across.

In fact, Hamer refused to define herself by personal circumstances and what others thought about her. Hamer had the courage to be herself, even with her limited English vocabulary. Hamer wanted her audiences to be prepared to hear the truth, as she held nothing back in her speeches when clearly explaining how black people were being manipulated and mistreated by members of the dominant group. But it was more important for audiences to see exactly what Hamer stood for, especially regarding those things which would benefit blacks politically and socially. All this was enough to make some whites in Mississippi feel extremely nervous and uncomfortable.

Hamer would also give to-the-point advice to your sometimes disagreeing and disbelieving face. And there was often an intense level of enthusiasm among the black people of Mississippi, given Hamer's involvement and leadership. You watched her, riveted by everything she did and said before you, intrigued by her unique style, knowledge and seriousness. For some, listening to Hamer's speeches was almost like a religious experience. Indeed, Hamer had a saintly quality about herself when she spoke, with her dark brown, oval face, serious eyes and proud and mystical disposition. Ultimately, her speeches before enthusiastic crowds allowed her personality to come through. As Hamer so eloquently put it once, "All my life, I've been sick and tired.... Now I'm sick and tired of being sick and tired."[6]

As an orator, Hamer was extraordinary — a black heroine who gave "hair-raising speeches against the Mississippi political establishment all over the country."[7] Her famous speech at the 1964 Democratic Convention in Atlantic City, New Jersey, where she stated, as a Mississippi Freedom Democratic Party (MFDP) delegate, "We want to register [to vote], to become first-class citizens, and if the Freedom Democratic Party is not seated now, I question America, is this America?"[8] would define Hamer for years to come. She spoke with the sentimentality and dignity of a proud black woman who had suffered much. According to novelist June Jordan, "When they heard her [Hamer] speak, all good people of America were shocked by her suffering, White people felt a deep shame. Every one respected her."[9]

Hamer also sought to set the record straight about the inhumane treatment of blacks by whites in Mississippi and elsewhere. She simply wanted to lend her considerable voice to the civil rights movement for black Americans. And her big voice won her a serious political following. Hamer was eventually accepted as one of the leaders of black Democrats in Mississippi. Moreover, she always spoke personally and uniquely, and mostly her audiences paid rapt attention because it was Fannie Lou Hamer speaking. And what she said was always interesting and engrossing. Just her mere presence gave many blacks confidence, because she was indeed outspoken about all those things that were good, fair, and decent. Should we also point to Hamer's infectious, upbeat message about racial equality? Hamer once wrote in 1964, concerning her actions in the civil rights movement, that "we're doing something that will not only free the black man in Mississippi but hopefully will free the white one as well. No man is an island to himself."[10]

Hamer's involvement with the Student Nonviolent Coordinating Committee (SNCC) in the 1960s catapulted the relatively unknown and somewhat demure but charismatic Fannie Lou Hamer into the political limelight. Members of the civil rights movement were thrilled at the publicity given Hamer. Hamer started off as somewhat tentative in the movement, but by the time she got her political legs under her, she was able to connect with almost anyone, and she was able to help put out the many political fires that needed putting out during the modern civil rights movement. But Hamer was always honest about her shortcomings and limitations.

When Hamer later became a part of the Mississippi Freedom Democratic Party (MFDP), which was the first interracial organization that seriously challenged segregation by standing up against the white democrats of Mississippi (who essentially excluded blacks), she became even busier. More importantly, the MFDP demanded adequate black representation in state government, as well as the right for blacks to vote and elect other black politicians as their representatives. So Hamer was heavily involved in the black community, and was active with several civil rights groups. Indeed, it was Hamer's unique ability to work with others which made her special. Hamer's genius resided in her ability to get things done — to make people follow her, no matter what. There was just something about Fannie Lou Hamer that attracted people to her cause.

Hamer, of course, was a shrewd operator, an activist of notable skills and repute. Her ability to implement and make things happen seemed to be founded on her limitless drive. Hamer was always a people person, too. Many white Southerners, however, made critical and inappropriate comments about Hamer and other black activists in the State of Mississippi, creating additional conflict and tension. Moreover, the racist beliefs, uncouth actions and draconian attitudes of some whites became enormous obstacles in achieving racial parity for blacks. The fierce opposition and monstrous assaults by white hate groups, like the Ku Klux Klan, also made things extremely difficult.

Furthermore, some white Americans, especially in the South, didn't hide the fact that they held black people in contempt. But many black Americans still wanted and expected to be treated fairly and with dignity; and as white Mississippians found out, blacks would not back down. In fact, as the late white Southern novelist Walker Percy once wrote, "There was no one to head off the collision between the civil-rights movement and the racist coalition between redneck, demagogue, and small-town merchant. The result was [black] insurrection."[11]

Hamer simply wanted whites in Mississippi, and other places, to realize the error of their ways, which sometimes put her patience and tolerance to the test because the political thoughts and ideals of blacks and whites in the South differed considerably. But Hamer also knew that wishful thinking ultimately wouldn't solve the intractable problems faced by blacks in the United States. Indeed, she believed that only direct action would rightly force the dominant group to do the right thing in terms of providing justice and equality. In the final analysis, the outspoken Fannie Lou Hamer's goal was to secure social justice. In the end, blacks in Mississippi and throughout the nation would gain political strength — but not necessarily economic strength, which still has yet to be totally realized, even today. And for many black Americans, the civil rights struggle goes on.

Fannie Lou Hamer was a particularly important personality of our time. She could have settled for an easier path, but that was not to be. She certainly experienced her knocks in life. And for a while, Fannie Lou Hamer was a cultural phenomenon. Indeed, the scope of what she accomplished in terms of supporting the civil rights movement in the South was absolutely amazing. What Hamer did for the freedom movement is worthy of recognition and celebration. Hers is a story worth telling, one that should always warrant our attention. It was like she was born to give testimony to the truth regarding the relationship between blacks and whites during the Jim Crow period. Hamer knew where she was going in a world that tried to marginalize and limit her. But she stood up for her constitutional rights to the very end. To her credit, Hamer was always persistent in what she did or tried to accomplish.

Nonetheless, Hamer never expected anything to which she felt she was not entitled. And she held no illusions about White Supremacy in the South suddenly changing overnight. While she lived, Hamer represented many things to black people and white people, and perhaps no one got the same kind of respect as Fannie Lou Hamer — that is, at least in Mississippi. Indeed, Hamer's charisma and arresting qualities inspired the fierce loyalty and admiration of many, especially in the South.

Although Hamer wasn't a highly educated person, underneath her tough exterior she was extremely thoughtful, generous and wise. She was a smart black woman who galvanized a generation of black people during the civil rights movement to act against the forces that wanted to silence them. Hamer was never concerned that people would think less of her because she didn't have a high school or college education. But she was not an ignoramus or someone who didn't know their way around the political block, especially when she eventually became involved in Mississippi politics and served as a powerful voice for disenfranchised black people and other minorities. In this regard, Hamer was abnormally clever.

So for many, it was not only Hamer's personal charm, but it was her verbal victories that made her a figure for the ages. As a black activist, she became a champion spokeswoman for the voiceless and powerless. Indeed, the barely literate Fannie Lou Hamer was very deliberate in her wonderful speeches when she spoke her mind, and remained unapologetic about her speaking voice. Her booming, rough voice was unmistakable, unhurried and without flourishes. And Hamer never stopped speaking out about racial injustices, inequality and racial issues that mattered to her and the beleaguered black people of Mississippi. In fact, Hamer remained an outspoken fixture in public life until the day she died, March 14, 1977, in Mound Bayou, Mississippi.

Hamer's good deeds are legendary, and during her adult life she gave testimony to a great understanding of what was good and just and truthful. In the end, white Southerners grudgingly admitted the importance of Fannie Lou Hamer. But she was everything that racists despised. During the later part of her life she moved in high circles, traveled widely, had her ups and downs, met lots of new people, and stood shoulder to shoulder with presidents, prime ministers, foreign leaders and other national and international dignitaries. In the end, Hamer never regretted anything because she felt that she had accomplished everything she had set out to do, or what she thought she was supposed to do during her life. Hamer had followed in the estimable footsteps of Dr. King and Rosa Parks, as well as other civil rights greats.

Hamer earned her status as a civil rights icon. And it is not an exaggeration to say that Hamer, as a strong, formidable black woman who lived an extraordinary life, didn't live to reap all of the possible rewards of her hard work during the modern civil rights movement. In the end, however, Hamer's prowess as a civil rights worker helped her gain a national and international reputation, as she became "an uncompromising political dynamo who would become one of the most powerful leaders and symbols of the Southern civil rights movement."[12]

1

Birth, Cotton and Childhood

Fields of white fruit, row after row, rolled for miles to and from the river, flowing like the river itself. Rolling like the river. It [was] hot and suffocating ... even for Mississippi, where summer had an awful habit of coming early and staying late and always wearing out its welcome. Summer was in love with Mississippi.[1]

— John Oliver Killens

When Fannie Lou Townsend was born on October 6, 1917, in rural Montgomery County, Mississippi. The Townsends soon moved to Sunflower County, to a Mississippi Delta plantation owned by W.D. Marlow, where Fannie Lou came to know her parents, Jim and Ella, and her other nineteen siblings in due time as she grew older. Such large families were an absolute necessity for blacks living in Mississippi. Having so many children worked on several levels — they could help with hard farm work and, of course, provide many more hands to pick cotton. Life, however, was exceedingly difficult, and it was expensive feeding so many mouths. Nonetheless, having twenty children was considered an economic asset. According to journalist Rochelle Sharpe, "Children were considered a financial asset to the poor in the 19th century [and beyond], providing a cheap source of unskilled labor and the potential to bring additional income to the family."[2]

Fannie Lou, at two years old, didn't know that she was black and poor, the descendant of African slaves, and that her large family lived a life of abject poverty as sharecropping cotton pickers. But when she reached the age of thirteen, Fannie Lou would come to know about all of these things.

Fannie Lou was a bright child with a precocious and serious interest in why things were the way they were. The cotton field landscape provided the young Fannie Lou the perfect canvas for her imagination, as the older black folks' voices floated over the dreaded cotton fields and beyond with sad and hopeful Negro spirituals. It was here and at the churches she attended that Fannie Lou learned the words to important songs, religious songs during freedom-ride fields trips in Mississippi and elsewhere. While picking cotton, Fannie Lou would tune in to the various sounds around her. Indeed, she learned the art of listening by observing birds and insects and the peculiar sounds they made while she would frolic in the forest next to the prodigious cotton fields. Listening to the creatures outdoors allowed her to focus on the work of picking cotton; and Fannie Lou had a remarkable ability to focus and concentrate, even at the tender age of thirteen.

At Strangers Home Baptist Church, Fannie Lou would sing along with the black congregation. While picking cotton, however, she didn't have much to sing about. Still, Fannie Lou enjoyed hearing her mother's strong singing voice in the cotton fields, especially when she sang hymns, songs of captivity, or gospel songs that touched the heart and made her dark eyes sparkle with joy. This was the time when Fannie Lou developed her listening and speaking powers. According to Professor Linda Reed, "Fannie Lou Hamer abided by strong religious teachings and often expressed that religious zeal through a sacred hymn before each of her speeches. She opened many gatherings with 'This Little Light of Mine,' one of her favorite songs."[3]

As a child of six, Fannie Lou took to picking cotton as if it were a natural thing. But working in the cotton fields of Mississippi was probably the worst thing for her. Or so she would later think. However, picking cotton was how blacks in the delta made their living. They were immersed in difficult circumstances in which survival was the most important thing — blacks in this part of the state had no choice but to

A map of the state of Mississippi with the location of Fannie Lou Hamer's birthplace and other important places relevant to the civil rights movement.

work the rich, red-dark earth. Accordingly, "Cotton was pretty much all that [black] farmers knew how to do and they were determined to keep right on doing it, whether or not it drove them to an early grave."[4]

Picking and cultivating cotton was certainly a terrible way of life for blacks living in the Mississippi Delta. And for all their work at cotton picking, Fannie Lou and many other blacks in the area of Ruleville didn't have much to show for their efforts. But Fannie Lou Townsend's response to hard work, and her precocity as a cotton picker, was to spit in her hands and keep moving toward the objective. And she was very serious, trying always to do her best. Fannie Lou also exuded remarkable patience as a young girl. She was a hard worker and good at almost everything she did.

Fannie Lou eventually deduced that she had been duped by the plantation owner, W.D. Marlow, who dared her, when she was six year old, to "pick some cotton," trapping her in the beastly work that she would have to keep doing because of sharecropping debt.[5] And Fannie Lou "worked many long years chopping and picking cotton" for W.D. Marlow.[6] Hamer explained it this way: "I started pickin' when I was six. The [white] man [W.D. Marlow] told me if I'd pick thirty pounds I could come to his commissary store and get cracker jacks and candy, and I'd never had all that, so I picked the thirty pounds, and then the next week it was sixty, and by the time I was thirteen I could pick as much as a man."[7] Of course, the wide-eyed little black girl Fannie Lou was perhaps too naïve and innocent to think at the time that she was being bamboozled.

Soon enough, cotton had become the pervasive feature of her childhood. This was her rite of passage, as she hummed church songs to herself, or along with everyone else in the fields, and dreamed while laboriously picking cotton. For the most part, blacks laborers on the W.D. Marlow plantation were trapped working there for the length of their brutish lives. Most blacks in the Mississippi Delta, however, had the mental toughness and physical where-withal and strength to survive the stress, hunger and other hardships, no matter the circumstances. Indeed, while picking cotton, blacks had to essentially shrug off their fatigue. Many would pick cotton under the morning and noon-day sun, and sometimes late into the evening.

It often would seem quiet at dusk, as black sharecroppers headed home for a light supper. Afterward, many would go back into the cotton fields, with kerosene lanterns and tin buckets of sulfur-infused cotton fires, which were used to ward off mosquitoes and light the way so that the sober work of picking cotton could continue after the sun finally set. Contrary to the belief that blacks were lazy and shiftless, black families worked harder than most. The young Fannie Lou wanted to know why black people had to work so hard, more so than the white people she saw around the W.D. Marlow plantation. She certainly didn't want to pick cotton the rest of her life. Didn't blacks have any other options? Or would they always be economically and emotionally marginalized?

The sad and unhappy lot of blacks in Mississippi didn't offer much of a life. Despite this, Fannie Lou always tried to be brave. For a long while, Fannie Lou didn't know what she was going to do with her life, apart from helping her parents. Consequently, she "learned very early not to complain, but to work hard to make a difference."[8]

Fannie Lou's physical appearance was average and unremarkable. Fannie Lou was an intelligent little black girl who radiated practicality and wholesomeness, but she was not a beauty. As a young woman, Fannie Lou had a full-lipped mouth, with penetrating, deep-set eyes and dark, coarse hair, usually tied taut upon her big head. The authors of *American Hero* described the fourteen- or fifteen-year-old Fannie Lou as:

> Full-busted and wide-hipped, with long thin legs, she was beginning to develop the physical features that would characterize her looks in adulthood. She was a big girl, but her bigness reflected a solid bull-like strength, rather than the soft flabbiness of someone who was merely overweight.[9]

Fannie Lou was an average, plain, self-deprecating young girl, and extremely likable. She wasn't concerned about winning beauty contests, but she wasn't always comfortable with her body, either. For example, as a young girl she didn't like that her coarse and unruly hair was cut and kept short to prevent head lice and tatter. Furthermore, she was rather awkward and uncoordinated because of a bout with polio, a disease which could be a death sentence for some blacks in the Delta. Of course, "her leg had been broken during infancy and never professionally repaired," so she "ended up with a life long limp," which perhaps had something to do with her ungracefulness.[10] Though Fannie Lou never really saw herself as beautiful she had an inner confidence in herself, even during her vulnerable teenage years.

She was also a daydreamer who would escape her day-to-day drudgery picking cotton on a plantation by thinking about better days to come, or another life in which she never went hungry. She fantasized about growing rich one day, as well as being able to afford decent clothes. At this time in her life, Fannie Lou knew that there was a whole other existence outside her poverty-stricken world. Picking cotton in the hot Mississippi sun all day gave the young Hamer a lot of time to think, especially about her life to come and who she wanted to be. Fannie Lou wanted a life without limitations.

Fannie Lou also intuitively understood the angst and sadness of what her ancestors experienced as black African slaves working on various Mississippi plantations. In the 1920s and 1930s, many black farmers and sharecroppers in the Mississippi Delta were undereducated and impoverished, and closely supervised because of the legacy of slavery — and because the order of the day was "white rule." As Fannie Lou grew older, it became very difficult for her.

Fannie Lou spent a lot of her time trying to understand what her life was all about. Fannie Lou hated the assumption that other people were in control of her life. She often asked herself: Why am I doing this? Picking cotton for almost nothing? Was it because white people thought she was inferior? As she continued to grow, it just didn't make sense to her anymore. She even began to hate herself for a while. Fannie Lou recalled seeing how the black people around her lived in extreme poverty and misery, and how they suffered, and she would both sigh and cry. Would being white offer her a better life? Fannie Lou wondered about the opulence of wealthy white folks. She knew that whites had a bigger and better way of life than most blacks in Mississippi.

Fannie Lou would later realize that white southerners were unwilling to accept equanimity with blacks. Often whites resisted the notion that black people were being treated unfairly; or they were in denial that racial problems ever existed. At that time the young Fannie Lou was emotionally ill-equipped to deal with her feelings of jealousy and resentment of whites. Only later was she able to deal with her emotions and misgivings. About wanting to be white, Fannie Lou Hamer once shamefully admitted:

> At the beginning of my young life, I wanted to be white. The reason was that we worked every day, hard work, and we never did have food.... I asked my mother one time why I wasn't white, so that we could have some food. She told me, "Don't ever, ever say that again. Don't feel like that. We are not bad because we're black people.... You respect yourself as a black child. And when you're grown, if I'm dead and gone, you respect yourself as a black woman, and other people will respect you."[11]

In the end, Fannie Lou learned to be proud of who she was. And never would she feel sorry for herself or resent being a black person again. And Fannie Lou learned to love everybody. But even then she thought that *everyone* should be equal with everybody else, regardless of their skin color. And despite seeing some whites having so much more, Fannie Lou was not hateful, nor did she begrudge them, because she was a person of faith who was raised as a good and loving Christian. Besides, Fannie Lou wanted to make her parents proud.

As a young adult, Fannie Lou Hamer helped eke out a living for herself and other family members by "cleaning the boss's house." One day, while scrubbing one of the many bathrooms in the big, white house, Fannie Lou was told by W.D. Marlow's daughter not to clean the place as well as the other rooms because that particular bathroom belonged to their dog, named Old Honey.[12] Though shocked by this revelation, Fannie Lou didn't let on to the plantation owner's daughter. She especially didn't voice her feeling that blacks in Mississippi were treated worse than dogs, or that many blacks didn't even have indoor toilets.[13] Equally important, Fannie Lou didn't tell the white people around Ruleville that she too appreciated some of the finer things in life, like partaking of a good meal, or the luxury of taking a hot bath in a real bath tub, which was almost impossible to accomplish during her youth, given her situation as a poor black girl child.

Fannie Lou, of course, had big dreams and other aspirations, as we shall see. Perhaps she hoped that she could change things for black people, helping them to escape the harsh life of cotton picking. Fannie Lou also believed that hard work and an underlying belief in yourself could make *anything* possible. She also knew that some white people were capable of kindness. Furthermore, how would things be like if *everyone* got along, especially in Mississippi? And was there really a God out there anywhere? In the end, Fannie Lou made herself a promise to find out, if she could, or find another world outside the Mississippi Delta.

2

The Slavery of Sharecropping

They spent their days exhausted, hungry, and shabbily garbed, but her family never earned enough to break the cycle of debt and remained trapped in the usurious latter-day slavery called sharecropping. But [Hamer] was not angry: A deeply religious person, she focused her energies on helping others and eagerly awaited the day she would have her own family.[1]

— Harriet A. Washington

Fannie Lou Townsend's childhood really defined her character as a young woman. At that tender age everything was fraught with pain, hunger, and suffering — for herself and her family. And she would feel the repercussions of her hard family upbringing throughout her life. It was certainly a dark time. The white plantation owner W.D. Marlow wasn't as straightforward as it might have seemed. And being tricked into becoming a cotton picker was a painful lesson for Fannie Lou. But it was, nonetheless, a prerequisite, or *required* training for black youngsters to learn how to efficiently pick a lot of cotton at an early age. Hamer's family worked like animals, unfailingly but dissatisfied. Blacks were in extremely tough situations that they couldn't overcome because of sharecropping. It was a constant struggle to survive.

Few blacks in the Mississippi Delta, though working for many years, had made it financially. Many black Mississippians at that time, during the 1920s and 1930s, were "sharecroppers struggling from year to year to eke out a subsistence."[2] Black sharecroppers usually lived near the big plantation house in several ramshackle, clapboard shacks, especially during the 1920's, '30s and '40s, where they "continued to produce the majority of the crops on [white] southern farms."[3] Black sharecroppers produced the blood, tears, pain, sweat and labor that kept the plantation system thriving long after black American slavery, the Civil War, and Black Reconstruction.

Blacks in Mississippi beat impossible odds, but many were desperately poor, which deepened their misery. Some could barely live off the land to support themselves. The Townsend family, as well as other blacks, had to cope with many pecuniary hardships because "throughout the Deep South, the plantation owners kept their [black] sharecroppers in constant debt, claiming that advances made for seed, food, or clothing exceeded whatever had been earned from [cotton] picking."[4] Black people in Mississippi lived in a world of extended periods of privation, as many were unable to work their way out of such predicaments.

Clearly, the hardest part of being a poor sharecropper was the feeling of hopelessness, failure, and being trapped. Meanwhile, the back-breaking work on plantations continued unabated. Although there was always the certainty of respective holiday breaks, it was never enough to lift the spirits of the young Fannie Lou Townsend. To be sure, "sharecropping was bad for poor blacks," but it was lucrative and "very good for the white landowners."[5] According to Hamer's biographer, David Rubel, "It was almost like being a slave again."[6] In other words, "Whites still owned the land and blacks still worked it for them."[7] Furthermore, sharecropping provided "a cheap work force" and an effective means "to control blacks."[8] Black sharecroppers "were producing for the white landowner, and little went to them."[9]

Furthermore, by denying black sharecroppers "the right to vote, whites in the South were able to keep poor blacks down."[10] Equally important, "The laws of the South kept the races apart and placed very certain chains on [black] Americans."[11] As Fannie Lou Townsend was growing up in the Mississippi Delta, she became increasingly conscious of the *Haves* and *Have-Nots*. The Mississippi Delta, of course, was a place where black people struggled to make ends meet. Indeed, many were living on the precipice, but worked hard to make ends meet. Still, there was no way of getting around the simple truth of their poverty-stricken existence.

Fannie Lou Townsend thought that black people were more than just beasts of burden. Although she didn't begrudge anyone having wealth or prosperity, Fannie Lou "could not understand why everybody was not white, with plenty of food and clothes, [a] big house and little work, while those like her and her family did not have shoes and had to wrap their feet in rags to keep warm."[12] Indeed, Fannie Lou Hamer's mother would sometimes sit up late into the night, dead-tired, after a hard day in the cotton fields, sewing scraps of cloth she collected to make clothes for their family. Most of the clothes the Townsends owned were made from rags by the hard-working, no-nonsense Ella.[13]

Some saw escape from the plantation as the panacea for their problems in the South. But this was not possible for many blacks, even those who desperately wanted to leave the Mississippi Delta. To the plantation owner, "the very decision of a black southerner to leave constituted a threat to the [very] fiber of social and economic relations in the South" because "legitimacy and order relied upon the assumption that blacks were by nature docile, dependent, and unambitious."[14] Nothing could have been further from the truth, however.

It was against this grim, racist background that black people *existed* in Mississippi — because they were not really *living*. And there were no good reasons why blacks in the Delta should have been lagging so terribly behind. Poverty-ridden black families like the Townsends didn't have a lot of money because they were being cheated out of fair wages. Hamer's family was typical of the majority of hard working black sharecroppers who rarely got paid for their efforts. According to Litwin, black Americans "who lived in the [Mississippi] Delta were among the poorest blacks in the South."[15] Fannie Lou Townsend understood the unexpressed anger and worry of black people through her own family's suffering. Indeed, nowhere was poverty more evident than in Mississippi.

Still, Fannie Lou, as an impressionable young girl, believed that life was worth living. And that their family would always find a way to survive. Starvation was of primary concern. Hamer's mother would beg for scraps of discarded meat and broken animal bones from black and white neighbors who slaughtered pigs, hogs, sheep, and cows, looking for *any* leftovers to feed her large family. And when there was no discarded meat or bones to be had, her mother fed her children sweet dirt, collected from a special dirt hill, to keep them from having to think about food and the pain in their empty stomachs.

Black novelist Edward P. Jones writes about how black people in the South ate dirt in his Pulitzer Prize–winning novel *The Known World*:

> Moses closed his eyes and bent down and took a pinch of the soil and ate it with no more thought than if it were a spot of cornbread. He worked the dirt around in his mouth and swallowed.... [The black man] ate it not only to discover the strengths and weaknesses of the field, but because the eating of it tied him to the only thing in his small world that meant almost as much as his own life.[16]

So whether they liked it or not, poor black people were tied to the soil, the dark earth, the cotton fields of Mississippi. And they ardently picked cotton under the worst possible conditions imaginable. Many black sharecroppers were overwhelmed by the sheer amount of cotton they were expected to pick in a given season. As an adult, Fannie Lou Hamer once recalled:

> My parents would make huge crops of sometimes 55 to 60 bales of cotton. Being from a big family where there were 20 children, it wasn't too hard to pick that much cotton. But my father, year after year, didn't get too much money and I remember he just kept going.[17]

In that very early time in Fannie Lou Townsend's life, the idea of being alive was probably the only thing blacks like herself in Mississippi had to be grateful about, because sharecropping had hampered their ability to be happy and prosper. The nation, it seemed, didn't concern itself with the ubiquitous injustices faced by black sharecroppers in Mississippi. Life for the young Fannie Lou and her poor family was a hand-to-mouth existence, but she didn't want to just dwell on how things she thought should be for poor black people. Indeed, Fannie Lou wanted one day to right the wrongs for all oppressed people. She was open to certain life possibilities other than being a poor black sharecropper. During her teenage years it was all about acquiring the skills necessary to survive and be counted.

The quality of life for black sharecroppers in the Ruleville area was declining. It might have been hard for some to comprehend or believe that some black sharecroppers did not even have enough to eat. According to author Penny Colman, Hamer's family "survived by walking miles and miles through cotton fields looking for scraps of cotton left on a bush or lying on the ground, to pay for a family meal."[18] Later in her life, Fannie Lou Hamer recalled their struggle to pick over the cotton fields, to buy food, in this poignant way: "My mother would go around to the plantation and get them to let us scrap the fields, and sometimes we'd walk twenty miles a day just to get a bale of scrappin' cotton — you know, what's left when the field has been picked over."[19] Such drastic and desperate measures helped them survive.

Many black sharecroppers in the Mississippi Delta grew most of their own food. Black families ate what they were able to hunt and raise in their vegetable gardens. Collard greens or turnips boiled with fat back or salt pork was their standard fare. A simple meal for the Townsend family might consist only of "some cornmeal and an onion cut up with some salt on it, or maybe flour gravy."[20] Her accomplished father and fourteen brothers would also hunt for venison and fish, when possible, to supplement their meager meals. It was not unusual for them to eat whatever they could find, like wild dandelions or wild salad greens, which were always delicious in salads and found throughout the area where they lived. Some black families thought that dandelions were only weeds to be eradicated, but the Townsends knew better. It was food, theirs for the taking, because all parts of the dandelion plant were edible. As a treat for the many Townsend children, the roots of the dandelion were eaten with sugar, when available. Or Fannie Lou Townsend's mother, Ella, made dandelion fritters. The leaves of the plant were sautéed like spinach, or boiled in a big iron pot and eaten like turnip greens. The Townsends also learned how to find, cook and eat wild mushrooms. Or they would sometimes pickle the mushrooms or some of the vegetables from their garden. Finally, they would scour the forest for wild berries in the summer to make preserves for the winter.

Fannie Lou wasn't quick to excite; but it seemed food was *something* for her to get excited about. As a child, she wanted to eat sumptuous food, all that she could eat. Anything to prevent starvation. Fannie Lou would occasionally suck slowly on the ends of honeysuckle flowers to stave off hunger. In this sense, she was very practically-minded. As Fannie Lou recalled, everyone in her family was expected to pitch-in wherever and whenever it was necessary. And they certainly had to pinch pennies, because the Townsend family had enormous living expenses, with twenty-two mouths to feed. They also had to pay the exorbitant price for farming equipment and seeds for planting each year. But, as already mentioned, the Townsends were constantly being short-changed for the numerous bales of cotton they picked. It was a vicious cycle, a revolving nightmare called *sharecropping.*

3

Cry the Beloved Parents

The birth cry of some children may not be the cry for which some [parents] are constitutionally prepared, and the quality of the [parent-tie] may be determined by interaction between mutually reinforcing and releasing mechanisms, on the one hand, or by mechanisms which negate, mute, extinguish each other, on the other.[1]

— Margaret Mead

The world in the state of Mississippi operated very differently for black people. The young Fannie Lou Townsend grew up extremely poor and uncomfortable, never knowing why and for what purpose she was born, until much later. Despite claims to the contrary made by some scholars, Fannie Lou did not have a healthy, happy childhood. It was no fairy tale. Indeed, Fannie Lou couldn't recall a time when she was totally content, and she often cried herself to sleep. If she had had her way, Fannie Lou would have had a wonderful, beautiful time being a child. But it was not to be.

In fact, merely surviving was a very real challenge for the Townsends and many other black families in the Mississippi Delta. For Fannie Lou, there was nothing quite so frightening as not knowing where her next meal was coming from. Blacks in the state, of course, were living in a time period in which they were socially and economically depressed. Many black farmers and sharecroppers were beginning to wonder if they could even survive in Mississippi. The Townsends were living an unglamorous life, on the very margins. But Fannie Lou had always been aware of what was going on in the world outside the Delta by reading discarded magazines and strips of old newspapers.

Fannie Lou had also tried to write down the lyrics of church songs, chants, or whatever was on her mind. And although she didn't have any inflated ideas about herself, Fannie Lou could think for herself. As a child, she was mesmerized by the simple pleasures of having free rein of the surrounding countryside where she lived — that is, when she wasn't picking cotton or performing household chores. Fannie Lou often tried to put the bad things out of her troubled mind. Indeed, she was a very serious, contemplative little girl, with an energetic personality. So she tried to understand many things about life and race.

She knew, for example, that the entitlements of white people ran very deep in the Mississippi Delta, because many didn't say a thing about the terrible situation regarding black sharecroppers. Whites in Mississippi had also fought hard to relentlessly keep blacks down and illiterate, while directing them along a "slave-like" path whites had chosen for them. Of course, there was a widely held view that black people were stupid or ignorant, and somehow deserved the way they were being treated. Indeed, many had been relegated to the dung-heaps of society. Poor black families were forced to do more and more with less and less. One only has to read the famous black writer Richard Wright's books, like *Black Boy*, or *Uncle Tom Children's*, to get a sense of the racism and how awful things must have been for the Townsends and other blacks families in the Mississippi Delta.

Black families also had to deal with serious health issues, like heart and liver diseases, cancer, diabetes, infant mortality, and premature death. The reasons for all the health troubles that beset black people during this time weren't always clear. But the Townsends survived the various childhood diseases and illnesses without any medical insurance — by their faith in God. Many black families could not afford health care, or they didn't have access to a medical doctor during the 1930s and 1940s. And the Townsend family was no exception. Fannie Lou limped as a young girl, probably because she didn't receive prompt medical attention after a childhood accident.[2] Home remedies were used prodigiously to take care of the sick and ailing black people of Mississippi. Perhaps Fannie Lou Townsend's mother, Lou Ella, made medicinal tonics to relieve some of the aches and pains of her beloved children, like when they would contract *chilblain* because of the severe cold and lack of shoes, gloves, and other winter clothing.

Fannie Lou's parents, James Lee and Lou Ella Townsend, were salt-of-the-earth black people working extremely hard to survive and make an honest and decent living for themselves and their twenty children. Indeed, James Lee and Lou Ella were continually sacrificing for the fourteen Townsend boys and six girls, as they wanted a brighter future for them. But the Townsends had only the absolute necessities. The Townsend children didn't get much in the way of toys, leather shoes or pretty clothes. Fannie Lou often wore hand-me-downs from her older sisters. But her parents would do almost *anything* to make things better for their children, despite the hardships. Both James Lee and Lou Ella spent a lot of time watching over their brood, while trying to find unique ways to feed and cloth them. And they both did their very best, all things considered.

Lou Ella Townsend made patchwork quilts from discarded cloth and clothes that they found or no longer used, as she was skilled with a needle and thread. Lou Ella was even able to create makeshift shirts for the boys and skirts for the girls using discarded fifty-pound flour sacks. The Townsends wrapped themselves in old cotton sacks, heavily patched, instead of winter coats. Fannie Lou drew her strength from her mother Lou Ella; and she determined that some day her mother would no longer have to suffer, or wear patchwork clothing. Fannie Lou Hamer later recalled: "I'd look at my mother and say to myself, if I ever live to get grown, I'll never see you [her mother] in patched clothes or workin' [so] hard."[3] Their mother was a ferociously smart and strong woman. And her generosity of spirit was second to none in that she was extremely affectionate to her many children.

Indeed, Lou Ella Townsend was generous to a fault, a good person and a hard-working black woman. She was a dynamo who gave birth to twenty children. Having been pregnant for almost all her adult life, Lou Ella was strong, but not necessarily happy or content. Indeed, Lou Ella Townsend was overwhelmingly sad, but endeavored to never let it show around her children. She never dared cry, even when she wanted to. Fannie Lou remembered that "her mother used to come in from the [cotton] fields wearing tattered and torn clothes, too tired to walk. She had worked herself nearly to death, but she did [it] for family survival."[4] When all was said and done, it was the sheer bullheadedness of her mother and father which allowed the Townsends to survive.

The Townsends were a simple black family, with less than modest means, eking out a livelihood in an area that was unsophisticated and underdeveloped, where black people were less than educated and prone to die at an early age. For Fannie Lou and the rest of her siblings, the key to survival was being able to latch onto the exceptional guidance their parents gave all the Townsend children. When Fannie Lou was growing up, Lou Ella would often tell her daughter that she was doing the best she could to raise them — all her babies, she called them — especially given their awful situation. But Fannie Lou continued to ask her mother why black people lived in such abiding discomfort. Her proud mother would often try to allay her youngest daughter's concerns and worst fears. And it was probably because of her mother's sage words of wisdom that Fannie Lou thought her mother was the greatest mother who had ever lived, especially as Lou Ella was known for doing creative things to help her enormous family make ends meet. For example, she made the family's own soap for washing and bathing, with lye and the animal fat she stored after using it for cooking.

Fannie Lou Townsend's father, James Lee, stood tall among men. Fannie Lou thought her father was indeed a giant, as he was immense in stature and the manner in which he carried himself. James Lee Townsend watched over his big family, with affection. The stalwart James Lee Townsend was a good storyteller who never failed to delight and entertain, no matter how far-fetched a story might sound. In so many ways he challenged his brood with his sense of humor. Fannie Lou loved him dearly, even as old age robbed him of his vitality and strength. When possible, her father made furniture for their ramshackle home with tools he borrowed, scrounged or bought with the little money he had. However, despite his best efforts, their tiny, unpleasant tumbledown house was never quite a real home because it didn't have workable indoor plumbing, or even "electricity, heat, or running water."[5] And the Townsends slept mostly on raw cotton pallets, which were coverings filled with cotton or cornhusks, in one large communal sleeping room.

From her father, Fannie Lou learned about different trees growing in the forest. She also learned of the various wild plants that could be used for healing purposes or edibles. James Lee knew how to recognize different herbs and edible fungi, and he assiduously taught Fannie Lou about these important things. James Lee did whatever he could to make do for the family. And he was always proud that he was able to feed his offspring, no matter the hardship.

Fannie Lou had a sense of wonder about life. Neither James Lee nor Lou Ella Townsend, however, could answer the big questions about life, such as the nature of evil or death, but Fannie Lou loved the parenting advice she received from them because they were practical and had a lot of common sense, and gave good counsel. Fannie Lou had to mature in a hurry. She had to be strong to get through a difficult time. Fannie Lou Townsend's early childhood instilled in her the mentality of a hard-nosed pragmatist.

Her parents essentially told their many children that as long as they didn't do anything self-destructive or harmful to others, they would be okay. James Lee and Lou Ella Townsend always tried to push them in the right direction. They taught their offspring to always respect the elderly, calling them Mr. and Mrs. or madam and sir. Her parents never stopped inspiring Fannie Lou and her siblings. But in the final analysis, James Lee and Lou Ella Townsend could not reasonably expect the young Fannie Lou and her brothers and sisters to advance in the world or escape poverty when they were being limited and marginalized by the dominant group at every turn. Even as a child, Fannie Lou resolved to look deeper into the differences among people of racial groups. Unfortunately, she would later learn to see people in terms of their skin color.

Fannie Lou learned about the "golden rule," and right and wrong, from her parents. Indeed, they inculcated strong morals, a sense of purpose, and other religious values in her. James Lee and Lou Ella Townsend also told Fannie Lou to trust her instincts and act on them if necessary. Consequently, she became a strong-willed little girl with a sweet disposition (unless provoked). Fannie Lou never went through a rebellious stage, as she certainly didn't want to be a burden to her parents. James Lee and Lou Ella Townsend were always there for their youngest daughter, even when Fannie Lou would stub a toe or cut a finger. But as a little girl, Fannie Lou just wanted to know why life was so unnecessarily hard for black people in the Delta.

When all was said and done, Fannie Lou had to figure things out for herself, because no one would give her any real answers to her questions about race — except her mother, who only suggested she not waste her time thinking about such matters. But in her heart of hearts, even then, at that early age in her life, Fannie Lou knew things could be different for black people. For a time, Fannie Lou was rather introverted, but "race hatred always made her angry."[6] When she was seven years old a white boy in the neighborhood called her a "dirty nigger" when he discovered Fannie Lou playing with his sister one day.[7] According to black writer June Jordan, "Fannie Lou had punched him [the little white boy] in the mouth. But she had learned that white hatred was so powerful, she would have to use more than just her two fists to stop it."[8]

Her parents had raised her to be compassionate and sensitive to others. But in challenging the little white boy, Fannie Lou showed gumption, as she was not some frightened child with low self-esteem. Fannie Lou, of course, cherished both her parents, especially her mother, who had always been special to her, so she tried to abide by her wishes. After all, Fannie Lou was taught not to harm anyone. Of course, her mother knew that her young, ambitious daughter wouldn't be able to become what she wanted to become because of a segregated Mississippi, but at least she could provide Fannie Lou with a spiritual life. Haunted by the prospect of going to Hell in childhood, Fannie Lou was an exceedingly well-behaved child.

At the age of twelve, Fannie Lou "was baptized in the Queen River," under the auspices of the Strangers Home Baptist Church.[9] Fannie Lou loved going to church because she liked listening to gospel music. It was music that gladdened her little heart, and she would clap for joy. Their little church was a way to mark the passing of hard times. It must be remembered that the black church, especially in Mississippi, provided a sanctuary for black people, particularly those being abused and oppressed by the dominant group. According to the late Julius E. Thompson, former professor of history at the University of Missouri, Columbia, "The church offered blacks solace and spiritual comfort from the daily burdens of segregation, lynching, racism, and oppression in Mississippi."[10] The Strangers Home Baptist Church taught the young Fannie Lou something about character building, mercy, and love of family and other human beings. Her mother would often straighten her coarse hair into a neatly coifed style on Sundays before going to church, and Fannie Lou loved her for that too.

Attending church struck a chord with the young Fannie Lou, who would never forget the life lessons inculcated in her by her church and parents. She would later instill her commitment to God, and her strength of purpose, in her own adopted daughters. Unfortunately, at the age that she was baptized, Fannie Lou "went to school for the last time."[11] Although James Lee and Lou Ella Townsend desperately tried "to keep their twenty children in school, which proved to be no easy task, despite the sessions of only four months for blacks,"[12] they couldn't raise the extra money needed to buy them school clothes. ("School for black children was in session only four months out of the year, and the rest of the time was spent 'making' the cotton crop.")[13] Annelise Orleck, professor of history at Dartmouth College, writes, "There was little chance that education would offer a way out"[14] of their miserable existence. Nonetheless, if the black students managed to learn and go on to finish high school and even college, many would come back home to help. So these things really did matter to black families in the Mississippi Delta. Orleck goes on to write:

> Children in black sharecropping families were able to attend school only after the cotton crop was picked. That meant, in effect, that school was open only during the winter months. Finishing elementary or middle school was the best that most black children could hope for.[15]

Unfortunately, by the time Fannie Lou realized that she really liked school, her parents had to tell her the sad news that she was needed in the cotton fields, and that she probably wouldn't be able to finish her primary education. This was a terrible blow to the young Fannie Lou. Although her parents encouraged Fannie Lou to do well in school when she did attend, or "when the crops were in,"[16] she was disappointed. Fannie Lou always took pride in the fact that she could read and spell better than the other black children in school. Generally, she was a fast learner, a quick study. And Fannie Lou had a reverence for learning new things.

Unfortunately, many of the other black children at school were jealous of Fannie Lou Townsend's initial academic success. She was able to connect the dots regarding important academic things, and excelled at basic math, which would later make a tremendous difference in her life. Classes were short in any given year, and several grades were taught simultaneously, with different seating divisions in the same school room. Consequently, Fannie Lou was able to listen to all the other lessons given in each class section. Fannie Lou was always excited about starting classes during the school year, short as it was.

However, many of the young black students were unable to keep pace; with all the hard school work, many failed. Fannie Lou, however, strove to excel at everything. And she often gave the misleading impression of being pleased with herself. Fannie Lou spent much of her adolescence apart from the other black students, but it was not because she was arrogant or full of herself. Difficult circumstances and family matters took up much of her time. Even at that young age, Fannie Lou would stare at you intently, soaking everything in, especially when you spoke to her. Was there ultimately something in her personality that said she was going to make something of herself?

4

Death of Her Parents

What happens to the history of a people not accustomed to writing things down? To whom poverty and illiteracy makes wills, diaries, and letters superfluous? Birth and death certificates, tax receipts — these occasional records punctuate but do not describe everyday life.[1]

— Theodore Rosengarten

As a student, Fannie Lou was someone you wanted to get to know. Many trusted her, as she seemed much more mature than the other black children at school. And her intellectual energy was something to be admired. Of course, her parents deeply influenced Fannie Lou's mental development. Her mother, for example, always told her to learn from other people, if possible. Fannie Lou was an astute and determined student, sharp as a tack, as they say. With her obvious ambition, she was born to lead. In addition, she was never intimidated by the other black school children because she felt that she was just as strong as the next person. But her zeal for learning was not shared by all the black students, because they probably didn't see the need. Fannie Lou, however, believed in herself and didn't hesitate to learn new things in school, no matter how difficult the lessons. She also learned from her mistakes and got better as time went on. Indeed, she was academically hungry, desperately looking for *something*.

Fannie Lou Townsend's parents were very protective of their children, and stood up to anyone that would do them harm. The Townsend children were instructed *never* to grovel in fear, and self-loathing. Still, Fannie Lou's parents had mixed feelings about all of their children going to school full-time, with all the work to be done in order to live. Someone had to work the cotton fields, and they didn't have the money to buy school clothes for everybody. Many of Fannie Lou's siblings couldn't read or write, as they had never been to school, although they possessed adequate intelligence.

As far as school was concerned, Fannie Lou would never realize her full potential as a student. But when she did attend school, Fannie Lou was always attentive and engrossed by what her teacher, Professor Thornton Layne, a black man, told them. Professor Layne worked to give his charges at least the basic rudiments of learning, like reading and basic mathematics. And Fannie Lou was an excellent reader. Indeed, she was obsessed with reading, and it became her favorite subject in school. Professor Layne also taught them other things of value, which held Fannie Lou Townsend's interest, like social relations and citizenship. Full of life, Fannie Lou was unafraid to speak her mind when she felt the need to. However, Fannie Lou abided by the rule of not speaking to Professor Layne (and other adults, as well) until she was spoken to. In this sense, she was a well-mannered child.

Fannie Lou was also farther ahead in her studies than the rest of the students her own age. And Professor Layne recognized that she was someone special. Fannie Lou thought Professor Layne, "was a good teacher, and she tried hard to learn all she could from him."[2] Fannie Lou liked hearing her teacher talk about his misadventures, personal struggles and life experiences. He was also quite amusing. Fannie Lou remembered Professor Layne as fair, happy about teaching, and consistent in his push for excellence from his students. Professor Layne wanted his charges to be the best, including Fannie Lou. She was grounded and could be outgoing when she wanted to be, but never demonstrative. And sometimes she could be annoyingly precocious. Fannie Lou was also buoyant, funny and opinionated.

Fannie Lou even imagined herself a school teacher. She also had vivid dreams of being someone important one day. Later, her enthusiasm waned because she wasn't allowed to complete her education. Her dreams were shattered because "she had to leave school, at the end of the sixth grade."[3] Fannie Lou had to work in the cotton fields on a full-time basis to help with her family's finances. She wished that she could have stayed in school and learned more, because Professor Thornton Layne certainly made a big impression on the young Fannie Lou. But it was not to be. She found out that there were things that she just couldn't control. Still, Fannie Lou continued to read on her own, especially from the Holy Bible.

Moreover, with very few resources, Fannie Lou tried to improve herself by reading old magazines, paper advertisements, and even outdated newspapers used as wrappings for cooked and perishable foods. Life lessons came easily to Fannie Lou. As mentioned, she had a hunger for learning, especially about the world outside the plantation. Additionally, Fannie Lou would never forget her studies and the important lessons she learned from Professor Thornton Layne. It was around this time that she also developed a gift for oratory. Fannie Lou forced herself to practice words, intensely and by rote. In this way she was able to remember much of the lessons and school materials — especially after dropping out of school. Nevertheless, as she grew older, and maybe because of bouts with depression, Fannie Lou would sometimes forget some of the heady things she had learned in school, like proper grammar.

In a recent study in the May 2009 *American Journal of Public Health*, it was found that minorities "who feel they've been mistreated because of their skin color are much more likely ... to have symptoms of mental disorders, especially depression."[4] Perhaps this was why Fannie Lou felt sad most of the time. But growing up in the Townsend family taught Fannie Lou that sometimes what they saw as a problem in life was just a challenge that could be overcome. And she would never chafe against her parents' moral teachings. More importantly, Fannie Lou wasn't able to pick and choose her life trajectories, especially as a dark-skinned girl, who dreamed bigger dreams than a hard life in the Mississippi Delta.

Although Fannie Lou was encouraged to read from her Bible, she could not pursue her education, or some other career, because of abject poverty. The Townsends did the best that they could under the circumstances but her parents told her that she had no choice other than to work in the cotton fields for the family's sake. Fannie Lou did what she was told because she was never a difficult child. Still, despite their best efforts to make things better, Fannie Lou and her family sometimes went to bed hungry.

Fannie Lou's parents eventually saved enough money to buy some farm animals, which would make their lives a little easier. James Lee spent his life savings on such things as "mules, wagons, cultivators, and some farming equipment."[5] The Townsends scrimped and scraped to get by, and purchasing these farm animals was supposed to make all the difference in the world in improving their family's standard of living. According to journalist Elton C. Fax, the Townsends were also able to rent some land; this too would afford them a measure of independence and success.[6] The farm animals presented a tremendous opportunity to increase the livelihood of the Townsends; with the new animals and farm equipment, perhaps their family could turn the tables. Unfortunately, James Lee and Lou Ella Townsend made the mistake of sharing their good fortune with others in the neighborhood — both blacks and whites. And their efforts to get a leg up were sabotaged because of racial jealously. Apparently, "a white man living nearby placed some poison in [their] animals' drinking water and killed them."[7] According to Fax, "Someone determined that they [the Townsends] would not 'get too uppity,' and put Paris green in their livestock's feed trough, killing their mules and cows."[8]

Fannie Lou always tried to focus on the positive side of things, but she just couldn't understand why someone would kill their favorite cow, Della, from which the Townsend children got almost all of their drinking milk.[9] How could someone be so hateful and mean?, Fannie Lou wondered.

But other black people had been down this road before. By that time, blacks were used to dealing with white racism. According to historian David Rubel, "White plantation owners often made up new rules to keep the blacks down.... [If] a black family began to raise some hogs for meat, the plantation owner would issue a new rule against raising hogs on the plantation. The [black] sharecroppers were thus forced to buy their pork at the high company-store prices."[10] White southerners always seemed to want to change the rules if the rules didn't favor whites in some way. After the deliberate killing of their farm animals, the Townsends struggled to get back on their feet. Indeed, the poisoning of their farm animals further eroded their family life, especially since they didn't have the resources to buy additional animals or pay for the seeds they would need for planting. It was an enormous setback. It was like Fannie Lou's family was being punished for some intransigence.

The Townsends could barely feed themselves, so they did not prosper. Clearly, Fannie Lou had a first-hand look at evilness. The death of their farm animals underscored the mistrust that persisted between blacks and whites. And "following the loss of the livestock, things were very tough for the Townsends."[11] Still, Fannie Lou's father and mother were imperturbable, as they would try to rebuild their lives regardless of what had happened, confident that they would somehow survive. And Fannie Lou's father never failed in his resolve until he was struck down by illness, perhaps as an indirect result of the animal poisoning incident. It was as if he couldn't come to grips with the fact that someone would do such an atrocious thing to his poor family. James Lee had taught his children that people, regardless of their color, were all neighbors and connected, and that they should love and respect one another. But it was hard for him to do either after someone killed his animals.

Fannie Lou often wondered why whites in Mississippi didn't have it in their hearts to treat blacks like human beings. Her father could only emphasize that what some whites did to blacks "wasn't right." Something was seriously eating at her father, however. He certainly was upset and angry about the death of his prized farm animals, until "his general health began to deteriorate" and he died from a massive stroke in 1939.[12] Fannie Lou Townsend's father often thought that he had only himself to blame for being trustful of white folk. It was a sad state of affairs. After Fannie Lou's father died, her mother, Lou Ella, lived a solitary life, as she was never interested in getting married again or having a relationship with another man. By then, Fannie Lou's mother's health also began to deteriorate rapidly.

But Lou Ella continued to work as hard as ever, as Fannie Lou Townsend's family continued to struggle. Gradually, and perhaps to the chagrin of Fannie Lou, the older children left home, one by one, usually in widespread directions to the North and West, scattered to the proverbial winds, seeking a better life and eager to begin their own families. It must have been hard for the Townsend children to leave their household, but many of Fannie Lou's siblings felt that the day had come to leave the fold after the death of their father. Fannie Lou stayed home while her siblings left, to help take care of their sickly mother. The love and support of her mother was always important to her, and Fannie Lou felt particularly comfortable with her mother around. It seemed that Fannie Lou subsumed her own need to care for her ailing mother, and her siblings appreciated that the young Fannie Lou would be there for her. Still, Fannie Lou was determined to become more than what others thought she could be. Fannie Lou looked after her beloved mother, "an invalid, until she passed away in 1961."[13] After Fannie Lou's father died, her strong mother became the sole provider for their family, working more like a man, "valiantly trying to make up the loss" of her husband. Apparently, a flying splinter had struck Lou Ella in the eye while she was wielding an ax, "an accident that eventually led to [her] total blindness."[14] Fannie Lou resolved, before her death, "to get something for my mother."[15] Unfortunately, Lou Ella died before Fannie Lou would become an important civil rights activist. But Lou Ella did see her youngest daughter secure a job as a sharecropper and timekeeper on a plantation she would eventually be fired from.[16] Because of their past experience, Fannie Lou had been taught by her parents to be circumspect when it came to white people. And she especially remembered this when she became a timekeeper at W.D. Marlow's plantation. Fannie Lou was a stickler for bookkeeping, and she had an impressive ability to remember and count accurately. It was a gift that the white plantation owner would recognize in hiring her.

Fannie Lou took on three jobs to support herself and her blind mother, without any help from her siblings, or anyone else for that matter. Fannie Lou "picked cotton ... [and] was a timekeeper, which meant that she kept the records of how many bales [of cotton] each worker picked."[17] Fannie Lou worked extremely hard for her ailing mother, who was still full of love and endurance, and dealt with her blindness. Maybe an eye operation or attentive medical care could have saved her mother's sight, or even extended her life; but they were too poor to afford the necessary medical procedures. Fannie Lou, however, made personal sacrifices to take care of her mother. It certainly wasn't a normal life for a budding young woman, but it was the one life that she knew.

When her mother finally passed away, Fannie Lou was devastated. She cherished the little time she spent with her dying mother, especially at the end. It took Fannie Lou a while to recover from such a loss, as Lou Ella Townsend was helping her come into her own. Indeed, Fannie Lou thought her mother was right all the time. How exactly could she live without her mother, who had made a vital and lasting impression on her during her entire life? Fannie Lou continued to work hard, constantly doing more and more, because she had always been afraid of failure. Unfortunately, at this particular time, Fannie Lou's understanding was that only if you were a white person could you get what you wanted out of life. Ultimately, Fannie Lou knew that she would have to use guile and cunning to get what she wanted.

5

Marriage, Eugenics and Adoption

It is important to reiterate that the history of eugenics in America was a time period that was something more that a little crazy. It is not difficult to understand what happened. Maybe we expect more of an explanation? We should at least demand elucidation on the part of surviving eugenicists. Or any answers must begin by first acknowledging that the American eugenics program happened, because it can never be erased from our inglorious history.[1]
— Earnest N. Bracey

In many ways, Fannie Lou never had a clear picture of what her life was supposed to be. But she tried to be honest with herself, and she always tried to deal with the reality of her sad and hard life. Also, it should be clearly understood that Fannie Lou didn't really complain a lot about the terrible conditions that still existed for blacks during the 1940s, even though she thought things were unfair and demeaning for people of color living in the Mississippi Delta. Still, Fannie Lou wanted things to be better for herself and her family. After the death of her father in 1939, Fannie Lou and Lou Ella continued to work to get the Townsends back on their tired and worn feet. Her late father had been the backbone of the family, and Fannie Lou had loved his company and wisdom, which became a big factor in shaping her young life. But now he was gone.

The days, months and years dragged by as Fannie Lou desperately waited for things to change for black people. But she finally realized that things wouldn't change for blacks until they stood up for themselves against the tides of discrimination and racial segregation. And as a young woman, Fannie Lou felt that she was without any sense of direction. One of the things that was lacking in her life was intimacy with another human being. She couldn't imagine being alone in her life forever.

But Fannie Lou didn't just want to live with a man. And she wasn't seriously looking for a husband. Her heart didn't rule her head. Fannie Lou, of course, was a practical black woman. As far as she was concerned, there was no time for fooling around. Fannie Lou was extremely shy around men (other than her fourteen brothers), especially when it came to matters of the heart. Of course, the young Fannie Lou was never a great looker. But she was not especially concerned about her looks. When it came to men, Fannie Lou just wanted companionship. Fannie Lou became attracted to a man named Perry "Pap" Hamer. Pap Hamer was considered bull-headed by some, and more than a little mean-spirited, but he certainly wasn't some cock-of-the-walk wise guy. Hamer knew how to survive, because he was a hard-working "tractor driver and share-cropper" outside of Ruleville, Mississippi, on the W.D. Marlow plantation.[2]

Fannie Lou thought of Pap as a bit of a suave rogue. He was also level-headed and had a pleasing disposition. The two often traded playful banter in the cotton fields. Pap could be something of a prankster, especially when he tried to endear himself to Fannie Lou. Moreover, Pap was willing to laugh at himself. Often, when her mother and Fannie Lou were planting a particular cotton field, Pap "would plow the row next to them, as fast as he possibly could, hoping to catch up to them,"[3] so that he could get a glimpse of Fannie Lou. At first, Fannie Lou gave Pap a hard time. She remained reserved because she didn't want to compromise the morals that were instilled in her by her parents. Pap would sometimes smile and try to get Fannie Lou to look at him. But most of the time she averted her gaze. Pap, besotted with Fannie Lou, persevered and ultimately found her to be the love of his life. Pap thought that Fannie Lou was one of the most loving women he had ever met.

Perry "Pap" Hamer was, more or less, a meat and potatoes man who loved life, no matter the hardships and difficulties. Indeed, he treasured the simple things, like taking a walk, enjoying the sun, and fishing on a hot summer day. Pap was very organized and precise in what he was trying to do — start a new life with a woman he cared for. And Hamer loved being around Fannie Lou. Fannie Lou fell in love with the good-humored black man, attracted not only to his easygoing manner (and the fact he wasn't a hard-drinking man), but also to his charm and intelligence.

Pap Hamer had been full of love for Fannie Lou for quite a while, even though he was a poor man. He had a big heart underneath his massive body, and inexhaustible energy. For Fannie Lou Townsend, who was in full flower, the very appealing Mr. Perry "Pap" Hamer would become the first and last man she would ever intimately know. Indeed, Fannie Lou gave her heart to Pap. But there were lines that Fannie Lou believed she should never cross before marriage. Fannie Lou and Pap Hamer were old-fashioned when it came to dating. Fannie Lou brought out the sensitive side in the hard-muscled Mr. Perry Hamer, who would become her husband. And she believed that sensitivity was an important ingredient in a good husband.

Fannie Lou and Pap married in 1944, when Fannie Lou was twenty-seven years old.[4] There wasn't a lavish wedding. It has even been speculated that it was only a common law marriage.[5] Chana Kai Lee, professor of history at the University of Georgia, writes:

> There is some confusion as to the exact date of their marriage. Some short biographical sketches of Hamer record a marriage date as early as 1942, and some document it as late as 1945. (Hamer often cited 1944, but there are no marriage records that document this claim.)[6]

Nevertheless, Fannie Lou and Pap were in love. Pap was the first man she had ever truly dated, and Fannie Lou became the center of his life. Pap was impressed by Fannie Lou's inner goodness and sense of humor, often noting that she was kind and compassionate, a great wife and mother to be. For her part, Fannie Lou was understanding of Pap's past indiscretions with other women, including a relationship that produced "a daughter by another woman at the time he began a serious courtship with Fannie Lou."[7] And Hamer made her feel good about herself.

Fannie Lou could have done a lot worse than Perry "Pap" Hamer, and by all accounts, she was happy with the arrangement. Apparently, the union worked like a charm, and they moved to another house on the W.D. Marlow plantation. Fannie Lou thought that her marriage to Pap would give her life purpose. Even more important, she couldn't wait to have children. Fannie Lou thought that Pap Hamer — tall and muscular, patient, kind and humble — was a good catch. The two adored each other.

When they set up house, Pap and Fannie Lou enjoyed each other's company above everything else, even though there were lean days. In later life, Fannie Lou would always credit Pap with her success in the civil rights movement, as well as attributing her happiness to him. Fannie Lou also praised Pap for his caring, understanding and patience (particularly given how often she was gone from their home in any given year). But she tried very hard not to talk much about her husband to the media. And as the years went by, Fannie Lou realized that the best thing that had ever happened to her was her marrying Perry "Pap" Hamer. Pap himself was averse to stepping in front of the cameras after his wife became famous, and he refused to bask in the light of publicity. Nonetheless, Pap would stand by Fannie Lou through thick and thin.

Unfailingly supportive to Fannie Lou in almost every way, Pap was her lover, friend, muse, confidante and confessor. Above all, he was a great listener. There were things about herself that Fannie Lou had been unable to change or talk about before — until she met Pap Hamer. Whenever Fannie Lou needed to get something off her worried chest, she would talk things over with her husband, who would often give her valuable and sound advice. In this regard, Fannie Lou and Pap Hamer were equal partners.

Pap provided Fannie Lou with a new home, but it was not substantial. According to Lee, "They had running water indoors (though no hot water), a bathtub, and an inside toilet, though it never flushed, so they still used an outhouse. This outhouse became a constant reminder of the indignities blacks faced."[8] In the end, Fannie Lou and Pap Hamer did well enough to survive.

The fetching Mr. Pap Hamer was attentive to Fannie Lou, as he remembered personal things that she liked, such as certain foods. Indeed, Fannie Lou had a legendary appetite. And Pap never let her want for good food to eat. June Jordan explained it this way:

> Life was different with "Pap." He saw to it that they always had food. He would do anything and everything to take care of his Fannie Lou. In winter he'd shoot rabbits and squirrels, so they would have meat to go along with the delicious hot potato salad that Fannie Lou whipped together once or twice a week. But they were still poor, and they were still living on a plantation.[9]

Pap had a sense of humor, and he made Fannie Lou laugh all the time with funny jokes and songs. And Fannie Lou thought that Pap Hamer was a big "softie." As far as Fannie Lou was concerned, there was never a dull moment with Pap. They were building their own life together. Surviving, however, wouldn't be easy, even as Fannie Lou kept her job as W.D. Marlow's timekeeper. Fannie Lou didn't make a lot of demands in life, but she did demand fairness, especially when it came to doing the right thing for the black farm workers and sharecroppers who had to bow and scrape when dealing with white land owners. Consequently, Fannie Lou covertly rebelled against the white plantation owner who "used deliberate miscalculations and various devices to cheat [black] sharecroppers who came to 'settle up' at the end of the cotton-picking season."[10] At that time the dishonest white Mississippi plantation owners often went unchallenged. Lee writes that Fannie Lou Hamer "began taking her own weighted instrument to the cotton field, and whenever the [white] landowner was not looking or had left the field momentarily, she added her own counterbalance to the scales so that workers got their fair share."[11]

This shrewd and audacious move on the part of Fannie Lou showed her independence and passion for fairness. But was it cheating? She was determined not to spend her life picking cotton on a plantation for next to nothing. Poverty always worried her, as it did her parents. And times were, to say the least, hard for them, as they were for every other black family in the Mississippi Delta in the 1940s. Pap Hamer, however, made sure that Fannie Lou was always comfortable, no matter what it took. In fact, Pap had his own liquor still for making illegal spirits. Of course, he felt that he didn't have any other choice other than to augment their meager income by making moonshine to sell. In other words, Hamer had to get involved in the unlawful liquor business to make ends meet. But Pap was not some hell-raising drunk or crazy hothead. He was primarily concerned about being a provider to Fannie Lou.

Later, when Fannie Lou took up the career of a civil rights activist, Pap Hamer loved her enthusiasm and energy. Fannie Lou was still able to make time for herself and her husband and later for her adopted daughters. Additionally, Fannie Lou might have never been a civil rights activist had it not been for her family. Pap had to deal with Fannie Lou's fame-related issues, and he pined for her when she was away from him at her many meetings, voter training sessions and civil rights events. But Pap would never talk about the rough spots in his long marriage to Fannie Lou. And over the years, and with all of Fannie Lou's absences because of her fight in the civil rights struggle, they stayed together. No doubt it was because Fannie Lou and Pap Hamer cared deeply about each other. Pap certainly liked the fact that Fannie Lou was so down-to-earth, especially when it came to matters of the heart.

When she did get pregnant, however, Fannie Lou worried about whether her pregnancy could be carried to term, given her poor diet, as well as her physical and mental health. But she kept trying to get pregnant well into her forties, having at least two pregnancies that resulted in stillbirths.[12]

Even into middle age the Hamers were unable to have a child, although they continued to try. In 1961, Fannie Lou Hamer was hospitalized for "a small uterine tumor"—a knot on her stomach, as she called it.[13] The non-cancerous tissue was supposed to be removed by "minor surgery." In fact, a white doctor "removed her uterus, so she would never be able to bear children."[14] Journalist Harriet A. Washington explained that "in the South, rendering black women infertile without their knowledge during other surgery was so common that the procedure was called a 'Mississippi appendectomy.'"[15] What happened to Fannie Lou Hamer was wrong, inexcusable. She had been robbed of her ability to bear children. And no one apologized for what was done to her, this sterilization without her consent. This affected Fannie Lou deeply. Fannie Lou was heartbroken, and her heart never really healed.

The forced sterilization of Fannie Lou was probably the most traumatic thing that had happened to her up to that point; and Fannie Lou was to stay an angry woman for a while. Washington writes:

> Some women, like Fannie Lou Hamer, were never told by their doctors that they had been sterilized, and others never found out. One of the few methodical surveys conducted revealed that at least 60 percent of the black women in

Hamer's native Sunflower County (Mississippi) unwittingly suffered postpartum hysterectomies.[16]

Although Fannie Lou could never reach her full potential in that she couldn't have the baby that she so desperately desired, she still knew that she was a bona fide woman. Therefore, the unauthorized and illegal sterilization of Fannie Lou was, in essence, her badge of survival. The treatment of poor women, especially black women, by medical facilities in Mississippi was repugnant. "It is crucial to remember that many of the black women, who were unknowingly sterilized, did not volunteer for these horrendous medical procedures. Indeed, these women were treated with utter disregard."[17]

It's a despicable thing that no one was punished, or even held accountable, for what they had done to her and other women, especially doctors violating their Hippocratic oath to "Do no harm." It was unconscionable and reprehensible what happened to black women like Fannie Lou Hamer, but no one was ever brought up on criminal charges. Did the hospitals in the Mississippi Delta who promulgated eugenic sterilization and the victimization of black women feel any shame for what they did? Probably not. As shocking as it sounds, white eugenicists thought that the sterilization of minority women was perfectly acceptable. But such inhumane measures can never be accepted or justified. In the final analysis, Fannie Lou "was one of many poverty-stricken African American women whose inability to have children was against their will."[18]

Ultimately, Pap and Fannie Lou Hamer decided to adopt. Indeed, they "realized after a period of time, that they would never have children, and they were saddened by the knowledge. But when the opportunity presented itself, they took in a child...."[19] Fannie Lou and Pap adopted two adorable little black girls named Dorothy Jean and Virgie Ree. Later they were given the Hamer last name. Apparently, Dorothy Jean was adopted because she was born to a single mother who was "too poor to care for her."[20] Her adopted daughters became precious to Fannie Lou. Fannie Lou stated that Virgie Ree, "the younger girl was given to her at the age of 5 months. She had been burned badly when a tub of boiling water spilled, and her large impoverished family was not able to care for her."[21]

Fannie Lou Hamer also recalled that when she took Virgie Ree in, "We had a little money so we took care of her and raised her. She was sickly too when I got her, suffered from malnutrition. Then she got run over by a car and her leg was broken."[22] Fannie Lou, of course, could empathize with her younger daughter's leg wound, because she too suffered a similar injury. Indeed, she was thoughtful and tender towards her daughter, as her motherly instincts kicked in. But Pap and Fannie Lou tried to treat the two girls equally, and as their own.

The relationship between Fannie Lou and her adopted children was heartwarming. And she was grateful for the opportunity to have children, even if they were not biologically her own. Fannie Lou became their rock, so to speak, in a complex and racist society; she was their anchor in the world. When all was said and done, Fannie Lou felt blessed to have her two adopted daughters. And they were able to thrive under the tutelage of Fannie Lou and Perry "Pap" Hamer, who were the only parents they would ever really know. Meanwhile, Fannie Lou continued to work hard.

6

Apartheid in Mississippi

The South's adoption of extreme racism was due not so much to a conversion as it was to a relaxation of the opposition. All the elements of fear, jealousy, proscription, hatred, and fanaticism had long been present, as they are present in various degrees of intensity in any society. What enabled them to rise to dominance was not so much cleverness or ingenuity as it was a general weakening and discrediting of the numerous forces that had hitherto kept them in check.[1]

— C. Vann Woodward

Mississippi during the 1940s through the 1960s was a closed, racist and *myopic* place where white people, ignorant in their separateness, controlled everything. White Mississippians, of course, used whatever rationalization they could to justify segregation and racial inequality. Like the *Dalits* of India, black people in the Mississippi Delta were treated by whites as if they were *untouchables*. Renowned economist, Marendra Jadhar writes that in a "system of graded inequality, the *Dalits* were so inferior that their mere touch was believed to pollute others. They were denied human rights and were forced to scrape together a living from denigrating chores.... [And] they were powerless to change their caste-based social status."[2] Black people were treated similarly in the Mississippi Delta, as they were viewed with repugnance and disdain — for no other reason than the color of their skin. Whites in the state wanted the black population to accept things without question, including abiding by "white rule." But this would never do, especially for Fannie Lou Hamer.

Whites had an almost resolute and ineradicable hatred of blacks. And in most cases, the feeling was mutual. White southerners could not recognize persecution when it was happening to blacks, so invested were they in their selfish and prejudiced beliefs, and the unrighteousness of their white supremacist purpose. It would be hard to exaggerate the pain and misery black people experienced at the hands of the dominant group in Mississippi. Many blacks in Mississippi questioned the insane arrogance of whites, as they created an untenable political climate that made it extremely difficult for black people to live their lives. White southerners' deep hatred of blacks was learned through their socialization. Not surprisingly, some whites in Mississippi were under the misapprehension that blacks were smelly, dumb, ignorant, and no-good low-lifes. This wasn't true, of course. But this misperception about black people was held by many whites because this was what they were taught to believe by parents and family members.

It was one of the things that baffled Fannie Lou Hamer, this total lack of compassion for blacks on the part of white people in Mississippi. Many whites in the state also conveniently forgot the fact that blacks were American citizens too. Moreover, the contemptuousness of whites, as they spat out words like "coon," "nigger," "monkey," "gorilla" or "darkie," was shameful. The scorn was palpable. Dehumanizing blacks with derogatory labels made it easier to abuse, denigrate and even kill members of the black community. Furthermore, blacks were considered, even at this period in time, to be subhuman and often treated like animals. Fannie Lou once commented that blacks in Mississippi were "treated worse than dogs!"[3] Fannie Lou Hamer, of course, didn't care if her opinions about white injustice hurt the feelings of white people in Mississippi. She was also on the same wave length as the other blacks in the Delta who were hoping for a better life, which actually exacerbated the long-standing tension between blacks and whites in Mississippi. Indeed, the white community was numbingly ignorant of racial matters, as these things did not directly touch their lives.

There is no way of getting around the fact that, fundamentally, many whites in Mississippi thought blacks were cursed in some way. It was a nightmare of white racism, as the white community thought of black people as ignorant beasts of burden. Their deeply ingrained racism was a characterization of that time and place, because the racial divide in Mississippi was not only acceptable, it was the order of the day in the 1940s and 1950s. It was very much like the situation in South Africa at the time, where racial discrimination was acceptable to the general white population. Black journalist Mark Mathabane explained such a racist and segregated society in this way:

> [Segregation] meant hate, bitterness, hunger, pain, terror, violence, fear, dashed hopes and dreams. Today it still means the same for millions of black children who are trapped in the ghettos ... in a lingering nightmare of a racial system that in many respects resembles Nazism. In the ghettos black children fight for survival from the moment they are born. They take to hating and fearing the [white] police ... and authorities as a baby takes to its mother's breast.[4]

Some whites even believed that blacks had no one to blame but themselves for their predicament. And there was no one to protect black people from the racism, hatred and ignorance of fearful whites in Mississippi. Moreover, some whites in Mississippi were uninterested in, or unmoved by, the human suffering of black people. And many scrupulously avoided the black community, as blacks were ultimately viewed as threatening and disruptive to the social order of the day (i.e., "white supremacy"). Many also felt, as we shall see, that educated blacks were always plotting and scheming to undermine their "white rule." Whites swept legitimate concerns of blacks under the rug. Whites in the Delta did not care about the broad, social consequences of their harsh and abusive rule. In other words, white Mississippians had "amnesia" for the concerns of its black citizens. It certainly reflected poorly on the state of Mississippi.

Admittedly, some whites were sensitive to the concerns of blacks and were respectful of their different culture and lifestyles. Indeed, some fairminded whites showed a willingness to listen to the concerns of blacks living in the Delta, as they believed in the humanity of mankind. But quite simply, it was unimaginable for most whites to extend a hand in brotherhood to blacks, lest they risk their own lives. Some whites had no idea what to do. Fannie Lou Hamer looked forward to the day when black people would be considered equal to whites, which at that time seemed like an impossibility. She also wanted whites to start looking at racial matters in a different, more favorable light; but that wouldn't come until much later. Of course, Fannie Lou Hamer believed that black people deserved honor and respect, too.

Blacks knew how things were in the Delta. Black parents "trained their children in the cruel realities of Delta life"[5] — they were at the mercy of hateful and racist forces that they could not predict, control, or do anything about. As children, blacks were well aware of segregation. And Ruleville, Mississippi, was a polarized, racist and isolated place, like many other small Southern towns. To be fair, some whites in Mississippi were ignorant of the mistreatment of black people, or they chose to ignore such unpleasant things. But white Mississippians demeaned themselves every time they accepted Jim Crow racism. Blacks had been made to suffer at the hands of the dominant group, and the white community as a whole was complicit in doing nothing to help the situation, even as they paid lip service to the myth of fairness and equality in Mississippi. It was obviously untrue. Some whites in the state believed that black people were all ignorant, and needed to be humbled before whites and put in their so-called place. Indeed, the notion that blacks were inferior and simple-minded was so pervasive among whites that they couldn't think of *anything* else regarding black people. "White rule" and white supremacy was deeply entrenched.

It was as if white Southerners had a total and absolute disregard for humanity, or at least the humanity of blacks. Their unwarranted and selfish feelings were inappropriate by any standard of human decency. Blacks in Mississippi were subjected to every kind of public humiliation, including murder and incarceration and the rancorous goings on in the state of Mississippi went unchallenged. It is therefore necessary to analyze and critique the dominant system of "white rule." Indeed, the history of inequality in Mississippi is a long and sordid story that must never be forgotten. Fannie Lou was of the belief that black folk must never turn a blind eye to what was going on around them. Blacks in the South only wanted to live in dignity, decency and respect, not as some brutalized animal. Whites in Mississippi were unable to truly understand black people, as there was no common ground on racial matters.

Blacks, however, could see that their freedom was being denied, as white folk put up roadblock after roadblock to stall the pace of political changes for blacks. All in all, Mississippi was a racially divided society that fostered an intolerable environment for black people. And whites terrorized and short-changed blacks politically and economically, so that they could have absolute control over the lives of the people in the Delta. Blacks didn't even have the right to complain. Whenever blacks said anything in protest, whites in the state of Mississippi refused to listen. The injustices going on in Mississippi were ignored by almost everyone in power. But Fannie Lou Hamer did not accept the racist Mississippi caste system of the time. Indeed, she was of the belief that people had a responsibility to others, to do right by everyone, no matter what ethnic group one belonged to. Fannie Lou Hamer would also come to believe that "the decision to fight against the humiliations of Jim Crow stemmed in no small measure from the feelings of guilt at having been so passive under the weight of oppression."[6]

Invariably, there was tension between the black and white communities, as the racism was dangerously overt. And white racists made no bones about their Jim Crowisms. Indeed, their obnoxious behavior knew no bounds. It was as if ignorant white people chose discrimination as a lifestyle, and racism as their battle cry. It was their skin color that gave them their entitlement. Thus, the opportunities made available to blacks were limited. Furthermore, blacks were trapped by unfair social conventions that forbade them from participating and speaking their minds. And the division between blacks and whites was extremely deep. W.J. Cash in his classic book *The Mind of the South* writes: "The South's perpetual need for justifying its [racist] career, and the will to shut away more effectually the vision of its mounting hate and brutality toward the black man, entered into the equation also and bore these people yet further into the cult of the Great Southern heart."[7] White privilege had for many years blinded white Mississippians from clearly seeing the injustices and inequalities imposed on the black population.

Fannie Lou felt that everything under the sun was possible if you didn't give up on pursuing your dreams. She remembered her parents telling her again and again that they would prevail, no matter what the circumstances. This echoed constantly in her mind as she assessed the economic scene and political landscape of Mississippi during the late 1950s. For segregationists, keeping blacks and whites apart maintained the status quo. Therefore, white leaders used a "divide-and-conquer" strategy against poor whites and poor blacks to keep them apart and racially compromised. In this way, poor whites were separated psychologically as well as physically, as many didn't want blacks to compete with whites or be completely incorporated into the larger white society. As C. Vann Woodward wrote in his provocative book *The Strange Career of Jim Crow*, "The black ghettos of the 'Darktown' slums in every Southern city were the consequence mainly of the Negro's economic status, his relegation to the lowest rung of the ladder. Smaller towns sometimes excluded Negro residents completely simply by letting it be known in forceful ways that their presence would not be tolerated."[8]

So poor whites in Mississippi came to believe that blacks were inferior too. Indeed, they had no problem spitting in the faces of black people while hurling insulting epithets. Blacks in the Delta had it drummed into them that they were not the best, and therefore not entitled to be a part of the dominant or ruling class. Many poor whites turned a deaf ear to the truth concerning blacks in Mississippi because of segregation policies. This is to say that whites viewed blacks in Mississippi through a totally different prism in terms of race. How blacks were treated by the white power structure was mostly hidden from the public. Many whites in Mississippi believed that blacks had no rights, and *in*equality reigned supreme.

A former governor of Mississippi, the late Theodore Bilbo, once made the racist comment that interracial relationships would corrupt the white race "with the blood of Africa, then the present greatness of the United States of America would be destroyed and all hope for the future would be forever gone."[9] What rubbish. But many whites in Mississippi believed this racist drivel. Some whites in Mississippi even believed that equal rights for blacks would undermind the very fabric of white society. It was essentially an "us-against-them" mentality, as many whites in Mississippi during the 1950s were trafficking in xenophobia. Nevertheless, Fannie Lou Hamer thought that treating people like human beings should have been a matter of basic decency. Perhaps it was presumptuous on her part to think that whites and blacks would automatically embrace each other when the truth of their existence was revealed.

The idea of racial superiority and segregation was rampant in the white community. Segregation was something that was unspoken, however, acknowledged by whites, as if everything was right in the world. Things in Mississippi, however, were not right, especially in the Delta. Segregation was a "suffocating hand" for black people, and blacks were often on the receiving end of white anger and mob violence. Former civil rights activist and historian Roger Wilkins described the legacy of segregation this way:

> [It] was the lasting humiliation thrown up by the enormous backlash mounted by Southern whites against blacks and white Northern "carpetbaggers" at the end of Reconstruction. Outraged at blacks participating in politics, serving in high office, and participating in law enforcement, the South struck back with a vengeance. A reign of terror ensued, carried out by such vigilante groups as the Ku Klux Klan and the Knights of the White Camelia. Blacks also knew that in many places Southern white law enforcement was often intermingled with, and indistinguishable from, these anti-black [and white] terrorist organizations, or from old racist thugs.[10]

Segregation was judiciously enforced. Whites supported segregation without blinking an eye and with overwhelming zeal. Whites in the state had immediate control of blacks and their lives, creating a repressive political system in Mississippi that personified racial hatred and unadulterated evil. It was whites' fervent belief that it was necessary to treat dark-skinned people in such an inhumane manner to keep the "nigger" in his so-called place. Indeed, some of the existing laws at the time were so arbitrary and unfair to black people, called Negroes at the time, that it was hard to believe. For instance, blacks in the South and in Mississippi couldn't be caught in a white neighborhood after a certain time — unless they were the domestic help — upon pain of imprisonment or even death. In an autobiographical sketch entitled "The Ethics of Living Jim Crow," the great black writer Richard Wright recounted:

> Negroes who have lived in the South know the dread of being caught alone upon the streets in white neighborhoods after the sun has set. In such a simple situation as this the plight of the Negro in America is graphically symbolized. While white strangers may be in these neighborhoods trying to get home, they can pass unmolested. But the color of a Negro's skin makes him easily recognizable, makes him suspect, converts him into a defenseless target.[11]

Some whites in Mississippi were closed-minded. It seemed almost nothing could change their hostile hearts. Fannie Lou Hamer wrongly believed that whites would treat her in the exact manner that she treated them; but there would never be found a happy medium between her and the white community in the state. She also believed that the judgment of whites about blacks was distorted because of their skin color, as she would come to believe that the concept of race was just a social construct.

Clearly, the United States has a history "steeped in [black] slavery, [and] terrorism by groups such as the Ku Klux Klan,"[12] and the very real fear (for blacks) of being lynched. Therefore, many blacks in the Delta were fearful of such despicable hate groups as the Ku Klux Klan and the Knights of the White Camelia because they were prone to violence against black people. Perhaps this trepidation sent a subconscious message to Fannie Lou Hamer: Her skin-color made her suspect and different. But she and other blacks were still sentient human beings. This notion that blacks are human was *not* necessarily shared by some whites in Mississippi, who thought their right to control was preordained.

Moreover, the death of many blacks in Mississippi at the hands of whites highlighted the problems of violence (with impunity) that continued to plague black communities across the South well into the 1960s. The important fact to remember is that absolutely nothing happened to many white terrorists/ racists, who literally got away with murder — usually involving lynching. The noose is indeed a symbol of racism. David L. Hudson, Jr. writes that the "noxious hangmen's noose depicts the horrors of racial violence perpetrated against African Americans." Hudson goes on to point out that "the noose not only symbolizes racism, but [it] also served as the actual murder implement for the lynching of people because of the color of their skin."[13] Usually the case against black men in Mississippi who were summarily lynched amounted to little more than small infractions or false accusations, or sometimes nothing at all. One has only to read the late Julius E. Thompson's book *Lynching in Mississippi: A History, 1865–1965* to affirm the validity of this assertion.[14] The Ku Klux Klan also staged mock (and sometimes real) lynchings throughout the South — including Mississippi — to frighten black people. They also lynched black men just for the fun of it. Of course, whites in the state didn't think blacks would do anything about it. Indeed, for the longest time, white politicians and people in power thought that blacks would not fight back because they were stupid and defenseless. It seemed the government of Mississippi turned a blind eye to such crimes as lynching, and failed to track down and prosecute those who murdered blacks. According to Anmelise Orleck, "Between 1930 and 1950, Mississippi had thirty-three reported lynchings of [black] citizens — a number that is almost certainly an undercount."[15]

Many white racists in Mississippi saw lynching as an answer to their "Negro Problem." Fannie Lou Hamer wanted whites to examine their own conscience and ask themselves if what they were doing was right and just. Unfortunately, many were secure in their prejudice and delusion, with no concern for the lives of black people in the state of Mississippi. Some white men, for example, suffered from delusions about black men wanting to rape all white women, which was nonsense. White Southerners, especially in Mississippi, always tried to rationalize their violence and evil actions. Journalist Scott Poulson Bryant writes that whites "needed a monster (the black man) against which to measure their own monstrous actions."[16] Whitfield points out that "interracial assault was the one crime that seemed to arouse bestial fears and primordial passions in otherwise law-abiding Southern white citizens."[17]

In any case, whites in Mississippi did not want to be reminded of their sins of injustice not only against blacks, but also against those who supported the black community. Furthermore, some white people in Mississippi desperately wanted to deny their racial hatred. They even became offended when someone pointed out their racist ways. Or they tried to refute the very existence of racism and discrimination. White leaders and politicians in Mississippi tried to downplay what was going on in the state. Indeed, many were remarkably uninterested in black people if they couldn't benefit from their labor in some way. In the final analysis, there was no real human connection between blacks and whites, because many did what was consistent with the drumbeat of racial hated, cruelty and vengeance. According to Kate Tuttle, lynching was based on "the sexual fears of white society," and it was to become "entirely a Southern, racial phenomenon."[18] Accordingly, "extreme brutality with which many lynchings were carried out" usually took place deep in a Southern forest; perhaps the black victim's neck was stretched taut with a thick noose before the heinous end, as the individual cried out with a blood-curdling scream, for help, for mercy, for God. Moreover, "It was not uncommon for lynching victims to be castrated. Many were burned alive." Tuttle goes on to write that "other common tortures were to have their eyes gouged out, their fingers severed, or their teeth pulled out — with the white lynch mob taking home various body parts as souvenirs."[19]

This sort of racial hostility and racist cruelty couldn't have come as a surprise to anyone who knew exactly what was happening in Mississippi. Indeed, as Whitfield writes, "Such Fierce acts of white violence [such as lynching] were putatively designed to secure a social order anchored in race and to affirm that the black criminals deserved whatever fiendish punishment the righteous could inflect."[20] But it must be clearly understood that white "mob execution was really about social control, not crime control."[21] Fannie Lou Hamer was sad that some whites had deluded themselves into thinking that blacks were inferior. But she never wished them bad luck for all their crimes and misdeeds, nor was she resentful of whites. Though changing the racist policies of Mississippi seemed at first an impossible challenge, as time passed, the racist apartheid system in Mississippi gave way to something else, something fairer.

Of course, blacks in Mississippi still have historical grievances against whites to this day. During the 1950s and 1960s, many blacks in the state were hateful and resentful of whites, psychologically traumatized, mentally dangerous, and emotionally paralyzed. Fannie Lou Hamer often commented that she would not rest until Mississippi had a democratic process in the state. "Obviously," as Professors Heribert Adam and Kogila Moodley write, "democratization, accompanied by political equality [even in Mississippi] for all citizens and the promise of greater material justice, can lay the foundations for a more stable and less violent political order."[22] Fannie Lou Hamer would come to understand the unbearable weight of black people's grievances against whites in the state.

7

The SNCC Comes to Mississippi

As an SNCC worker, Fannie Lou [Hamer] was smart, down to earth, a great speaker of sharp logic, a Scripture-reciting Christian, a singer, and a galvanizing field organizer.[1]

— Kennell Jackson

The fears of black people were exacerbated by accounts of blacks being terrorized by white hate groups. Black people in the Mississippi Delta had little recourse at that time. According to Kim Rogers, professor of history and American studies at Dickinson College, blacks "reported accepting the seemingly inevitable hardships such as poverty or the ill-health of family members."[2] But many were tired of banging their heads against the wall. Little did whites in Mississippi know that the racial and political landscape was slowly changing. Blacks in the state began speaking out about the challenges in finding ways to survive. At this time in the 1960s, Fannie Lou Hamer was not grandiose about it, but she knew that things didn't always have to be the way they were. As a child, Hamer had tried to make sense of it all. As an adult, she would try to make things right for blacks. Nevertheless, many black peoples' woes continued, as many lived in isolation and poverty. As Professors Joyce Allen-Smith and James B. Stewart point out, "The heavy concentration of rural blacks in specified areas, notably the Mississippi Delta and the Black Belt, [had] its roots in plantation agriculture and the systems of slavery and sharecropping that provided a cheap input, labor."[3] Unfortunately, as Stewart and Allen-Smith go on to write, many blacks in the Delta remained in these "impoverished areas because migration would not necessarily result in improvements in their economic position."[4] Furthermore, the Mississippi Delta was one of the nation's poorest rural areas.

Some blacks in the state of Mississippi were so poor that it was shameful they lived in the United States. The hard work put in by blacks could mean almost nothing for those living in the Delta. There was little gratitude or reciprocity on the part of white land owners towards black workers. Psychologically, economically, socially and politically, blacks in Mississippi were bankrupt during the 1960s. By then, as mentioned, Fannie Lou Hamer had married Pap, and had been abused by white eugenicists in Mississippi who had knowingly sterilized the great woman, and had become an adopted mother. A good mother to her adopted daughters, Dorothy Jean and Virgie Ree, Hamer, at the age of around forty, had plenty of life experiences at this time and was wise beyond her years.

Hamer and her family, from sunrise to sunset, did back-breaking work in the cotton fields of Mississippi for little pay and less appreciation. They continued to struggle in poverty. However, armed with the strong conviction that she could change things, she was now prepared to ask herself an important question: How long would it take for blacks in Mississippi to achieve equality, freedom and *parity* with whites. Of course, Fannie Lou Hamer wanted to give her adopted daughters the best life possible, but there were extraordinary racial barriers that held black people back. And Fannie Lou Hamer wanted to instill in her adopted daughters the idea that a little bit of kindness went a long way, no matter your social or economic status. But there were the constraints of white society imposed on blacks in the Delta. Indeed, black people were reminded of their low-class status every day.

It would be tempting to imagine that blacks were accepting of their second-class citizenship, but this assumption would be incorrect. The inexplicability of white racism was perfectly acceptable to the white community, however, because for them it was the natural thing to do — that is, segregate people along ethnic lines. But such actions required the suspension of logic, equal rights, convention, freedom and human righteousness. And the elimination of terrifying brutality by whites, as well as racial progress, was painfully slow in coming. Indeed, during the segregation era, white authority didn't buckle quickly. But the political climate would shift dramatically in the coming years in Mississippi.

Fannie Lou would not accept that the lives of her family — and blacks everywhere — would amount to nothing. Mississippi became a microcosm of the human condition concerning blacks and race throughout the United States. What exactly did black people do to white Mississippians that was so wrong, so damning, so awful or terrible? Blacks felt that their freedom and liberties were being sabotaged by some white people for no good reason, as they had to deal with extreme poverty, racism, discrimination and segregation. Fannie Lou Hamer would later learn that working against the forces of white racism wasn't for the faint of heart. Many blacks in the Delta found only heartbreak and despair.

Without any political power, blacks were unable to organize any large-scale demonstration at that period of time. Equally important, black people in the Mississippi Delta lived in fear because they never knew what might happen. This is to say that blacks, in Mississippi and elsewhere, felt general distrust for local government and other white organizations. And nothing could disguise the fact that they were treated in a lousy or despicable manner in Mississippi. In truth, most blacks in the Delta just couldn't understand why they were being treated in such disrespectful and hateful ways.

Some whites in Mississippi didn't like the idea of changing their southern way of life. Nor did they want to give up their sense of entitlement. But many whites didn't see it that way. Nevertheless, there were major disparities between the incomes of blacks and whites. Blacks lived in wretched, third-world conditions. And the lot of blacks worsened appreciably under "white rule." Moreover, the ignorance of black people inculcated by some whites was profound. And many whites were complicit in their marginalization of black people. It was a time of persistent segregation, as many blacks lived in squalor and isolation. Black people in Mississippi also feared white government reprisals. Fannie Lou and Pap Hamer and their two girls, like other blacks, had to tread a very fine line.

This sad situation is important to point out because many blacks in the Mississippi Delta were harassed at every opportunity, with obstacles deliberately put in their way. Maybe whites were under the delusion that blacks were happy with their lives. This was not true, however. Or some whites wanted blacks to be blissfully ignorant and accepting of their sad existence. It was outrageous, disastrous, and incomprehensible. Fannie Lou Hamer once stated that "life was worse than hard. It was horrible."[5] In other words, during the 1960s, blacks had descended into a state of economic depression across Mississippi. Furthermore, blacks resented whites in the state for dominating politics, the economy, and society in general. As one can perhaps ascertain, many whites had developed more than a bit of an entitlement complex. Certainly life in the Delta was worse for blacks than it was for whites anywhere in Mississippi. Question: How could whites in Mississippi stand face-to-face with a black people who acutely suffered violence and racial exploitation without really acknowledging such things ever occurred in the state? In this respect, many whites in Mississippi didn't want the truth to be told about how blacks were treated. Indeed, politicians of that era didn't want controversial racial issues to be highlighted under any circumstances. Nor did white political leaders want people outside the state of Mississippi to know the exact conditions. They were particularly sensitive to any comments about their racism. White politicians wanted only sanitized accounts of race relations and what was actually going on in the state. They were adept at dodging the difficult questions about race. White leaders in Mississippi, therefore, tried to sugarcoat what blacks were going through because of their unscrupulous actions and racist shenanigans.

Moreover, their insincerity and hypocrisy knew no bounds when it came to dealing with the black community. Whites in Mississippi often hid or disguised their true feelings when they were confronted by the media. By not saying anything to the media, whites were able to further their segregationist agenda, which insured their continued "white rule." White Southerners wanted to hear positive and poetic things about their rule instead of the truth.

Nevertheless, some white police authorities in Mississippi talked about how they handled unruly Negroes. They would go after those blacks who dared challenge the status quo. Some black men were sent to prison at Parchman State Penitentiary in Mississippi, sometimes for no other reason than they might have been disrespectful towards whites. After all, "Mississippi is famous for a past of police brutality, and for sure harassment, even death, of those who [would] defy the code."[6] Whites harshly suppressed dissenting blacks who bucked convention. Furthermore, police authority did what they wanted to do to black people, regardless of whether it was right or wrong. It was what made race relations in Mississippi so tenuous and trying during the 1950s and 1960s. Over several decades, some awful, hurtful things happened to blacks in the state of Mississippi. And although some whites did express their abhorrence of white racism, most whites in the South *never* really experienced racism in its ugly, unadulterated form. Even more important, many whites in Mississippi disregarded any and all historical understanding about how the brutalizing of blacks (by whites) played a profound part in the racist culture of the state.

Therefore, blacks lived in a world which was unnecessarily scarred by white racism, where the unthinkable could happen at any time to blacks living in the Mississippi Delta. And the demagoguery, hateful diatribe and fear-mongering by white politicians only fueled the fire. White political leaders knew full well that things were not equal for blacks. Indeed, many white politicians in Mississippi refused to address the black community, because facing them meant confronting the inequality and racism meted out by whites. Most of the white governors of Mississippi, for example, during the 1940s through the 1960s were fiery segregationists. Many laced their election speeches with racist rhetoric. And their hostile words were infectious in the white communities throughout the state. Members of the Ku Klux Klan assaulted blacks with impunity, with not only words but real violence, inspiring other white cowards to commit hate crimes galore, like house bombings, beatings, lynching and murder. Because blacks were maltreated and dehumanized, many never even dreamed that they could escape the Mississippi Delta.

Whites in the state took an astonishingly narrow view when it came to radical changes to their entrenched beliefs about equal rights. To change things, it was going to be extremely difficult. Those who fought against "white rule" and oppression paid the consequences. Still, black people in Mississippi showed great courage in the face of immense repression by whites, as many blacks never imagined that whites wouldn't be open enough to even consider racial changes. This would have meant that whites would have to make some fundamental changes in their attitudes toward blacks, because white racism ran deeper than the ideals of peace and racial equality. Also, white racists often worked themselves into a *frenzy* of racial hatred and misunderstanding, all caused by their fears and ignorance of black people. Finally, many blacks in Mississippi had no political voice. The state government should have played a more active role in helping black people, who, through no fault of their own, were experiencing extremely hard times.

Although Fannie Lou Hamer was taught by her parents to turn the other cheek and not to hate, "She did learn to keep an angry fire in her at those who thought that by keeping another human down, they might elevate themselves."[7] Fannie Lou wanted to know how she could help ameliorate some of the terrible effects of poverty, especially for black people in the Delta. She also wanted the white state politicians to step up to the plate and change things for blacks in Mississippi for the better. But perhaps this was an impossibility. Fannie Lou was tired of blacks being pushed around by whites so much. But she wasn't closed-minded about things, and was able to look at racial issues from a different point of view. Of course, Fannie Lou Hamer knew that blacks in the state of Mississippi at that time had a very narrow set of choices and opportunities. According to journalist Foster Davis:

> Hardship [had] long been a fact of life for the Negro in the Mississippi Delta. Typical housing [was] an unpainted shack with one leaky stove and no inside water or other plumbing. The [black] children often had bad teeth and swollen bellies. Such conditions [were] so commonplace that they [tended] to go unnoticed even among the Deltans who consider themselves concerned about the plight of the Negro farmhand.[8]

Blacks in the Mississippi Delta continued to struggle with poverty, unemployment, discrimination and racism in the 1960s. Such matters certainly violated Fannie Lou's sense of fair play and justice. Indeed, just surviving was no longer enough for black people in the state, she thought. But many blacks were ignorant about their rights. Perhaps there was something she could do about it. Of course, Fannie Lou Hamer had a widespread familiarity with black people in the Delta, so she could relate to almost anyone. And many liked her because she was honest and reliable. Fannie Lou Hamer was also of the belief that blacks were being taken for granted. She always wanted to look the problem of race relations squarely in the eye. As noted, the system of political power in Mississippi was rooted in white, European culture, where whites wouldn't give black people a second thought, especially when it came to providing equal rights. In so many words, "Most of the black people" in the state "were afraid to try and vote."[9] But if you had asked whites in Mississippi at that time — the 1960s — they actually believed that black people didn't even want to participate in politics. For example, a former governor of Mississippi, Ross Barnett, a white man and rabid segregationist, "repeatedly claimed that Negroes just didn't wish to vote," and that they could have voted if they had so desired.[10] None of Barnett's sentiments were true, of course, as will be demonstrated later in this book. In fact, Barnett's assessment was an outright lie. Historian Chris Myers Asch writes that "whites economically and physically harassed blacks who advocated voting rights."[11] And according to writer and poet June Jordan, "These were some scary times: in Mississippi."[12] Indeed, whites in the state of Mississippi were shockingly unfair in their overall treatment of blacks, especially when it came to registering to vote. And ensuring that blacks in the state could vote was all that really mattered to Fannie Lou Hamer.

Perhaps this was when she became interested in politics. Fannie Lou Hamer made friends easily, despite the fact that she was in her late forties by then. She was also able to inspire a kind of camaraderie among blacks. And the genial, quick-witted Fannie Lou Hamer didn't want to hold back if she thought she could do something for black folks. She also wanted to shock blacks in the Delta out of their lethargy, never imagining that her life was about to change forever. Indeed, Fannie Lou would eventually become a noted civil rights activist, as she was very good at swaying people to her way of thinking about things. Fannie Lou Hamer absolutely understood the frustrations that blacks were going through. Moreover, she felt that she had something important to impart. Hamer was prepared to act, to become a dedicated civil rights activist. But for most blacks in Mississippi, her abilities were not so apparent then. Still, she was eager for the new challenges to come. As Fannie Lou Hamer once commented, "But this white man who wants to stay *white*, and to think for the Negro, he is not only destroying the Negro, he is destroying himself, because a house divided against itself cannot stand and that same thing applies to America."[13]

In the past, Fannie Lou Hamer never really tried to make her feelings known to many people; but her loved ones and relatives knew full well how she stood on things. At that time, Hamer was at the cusp of morphing into a new black leader; later she would wield a lot of political clout. It was going to be a hard road ahead for blacks in Mississippi. However, Fannie Lou Hamer was taught never to give in to her fears. Therefore, she decided not to sit by and languish in obscurity. Hamer was planning to be seen and heard as much as possible.

When Fannie Lou Hamer heard about a meeting that would be held at a local church in 1962, it piqued her interest. Her curiosity was aroused by the very notion of a bunch of black civil rights men from the Student Non-violent Coordinating Committee (SNCC) and SCLC speaking openly and boldly about the civil rights of blacks in Mississippi. Until that time, Hamer had never *heard* of a mass meeting, and "didn't know that a Negro could register and vote."[14] She was certainly interested in what the young black activists, like James Bevel and James Forman, had to say. Indeed, Hamer was extremely impressed by everyone around her at that meeting, from the lively debate conversation, and the appeal from the black civil rights workers, to the way they looked and carried themselves. Hamer was beginning to believe that she, too, could make a difference. She had a high regard for these young black men, who were the *crème de la crème* of black activism in the civil rights movement, as she listened to and admired their pitch about citizenship, participation, and registering to vote. It was a beautiful thing. Hamer was flabbergasted and proud. These SNCC members were possessed by ambition and responsibility. And most of all, they had ideas about what to do that went beyond what black people thought was possible. So the mass meeting at the church was "about getting black people to register and vote that had been organized by two civil rights groups," the Southern Christian Leadership Conference (SCLC) and the Student Nonviolent Coordinating Committee (SNCC, pronounced *snick*).[15]

These "freedom-fighting organizations joined together to change Mississippi"[16] for the better. Fannie Lou Hamer ultimately wanted to find a way to contribute in a positive manner to the black freedom movement. Besides, Hamer had decided that it was time to try something different from picking cotton. In all honesty, Hamer just wanted to see what she could do, which was enormously important in helping her later achieve her goals. According to freelance writer Laura Baskes Litwin, the "SNCC appealed to Hamer for two basic reasons: It was concerned with the needs of ordinary citizens, and it believed that these citizens could and should make political decisions for themselves."[17] Fannie Lou Hamer was deeply impressed by these young civil rights activists. Besides, it was time for her to get serious about her ambition.

The young black activists would certainly point her in the right direction. So while she listened to these handsome, young, intelligent black men from the SCLC and SNCC at "a church down the street from where the Hamers lived in Ruleville, Mississippi,"[18] the activist seed was planted in the mind of Fannie Lou Hamer.

8

A New Political Activist

She tackled the job with a chaotic seriousness. She was a one-woman dem-
olition squad, since babyhood. She was Joshua at the Battle of Jericho, David
facing big Goliath. She seemed to think that fences, like straw men, were
constructed for her to bring to the ground. A kind of therapeutic calisthenics.
From birth, the child was some kind of a claustrophobe, whose theme song
might very well have been "Don't Fence Me In."[1]

— John Oliver Killens

At the time Fannie Lou Hamer attended her first "mass meeting," blacks
in Mississippi, especially in the Delta, were still suffering from a legacy of
racial oppression. Indeed, black people faced many particular challenges, such
as a lack of food, money, human dignity and respect from whites in Mississippi. Blacks also had difficulty paying off their sharecropping debt and health-
care issues. The root causes were poverty, isolation, the lack of access to high
paying jobs and education. Many, of course, were on the outside looking in
on all the riches and opportunities of many whites. Blacks today are still pessimistic about their futures because of this legacy. Whites in Mississippi during
the 1960s used fear, violence, fraud, repressive tactics and the threat of death
to control black people. They also used disingenuous measures to stifle black
dissent. It could even be posited that black people in Mississippi during the
early stages of the civil rights movement suffered from post-traumatic stress
disorders, given the frequency of deaths from untreated mental diseases.

The idea of social equality was considered an educated black man's disease. Whites did not want to cede power. Of course, whites in Mississippi in
the early 1960s did not care about the consequences of their decisions and
harsh actions against blacks because "segregation itself had not yet been out-
lawed by the federal government."[2] Many whites accepted the general view
that blacks were somehow less than human. But black people were undeniably
human beings. It was mind-boggling, the attitude of some whites. Such things
infuriated Fannie Lou Hamer.

61

Unscrupulous white men took advantage of uneducated black people who were extremely poor and less fortunate. White leaders certainly didn't pay enough attention to the concerns of blacks in Mississippi. And their racist thoughtlessness was creating unnecessary problems with the black communities. This is not to say that every white person in the state was a vicious racist or basically bad; but there were some vital differences. For example, whites in Mississippi knew that if you break the will of a people, you neutralize their ability to fight back. And whites in the state had enough power and authority to say what and how things should be done.

Fannie Lou Hamer was beginning to realize that there was no place for her and other blacks in the white Mississippi world. And because of these barriers, blacks and whites in the state could not live together. There were two different worlds — a black one and a white one. In his understanding of the white world, the great black writer from Mississippi, Richard Wright, once wrote:

> The words and actions of white people were baffling signs to me. I was living in a culture and not a civilization and I could learn how that culture worked only by living with it. Misreading the reactions of whites around me made me say and do the wrong things. In my dealing with whites I was conscious of the entirety of my relations with them, and they were conscious only of what was happening at a given moment.[3]

Fannie Lou Hamer felt the same way as the late Richard Wright regarding her relationship with whites in Mississippi. The palpable polarization of blacks and whites reflected the hard reality of racial prejudice. But the only obvious thing that differentiated blacks from whites was hair texture, and eye and skin color — *not* intelligence. Deeply religious, Fannie Lou Hamer firmly believed that God had a plan for black Americans.

Black people in Mississippi were finally at the point where they were forced to react against the white power structure, which generated mutual anger, conflict, and racial hatred at all levels in the community. Blacks had decided that they would not be silenced anymore. Still, black people continued to face difficulties. Indeed, blacks sought civil rights and equality in what they thought was a so-called democratic society. Civil rights actually pertain "to positive acts of government designed to protect persons [especially black people or minorities] against arbitrary or discriminatory treatment by government or [racist] individuals."[4] But government policies in Mississippi failed to protect *all* of its citizens.

Many whites in the state just couldn't embrace the idea of black people having the same rights as whites. So it was a good thing that the Student Nonviolent Coordinating Committee (SNCC) made its presence known in the state of Mississippi. The SNCC felt compelled to do something so that black people could empower themselves. Indeed, the "SNCC was different from the other civil rights groups for another crucial reason: It was the only one brave enough to take action in Mississippi."[5] Some blacks were fighting amongst themselves too, which the SNCC tried to ameliorate and resolve. Fannie Lou Hamer would come to respect the SNCC because she believed that "it was the only organization that did the hard work that had to be done in Mississippi."[6] The SNCC was not afraid of white terrorists and hate groups in Mississippi. According to Emily Stoper, young members of the SNCC "chose to concentrate their crusade against injustice in the rural counties of the Deep South, especially [in] Mississippi," mainly because "Mississippi ... had a reputation as the most racist state in the union.... Also, little work was being done there by other black groups, mainly because of the white terror."[7]

Fannie Lou Hamer was intrigued by the young black civil rights activists from the Student Nonviolent Coordinating Committee, such as James Bevel, John Lewis, Robert Moses and James Forman, who "all got their starts in political activity during the [renown] sit-ins."[8] The fact that black people were being denied their Constitutional rights, as well as their right to assemble and vote, enraged members of the SNCC. Professor Clayborne Carson wrote:

> SNCC staff members brought into the organization diverse attitudes drawn from their increasingly varied backgrounds, but at the same time a growing radicalism began to emerge from their intense involvement in the Southern black struggle. Day-to-day interactions with each other and with politically awakened blacks in communities with SNCC projects made staff members more willing to look to their own experiences in the struggle as a source of alternative values.[9]

The politics of Mississippi was definitely primed for change. However, things wouldn't improve for blacks unless there was a dramatic alteration in people's attitudes and the political environment. Moreover, organizing for change made some blacks highly nervous, as they were suspicious and full of trepidation. Some blacks even had the temerity to believe that the SNCC were leading them literally to slaughter, because "white Mississippians had a long history of 'taking care' of 'uppity' blacks who attempted to transgress sacred racial boundaries."[10] So, "being associated with [the] SNCC was dangerous,"[11] especially for black civil rights workers. But that fortuitous meeting in a local black church outside of Ruleville, Mississippi, set Fannie Lou Hamer on the path to becoming the great woman she eventually would become. It was at that time that Hamer glimpsed her future. When she arrived on the topsy-turvy scene, Hamer certainly enlivened the debate about black freedom and voting rights. And she helped establish and build the civil rights coalition in the state, from the ground up. According to journalist and science writer Harriet A. Washington, Fannie Lou Hamer "might easily have endured the life of quiet desperation dictated by her birth, then vanished without a ripple."[12] But such a dismal and dismissive life was not to be for someone like Fannie Lou Hamer.

Given the opportunity to become a civil rights activist and community organizer, Fannie Lou Hamer could not turn the job down when Bevel encouraged her to join the Student Nonviolent Coordinating Committee (SNCC). For half of her adult life, Hamer was content to sit in the background quietly, doing nothing, while others led the way. But not any more, as she finally decided she no longer had to suffer in silence. Therefore, "Fannie Lou Hamer became involved with the Student Nonviolent Coordinating Committee almost from its beginning."[13] But Hamer's efforts at that time consisted not so much of speaking out as of listening, especially at the beginning of her career as an activist. She became particularly interested and impressed when she heard talk of such courageous and daunting issues as guaranteed rights for all American citizens — something unheard of in the Mississippi Delta of that day. She was perhaps in awe of the serious young black men from SNCC. And these young leaders were very savvy. These shrewd members of SNCC changed Hamer's life, leading her to realize the importance of something greater than herself.

By joining the civil rights movement in Mississippi during the 1960s, Fannie Lou Hamer firmly believed she would achieve a greater understanding and appreciation for what these young SNCC members were doing for the cause of freedom, as well as what they were actually going through in terms of fighting racial discrimination on the front lines. Hamer, no doubt, believed that the people from SNCC were some of the greatest leaders she had ever encountered.[14] These SNCC members knew more about what it took to mount a successful protest against white supremacy in Mississippi than anyone. Given their wide experience in the ways of the real world, Hamer once commented, "Don't go telling me about anybody that ain't been in Mississippi two weeks and don't know nothing about the problem, because they're not leading us."[15] Fannie Lou Hamer was impressed by the black civil rights leaders, and even humbled by the presence of so many great people. And Hamer wanted to be on the same page as these black men from the SCLC and SNCC. Indeed, "the pitch of the [poignant] speeches," by the SNCC members, "stirred something in her (Hamer), though she had never seen a copy of the Constitution of the United States, nor that of Mississippi."[16] The SNCC made plain their position about black people utilizing their rights, civil liberties, and American citizenship. Perhaps Fannie Lou Hamer was like a fish out of water, but she certainly understood that the SNCC was game to fight for blacks against the "dreadful pockets of oppression throughout the South."[17]

At first, however, Fannie Lou Hamer had no idea about what to do with herself. Of course, she never had her career all mapped out. Later, she would come to believe that being an activist was what she was meant to do. She felt that she had the responsibility to effect changes in Mississippi. And, "seasoned by a society that systematically ... denied the Negro ... a right to self-assertion," Fannie Lou Hamer and other black women "had to take the lead in the struggle for dignity, as well as survival."[18] The intrepid members of SNCC were looking for someone bold enough to take the reins of the movement in Mississippi and run with it. And they didn't have far to look in Hamer. Hamer was plucked from semi-obscurity by calculating members of the SNCC to become the voice of the civil rights movement in Mississippi. They would have been hard pressed to find someone better. And the young black turks of SNCC liked the fact that Hamer demonstrated dedication and exactitude.

Fannie Lou's keen powers of observation and ability to pay attention to the little things made her an excellent choice. Equally important, she had practical wisdom. And her outstanding people skills were second to none. The SNCC leaders were extremely impressed with Hamer's personal story and experiences, which were deeply embedded in a world filled with gut-wrenching poverty, as well as her local knowledge about black people in the Delta. Moreover, the SNCC members were impressed with Hamer's off-the-cuff analysis of the racial situation in Mississippi, especially her knowledge of the layout of the surrounding towns and territory near Ruleville. She also knew the many black families in the area who feared the very act of voting because of white terrorism. Indeed, Hamer was at the right place at the right time, as her popularity among her peers was on the rise.

SNCC members Bevel, Forman, Lewis and Moses knew Fannie Lou was a very hard-working person. And like many black activists before her, she would bring to the table her considerable, albeit inelegant, communication skills. They also selected Hamer because many SNCC members lacked the necessary insight on how to deal with black people in the Delta. Fannie Lou knew from experience how to talk to ordinary black people in the region, which was expecially important when blacks starting registering en masse to vote. Hamer would eventually become their guide, as she wanted to console and direct them, like a modern-day Harriet Tubman. Hamer showed tremendous leadership potential. The confident SNCC leaders welcomed Fannie Lou's steadying input and influence. Many thought that she was the right black woman to do exactly what was needed — to energize the civil rights movement in Mississippi.

Of course, Fannie Lou Hamer did experience moments of self-doubt and inadequacy. At first, as Hamer thought about it, she needed more experience; nor did she know the proper activist etiquette. More importantly, she knew that the smart, young black men from the SNCC knew far more about civil rights than she. At the beginning of her activist days, Fannie Lou Hamer believed that she was insignificant when it came to the civil rights movement. She also realized that the responsibility would be extremely heavy, and being an effective activist would be the challenge of a lifetime. But in her heart, Hamer knew that she could do it, even though she didn't have the same pedigree or credentials as the young black leaders, some of whom had college degrees. Hamer would find her voice, however, while choosing her own way.

Fannie Lou was willing to commit herself totally to the civil rights movement. She thought long and hard about it, and decided it was in her best interest to become involved. And she was ready to stand by her convictions. Hamer knew that she would be doing something to help black people in the United States and Mississippi. Hamer was the kind of hard-charging woman who would roll-up her sleeves and pitch in with whatever needed to be done. She also wasn't bothered with what people thought of her, because Fannie Lou Hamer had a job to do. And she tried to put her best face and efforts forward as a newly-minted civil rights activist. Being an activist in the movement fired her imagination, as it allowed Hamer to reinvent herself as a champion for people who could not help themselves. The black leaders of the SNCC recognized Hamer's potential, and Fannie Lou Hamer would never let the SNCC down.

Although joining such a radical movement might have sounded intimidating in the very beginning — even a frightening challenge — Hamer was able to conquer her fears because she intuitively knew it was the right thing to do. She also had a real sense of her place in the scheme of things. Moreover, she had enough faith in her abilities to carry on. The SNCC transformed her life. Hamer's efforts would not go unnoticed by the white community, and soon she would incur the wrath of white racists in Mississippi. She would be later subjected to a barrage of harassment and death threats, including drive-by-shootings perpetrated by white, terrorist groups. Hamer was subject to many acts of terrorism by hateful whites who attacked anyone who dared question the status quo. Indeed, from the moment "Mrs. Hamer became an active worker for SNCC, mostly doing voter registration and literacy training jobs ... she was a prime target of white terrorists."[19] Whites were so upset with Hamer's activism that they arrested her husband and older daughter, while charging a $9,000 water bill to their house, which "didn't even have running water."[20]

Often using threatening actions and words to deter and dissuade the black community, some white Mississippians sincerely believed that black people were too ignorant to fight the status quo, and that they (blacks) were overreaching. Therefore, whites thought that blacks in the state would eventually back down from their budding protests. But as they (whites) would soon learn blacks in Mississippi would mount an unstoppable movement that would eventually change the way things were done. Fannie Lou Hamer believed in the inevitability of racial justice, and the idea that white racists would one day face a reckoning before God for their crimes and inhumane actions. In this regard, Hamer once angrily stated:

> This white man who is saying, "It takes time." For three hundred and more years they have had "time," and now it is time for them to listen. We have been listening year after year to them and what have we got? We are not even allowed to think for ourselves. They tell us, "I know what is best for you," but they don't know what is best for us! It is time now to let them know what they owe us, and they owe us a great deal.[21]

9

Voting Rights and Freedom Summer

Ninety percent of the Negro people in Mississippi have gone to church all their lives. They have lived with the hope that if they kept "standing up" in a Christian manner, things would change. After we found out that Christian love alone wouldn't cure the sickness in Mississippi, then we knew we had other things to do.[1]

— Fannie Lou Hamer

Being a civil right activist in the cause of black American rights, Fannie Lou Hamer vowed that her priority would be to stand fast against the racist onslaught of whites in Mississippi or elsewhere. Of course, Hamer was privileged to be part of a non-violent movement that would change things for black people. She was confident. Indeed, Hamer would discover (by her involvement) one great thing after another — and then something even better: Black people had *heart* and *courage*. Fannie Lou knew that you could not know what blacks were thinking without talking to them. But she didn't wish in any manner to impose herself on other people. Nor did Hamer want to get into any trouble criticizing other black people. Many were afraid and distrustful, and didn't want to upset white people. But obviously what Fannie Lou Hamer had to say to blacks was not meant to be disrespectful. She tried to tell things to those she disagreed with in a quiet, diplomatic way.

Fannie Lou Hamer often caused a commotion, but she was a down-to-earth Christian who counted her blessings every day. She had learned a great deal, and applied her home-style knowledge with all the profundity necessary. She would become a very diligent, determined and dedicated field operative for the SNCC. Hamer, by becoming personally and publicly involved in the "movement," did great things for the black community by raising awareness about the plight of blacks in the Mississippi Delta. Fannie Lou Hamer would work tirelessly in many rural counties in Mississippi, speaking directly to blacks to get out the vote. Charles McLaurin, who had volunteered to work for the SNCC in Ruleville in the summer of 1962 by setting up voter registration drives, remembered seeing the stocky Fannie Lou Hamer getting off a rented bus that was charted to take blacks to the courthouse in Indianola, Mississippi, to register to vote.[2] According to McLaurin, when the other black people, totaling eighteen, "from the plantations around Ruleville," were afraid to exit the vehicle, Fannie Lou Hamer bravely "stepped off the bus and went right on up to the courthouse and into the circuit clerk's office."[3] This type of boldness was typical of this burly black woman. It was then that McLaurin knew that Fannie Lou Hamer was special — and fearless — as she walked into a wretched den of angry whites who condemned this insubordination.

According to black Mississippi writer Anne Moody, most "old plantation Negroes had been brainwashed so by the whites, they really thought that only whites were supposed to vote."[4] But Fannie Lou Hamer's brazen nature often emboldened others, generating unwavering support. For some whites, it might have been fashionable to suggest that the time wasn't right for desegregation and integration, but Hamer didn't buy into such nonsense. She was able to push voting rights and racial equality to the political forefront, without giving it a second thought. Hamer refused to knuckle under to the white establishment. The biggest hurdle, perhaps, was persuading a fearful black population to go out and register to vote.

But Fannie Lou Hamer didn't try to manipulate black people for some self-serving purpose; no, she prodded blacks out of their political slumber for their own good. These were times of piercing fear, anxiety, sadness and danger. Hamer could be tough-minded and extremely clever when it came to civil rights involvement and strategy. The idea was to show black people in Mississippi that they had the right to vote in any election if they so chose, as granted by the Constitution. As a field worker for the SNCC, Fannie Lou Hamer "traveled the cotton fields by day and spoke at churches by night, recruiting others to register to vote."[5] According to Professor Molefi Kete Asante, Hamer's job was "to help register as many [black] people as possible."[6] And she was uniquely positioned to do so. In this regard, the "SNCC's work [was] done almost exclusively among the poorer and more deprived [black] people of the rural South."[7]

It should be pointed out that the average SNCC member was "a veteran of many civil-rights campaigns," unlike Fannie Lou Hamer, and many were in their "early or mid-twenties."[8] Most young people who wanted to be a member of the SNCC could do so "only by becoming a full-time member of its staff, which just about [meant] taking an oath of poverty."[9] According to the famous black sociologist Louis E. Lomax, the SNCC "operated on a budget of fourteen thousand dollars in 1961 and [was] out to raise thirty thousand

for its 1962 program."[10] Accordingly, in the mid–1960s the average SNCC
staffer got "between $20 and $35 a week in subsistence pay, although some
[were] bud-geted for $10," like what Fannie Lou Hamer was eventually paid.[11]
Hamer, of course, was a take-charge person who assumed responsibility for
everything she got involved in. But there were times when she was barely
paid. Hamer once proudly commented, "I worked for SNCC even when they
didn't have any money."[12] This showed absolute commitment on the part of
Fannie Lou Hamer, as she and other SNCC workers, "spurned all the trappings
of affluent America."[13]

During the 1960s, Hamer was determined to help make Mississippi a
better place, "where black people would be just as free as white people."[14]
Along the way, Hamer learned to talk to blacks in Mississippi, developing
specific tactics, and different angles and strategies during spare moments
"in the Mississippi countryside or on the weather-beaten porch of a shack
in a Southern ghetto."[15] She had a willingness on her part to dive into the
midst of things, without batting an eye, which would later help others.
She also had the ability to sway others to her way of thinking; and her honesty
and righteousness would serve her well. As an activist, Fannie Lou Hamer
conveyed strength and integrity, because working for the SNCC allowed
her to shed her doubts and insecurities that held her back from achieving
greatness. She obviously was maturing and learning how to become a
good activist. And yes, Hamer was willing to stick her neck out. Aside from
that, she obviously understood poverty, frustration, hopelessness and desperation.

Fannie Lou Hamer was focused, disciplined, relentless, and ultimately
ruthless when she needed to be. Indeed, Hamer had her mind set on what
she wanted to do as an activist, which was to push black people in Mississippi
out of their complacency. She didn't try to ingratiate herself to anyone either,
especially white folk. Nor did she tip-toe around the real issues, like race and
the human condition. And Hamer didn't care about platitudes. She once
stated:

> So many rumors have got out about me that you would think I was King
> Kong. A lot of people say I advocated violence. I've never been violent, you
> know, never in my life. But if I know I'm right you don't stop me. Now you
> might kill me but you will not stop me from saying I am right.[16]

Hamer believed that you either fully participated in the freedom movement, or you didn't. She certainly had *chutzpah* and demonstrated enormous
courage as she worked to expand the rights of blacks. Hamer became a uni-
fying focal point for civil rights for blacks in Mississippi. Things began to
fall into place, as the movement gave Hamer the ability to move forward in

her life. Hamer, of course, was a big influence on her young associates. She was able to help younger activists take the movement to the next level. Laura Baskes Litwin writes, "[Hamer] was older than many in the organization, and the students respected her wisdom and experience. They always addressed her as 'Mrs. Hamer.'"[17] Fannie Lou wanted to engage in public service earnestly and with humility. In this way, Hamer became a hard worker who pulled her own weight in the SNCC organization. Ultimately, she wanted to do something worthwhile and to challenge herself.

Hamer had a ferocious interest in things. And she was fastidious with details. All of which was grist for her expanding and important activist mill, so to speak. Fannie Lou Hamer was never a disappointment to the black community. And she was eternally optimistic. Indeed, Hamer was never discouraged, even during the dark days of the Freedom Summer in Mississippi. According to Asante, Hamer became "the symbol of courage, resistance, and defiance of the white South."[18] Hamer would be placed among the greats in the civil rights movement.

Some might say that Hamer had an oversized personality. Fannie Lou Hamer proved that she was as good or better than other black intellectuals and activists that made up the ranks. She also brought a unique perspective to the civil rights cause. Moreover, her demeanor as an activist was noticeably different. Politically, Hamer knew what she was talking about, but she could also be righteously concerned with peripheral issues, such as religion and living a moral life. Many of the black leaders Fannie Lou Hamer associated with had lived a far more varied life than she had. But Hamer wasn't embarrassed by her lack of sophistication. Besides, she thought highly of these young, black, educated people. But she brought energy and dynamism that many in the movement couldn't match. Hamer drew strength from the SNCC, which "was a tight band, which defined itself in the theological language of 'beloved community' and redemptive suffering."[19] Nevertheless, not everyone in the black community was enamored of the civil rights group. The late Roy Wilkins, from the National Association for the Advancement of Colored People (NAACP), for instance, "did not want to spend [registration] money through SNCC, which he considered irresponsible, and certainly not through SNCC in Mississippi, which he considered an NAACP state."[20]

Members of the SNCC's Mississippi delegation, nonetheless, were spending a lot of time wracking their brains to find easier ways to lead and help black people register to vote. Journalist Norm Fruchter, however, concluded that the SNCC should not have been able "to *lead* local people, or impose leadership, solutions, programs on them, but should [have] become the tool by which local people [could] begin to transform, and control, the organizations and institutions which presently dominate[d] their lives."[21] The SNCC, nonetheless, continued work and agitated with the local people in Mississippi. Fannie Lou Hamer never felt anything negative about her beloved SNCC organization. She was passionate about people and what she was doing. And Hamer seemed entirely comfortable in her own black skin. Being a part of this unique group showcased more of what she could do as a field-worker. Fruchter goes on to write that the SNCC accepted what seemed

> to be organizational confusion stemming from a refusal to utilize bureaucracies, hierarchies of responsibility, and all the mechanisms of rationalized decision-making, and an inefficiency which [seemed a] nightmare, because it [was] concentrating all its energies on reducing the gap between organizers and local people, and [attempted] to translate its own embryonic organizational structures into institutions which [evolved] out of local communities and [met] local needs.[22]

In the final analysis, the SNCC was still effective in recruiting blacks to register to vote. And "although the organization persuaded thousands to join the civil-rights movement, it encountered lethargy, and at times bitterness, from Negroes who had worked out at least a tenuous accommodation with the white man."[23] Some blacks felt desperate and hopeless, as well as psychologically crushed. Many blacks in Mississippi rejected the organization, because they felt they shouldn't have to make any more sacrifices, considering what they had been through. But blacks had long memories in Mississippi. And Hamer had met so many different black people along the way with their own unique struggles. Their hopes floundered almost every day as the years went by. Hamer showed a remarkable poise and maturity as she pushed hard against the almost impenetrable barriers of white racism and discrimination. Fannie Lou Hamer was able to make her presence known throughout Mississippi in a very short span of time. As an activist, she seemed to be making up for lost time.

Hamer decided to fight on, even when she didn't receive a salary from the SNCC, and even though she knew black people may *never* become entirely free. Besides, Hamer had a superstitious fear of being stuck on the Marlow plantation for the rest of her life — that is, had she not begun "traveling through the [Deep] South as a spokesperson and fund-raiser for SNCC."[24] Members of the SNCC were hoping that their actions might deal the final blow to white supremacy in Mississippi. Fighting against the tide of racial hatred was probably the hardest thing Hamer had ever done. But she wasn't intimidated a bit. Fannie Lou Hamer was "a devout Christian. [And] there were no niceties about separation of religion and politics for her, not even any fine lines of theoretical distinction regarding separation of church and state."[25] She also firmly believed that "doing what was right was doing what God wanted."[26] Without a doubt, Hamer knew that what she was doing was right. Many SNCC members appreciated her straightforward manner. Significantly, many of these black leaders would champion her, as they respected Hamer's incredible strength and iron will.

Fannie Lou Hamer won accolades for her work as an activist from the overall SNCC membership. She never hesitated in jumping into the fray. By this point, she had become well versed in the art of negotiation and racial cooperation. Furthermore, Hamer would use her intuition and gut instincts to handle political matters. Her increased exposure only whetted her appetite to become more involved. Hamer felt an unprecedented sense of legitimacy working for the civil rights movement and the SNCC.

Fannie Lou Hamer was energized by the civil rights movement in Mississippi, and later she energized others. She would no longer accept the role of victim, as her ability to speak out enabled her to finally do some things that advanced her ideas of equality and freedom. And serving as an activist gave Hamer a new confidence in herself and her judgment. And to her great delight, Fannie Lou Hamer was accepted as a true player in the fledgling civil rights movement in Mississippi. Hamer felt that John R. Lewis, when she finally met him, was a force to be reckoned with. Lewis was in his late twenties, slim, and with a head full of hair at that time in the 1960s (in contrast to his bald pate later in life). Lewis, along with other black college students, was one of the founding members of the Student Non-Violent Coordinating Committee (SNCC) in April 1960.[27] Hamer was thoroughly impressed by Lewis, who inspired real camaraderie through his cooperative spirit, especially among SNCC field workers. Lewis was definitely a man with a plan; and he knew that Hamer would become a very useful person. Fannie Lou Hamer, like Lewis would "join the Freedom Rides that the Congress of Racial Equality (CORE) sponsored ... to protest segregation," especially "at interstate bus terminals" throughout the South.[28]

Lewis, just like Fannie Lou Hamer, would be "assaulted several times during" their "protest activities." But they both continued to put their lives on the line for "a worthy cause," while practicing direct action and non-violent methods.[29] Fannie Lou Hamer and John R. Lewis had to work extremely hard to accomplish what they did. About Lewis's involvement in the civil rights movement, Professor David L. Chappell had this to say:

> Lewis's almost legendary willingness to get up after repeated jailings and beatings and go back for more is hard to account for without ... faith and conviction. Partly because of his battle stripes (there was a nonviolent macho in SNCC, where jailings and hospitalizations were tallied as badges of honor),

Lewis [eventually] became chairman of SNCC in June 1963, a post he held through the organization's most productive years until his [resignation] in 1966.[30]

As an older man and a survivor, John R. Lewis would go on to become a U.S. Representative from Georgia.

Some blacks were brutalized when they became bold enough to demand their right to register to vote. But black people in the Mississippi Delta were not dumb. They certainly could think for themselves. Fannie Lou Hamer knew that whites in Mississippi thought dissimilarly to blacks when it came to equality and the Constitution. Unfortunately, many whites thought that black people should be exterminated if they didn't abide by the wishes of whites.

Perhaps they were afraid. According to Elton C. Fax, "Outnumbered Mississippi whites became alarmed" because many wondered if these descendants of former black slaves would "take over the political and economic control of the state? And, after that, would they [blacks] not repay in kind the ill treatment they had received?"[31]

Hamer would eventually become the field secretary of the Student Non-Violent Coordinating Committee (SNCC). While she served in this capacity, "voter registration drives added thousands of new black voters to the rolls, virtually all of them Democrats"[32]— much to the chagrin of whites in Mississippi. Perhaps the biggest factor that increased the registration of blacks in the voting rolls was the selfless actions of students during Freedom Summer. That summer "volunteers came from all over the United States to register Mississippi's black population." Many of these volunteers were "mixed, in part because it was believed that violence against a mixed group would attract more attention than against an all-black group."[33] Later, this unique strategy "proved all too painfully accurate."[34] Historians Darlene Clark Hine and Kathleen Thompson put it this way:

> When white activists Andrew Goodman and Michael Schwerner and black activist James E. Chaney were found murdered, the press raised a huge outcry, and white sympathy in the country in general swung dramatically away from the white supremacists. The degree of violence the black people of Mississippi faced that summer of 1964 was horrifying. There were one thousand arrests. Thirty-five people were shot. There were eighty beatings, thirty buildings bombed, and three people ... were killed.[35]

It was extremely important to let the American people know what was happening in Mississippi in 1964, as many were out of touch with the dire straits of blacks in the state. As far as Hamer was concerned, it was long past due that blacks be given their voting rights. And she wanted to focus her attention and energies on activities where she could make a difference. Probably no one at that time shared her level of courage and commitment. Of course, Hamer had always been a spiritual, praying woman. She went to church as often as she could. Only that was not enough. Mississippi in the 1960s was an ugly place for black people. And this history can't be hidden or glossed over.

10

Enfranchisement and Training

Consciousness raising was at once a recruitment device, an initiation rite, and a resocialization process aimed at transforming group members' perceptions of themselves and society.[1]

— Nancy Woloch

Clearly, in the state of Mississippi there were "different standards of justice meted out to whites and blacks."[2] And for a while, it became almost impossible for black people in Mississippi to demand their Constitutional rights, including voting and the right to assemble. It was a ferocious power struggle between blacks and whites in the state. More importantly, "Whites often frightened and confused the local blacks, who had difficulty transcending an ingrained sense of inferiority and fear in their [whites'] presence."[3] But what many whites in Mississippi thought was a sense of inferiority was really a recalcitrant hatred by blacks for whites who had control over almost everything. According to Professor Susan Johnson, "Blacks had no other feasible alternative than to accept the Mississippi way of conducting their political affairs. Only in this manner could they gain the most within the system without having any political power."[4] Fannie Lou Hamer knew that black people had to create their own paths toward equality. Blacks from all quarters were taking a real interest in politics. And something was in the wind with regards to making social and political changes in Mississippi possible, which would prove beneficial to blacks in the Delta and elsewhere in the United States. However, according to Johnson, "Mississippi, like most other southern states, excluded blacks from positions of decision-making in all institutions, initiated the poll-tax bias in voting requirements, and used a variety of tactics to dissuade blacks from participating in the electoral system."[5]

With the tense racial atmosphere in Mississippi during the early 1960s, troubles for black activists in the state had only just begun. The time for change had come for the burgeoning civil rights movement. It must be clearly understood that "White officials in Mississippi had been doing everything they could to prevent black people from voting — especially poor black people like Fannie Lou Hamer."[6] And the same thing was happening, to varying degrees, across the nation. By this time Fannie Lou Hamer had discovered her niche. Hamer wanted to open the eyes of the nation to the terrible effects of poverty on the hearts and minds of black people. She felt like she had an obligation to tell people, especially black people, what was going on with their constitutional rights. Eventually, as the situation in Ruleville, Mississippi, became more volatile and dangerous, Hamer had to move away from her home.

In point of fact, white supremacists "relied upon violence as a potent weapon of intimidation to deprive Negroes [or blacks] of their rights."[7] According to former black activist Robert F. Williams, white officials in Mississippi "brazenly [slapped] themselves on the back for being successful in depriving great numbers of their [black] citizens of the rights of first-class citizenship." Whites in power were "determined to stay the hand of progress at all cost. [And] acts of violence and words and deeds of hate and spite rose from every quarter."[8] Nevertheless, Fannie Lou Hamer was a woman in constant motion. Her strategy was to get poor black people out of their homes and into the streets to protest and participate. Civil disobedience was something she advocated. Instinctively political, Hamer would follow her own personal convictions in getting blacks to register to vote in Mississippi. It was a notoriously tumultuous time for black people in the state. Fannie Lou Hamer wanted very much for blacks and whites to do the right thing. Indeed, Hamer was desperate for everyone to be nice — and non-violent. However, "Racial tensions escalated during the embittered summer when registration drives among blacks were at their peak."[9] And with her vast knowledge of the black community, Hamer's mission was to do whatever was necessary to help the movement, and to be there for other members of the black activist resistance.

Hamer was of the belief that all men and women were "created equal under God and that the privileges of citizenship must not be denied because of race, color or creed."[10] But Hamer also understood that white supremacists would never fully embrace such a lofty concept of racial harmony and togetherness. Being an activist meant that her job would have its downside.

Yet, to Fannie Lou Hamer's way of thinking, there was no task too difficult for her. It was a transformative time in her life. And Hamer was in a position of political prominence. In many ways Hamer became an expert community organizer. Hamer wasn't afraid of anyone. It was her defining characteristic. And although she didn't have any formal grooming for her leadership role, she wasn't ignorant about organizational matters. Hamer had stick-to-itiveness and was always willing to face controversial things head on.

She was certainly conscientious and committed to planning strategies for change and registering blacks to vote in elections in Mississippi. Fannie Lou Hamer was finally able to register to vote herself, but it had not been an easy road. According to Jessie Carney Smith and Linda T. Wynn, Hamer was "convinced that African American powerlessness was largely due to fear of white retributions." Therefore, Fannie Lou Hamer "tried unsuccessfully to pass the voter registration test" in Mississippi, in 1962.[11] Hamer remembered that she was unable to pass the convoluted, discriminatory and "infamous Mississippi literacy test" the first time because she didn't know anything about the state constitution of Mississippi. According to Colman, "Before people could register they also had to pass a literacy test, which meant that they had to 'read and interpret' the state constitution to the satisfaction of ... a white official who registered people."[12] Fannie Lou Hamer warned the white registrar at the courthouse in Indianola that she would come back every 30 days for the rest of her life until she passed the literacy test.[13] When Hamer returned after thirty days, she found out that she had passed on January 10, 1963.[14] But Hamer was still not able to vote because she didn't have the money to pay the poll-tax, which was another requirement for voting and an obstacle for blacks enfranchisement. Later, Fannie Lou Hamer would scrape up enough money to pay the unfair and unjust poll tax. Unfortunately, Mississippi law required that "the names of all persons who take the registration test must be in the local paper for two weeks. This [subjected] Negroes, especially Delta Negroes to all sorts of retaliatory actions,"[15] by angry white people.

Fannie Lou Hamer was no exception. She was exposed to "violent threats," by whites, "against her and the loss of her job,"[16] for trying to register to vote. White plantation owner, W.D. Marlow, III, who didn't believed blacks should have the right to vote, insisted that Hamer withdraw her name from the Mississippi voter rolls or she and her family would have to leave the plantation *post-haste*. Fannie Lou Hamer recalled:

> I was met by my children when I returned from the [Indianola] courthouse, and my girl [her eldest daughter] and my husband's cousin told me that this man my husband worked for was raising a lot of Cain. I went on in the house, and it wasn't long before my husband came and said this plantation owner said I would have to leave if I didn't go down and withdraw.[17]

W.D. Marlow went on to severely admonish Fannie Lou Hamer for her activities and actions to register to vote, demanding that she withdraw her name. But Hamer in no uncertain terms let W.D. Marlow know that she didn't go down to the courthouse to register for him, but for herself.[18] This back-talk from Hamer didn't sit well with W.D. Marlow, because she would have to leave the plantation and move "into Ruleville to stay with a friend, leaving her husband and two daughters behind...,"[19] because she was threatened. Journalist L.C. Dorsey described Hamer's predicament this way:

[Hamer] was fired from her job as timekeeper [from the Marlow plantation] after she attempted to register to vote. That night she and her family would not stay in their home because threats had been made on her life. Instead, she stayed with friends whose house was shot into 16 times. Miraculously, she escaped injury, but for two months she moved from place to place, finally settling in Ruleville, Mississippi.[20]

It was then that Fannie Lou Hamer decided to devote her entire life "totally to the struggle against oppression of her people,"[21] when before she had just wanted to work on the edge of the civil rights movement. Because of the long-standing racist attitude towards politics in Mississippi, black activists like Hamer were harassed mercilessly. Often, "cars full of white men armed with rifles ... followed them wherever they went."[22] Fannie Lou Hamer was also cursed at relentlessly by disrespectful, evil white men.[23] Nevertheless, political change was in the air, and perhaps that's all that mattered. Johnson explained that "Hamer's participation in politics was a violent experience." And "having greatness thrust upon her as a result of her involvement in voter registration," Hamer became "a charismatic grassroots organizer."[24] She was able to hone her skills as an activist by paying close attention to the way things operated within the SNCC and the SCLC, not caring if she revealed her ignorance about such matters. In this way Hamer was able to learn quite a bit about training and organizing. Fannie Lou Hamer would listen very carefully, learning everything she would later need to know to be effective.

Hamer's greatest strength was her ability to listen to anyone, no matter what their background, because she was able to rightly size up almost every situation. Fannie Lou Hamer was more formidable than people realized. As a political activist, she took a very active interest in the world. This was because Hamer grew up in the Mississippi Delta, which had psychologically prepared her to be an effective activist. And, as we shall see, Hamer's involvement and influence would spread nationally and throughout the world.

Hamer felt strongly that what she was about to undertake in Mississippi during the Freedom Summer of 1964 was extremely important. By then, Fannie Lou Hamer had been working "tirelessly to help local blacks become enfranchised."[25] But according to Fannie Lou Hamer, "There was no real Civil Rights Movement in the Negro community in Mississippi before the 1964 Summer Project."[26] Black and white people, students mostly, came together to make sure their voices were heard. Hamer also pointed out that "there were people that wanted change, but they hadn't dared to come out and try to do something, to try to change the way things were."[27] Of course, there were many blacks who believed that there was little chance of change happening, as they thought that racial equality was not possible at that time. But widespread disobedience by blacks was beginning to occur against "white rule" throughout Mississippi. Black people had absolutely nothing to lose and everything to gain. In this regard, Hamer "warned the northern students who went to Mississippi in the summer of 1964 (about four-fifths of them white) that they would find nothing ordinary in that state."[28]

Indeed, these young students were shocked by the savagery of what happened to black people in Mississippi during this time period. And these white students from the North hoped that their participation would heal some of the divisions between the races. "As they exercised their ingenuity to find ways of relating to the movement and of barriers, they also struggled to elaborate an understanding of community in which they could exist as equal persons, freed from both the passivity and the guilt of the internalized image."[29] Fannie Lou Hamer was intensely interested in the young people from the North — blacks and whites — who would help black people register to vote. She once wrote that "after the 1964 project when all of the young people came down for the summer — an exciting and remarkable summer — Negro people in the Delta began moving."[30]

Hamer would interact with people with truth, openness, and complexity. And when she was engaged in important work with others, she was all ears. Hamer saw herself as a soldier who knew what to do, and she was able to establish relationships with almost everyone. If things worried Hamer, you'd never know it. On the whole, she found her traveling and speaking engagements helpful, since it allowed her the opportunity to meet other civil rights activists, although Hamer's work demanded interaction among all people.

Many black activists like Hamer acknowledged it was an uphill battle. But Hamer also knew that "they started something that no one could ever stop. [And] these people were willing to move in a nonviolent way to bring a change in the South."[31] Which is to say, the political climate was shifting dramatically in Mississippi. In this racist era, white authority in the state would finally have to give way for the social and political demands of blacks.

Fannie Lou Hamer's resilience figured prominently in the next several years. Many of the students during Freedom Summer saw Hamer "as a symbol of ordinary rank and filerdom," as well as "an authentic representative of the down-to-earth reality they yearned keenly to understand and redeem."[32] Meanwhile, Hamer seemed to have been doing everything right. Hamer always thought that things would be accomplished through guile and street smarts, even though "she was an uneducated, poor, black, rural Southerner."[33] Fannie Lou Hamer was good at building coalitions to help accomplish her objectives. And she was always encouraging. But it was something always in the back of her mind to help ordinary black people. In the final analysis, Hamer "was local, from the grassroots, someone awakened to her own power to lead and to effect change, and strong enough not to be intimidated by her enemies."[34]

Fighting for the rights of blacks became Hamer's *raison d'être*, because the racism in Mississippi at that time was unmatched anywhere in the world. Black people voiced their contempt for white racists and their cowardly acts of violence, as many black activists were devoted to eradicating segregation in the state. And many whites would not bow to the deliberate campaign of violence and intimidation by other whites. They would no longer remain silent in the face of criticism of white terrorism. Fannie Lou Hamer certainly wanted to contribute in more meaningful ways, as she was well acquainted with the inflammatory rhetoric of whites in Mississippi. Increasingly, Hamer identified the conflict between blacks and whites with the social and political struggle familiar to all black people everywhere in the state. Basically, some whites in Mississippi were sanctimonious in their racial hatred of blacks, and they didn't mind attacking anyone that went against the established order. Journalist DeWayne Wickham writes, "What happened to the Freedom Riders is an ugly chapter of American history. Many of them were savagely beaten by Klansmen and their supporters with the complicity of local police."[35] Fannie Lou Hamer significantly enhanced the push toward integration and freedom in Mississippi. And the activism of local blacks and whites from outside the state embarrassed the leadership and other white government officials. Perhaps at first, whites thought the protest of blacks was much ado about nothing. But they were sadly mistaken.

Hamer impressed the members of the SNCC, who believed she "embodied what the Student Nonviolent Coordinating Committee hoped to achieve in Mississippi," and the SCLC, who arranged to have her assigned as an organizer and trainer for voter-registration drives.[36] Hamer shared her ideas and used her abilities to let everyone know what was good for blacks in the Delta and elsewhere. It was an auspicious start to her training and activities as a civil rights advocate. Fannie Lou Hamer exemplified strong character and leadership, especially to the many young volunteers who had come from all over the South and other places.[37] According to Professor Andrew J. DeRoche, Hamer "was just one in a long line of rural African Americans who [deeply] impressed" leaders of the Southern Christina Leadership Conference (SCLC), like the Reverend Martin L. King, Jr., and Andrew Young.[38]

11

The Arrest and Beating of
Fannie Lou Hamer

There is something wrong with this [country] when ... white [men] can beat
a colored woman [almost] to death and no one raises a hand to stop [them].[1]
— Rev. Thomas C. Jackson

Many blacks in the State of Mississippi hoped that the Freedom Summer
of 1964 would be the start of a new era. But white racism in the Delta and
other places was still like an impenetrable fog, because it was so hard to see
through it to an ending. It was the sad reality of things. But for Fannie Lou
Hamer, fighting racism had become a way of life. Indeed, she stepped into
the fray at a chaotic time during the early stages of the civil rights movement.
For a while, Fannie Lou Hamer stayed in the trenches, where her mettle was
often tested. She knew that everyone wouldn't be on her side, no matter how
much she planned and how hard she tried. Hamer was also realistic about
what she could do; and it didn't take her long to get her bearings about her
position in the movement. Additionally, Hamer tried to be nonjudgmental,
regardless of who she met in the movement during the 1964 Summer Project,
because she and others needed good relations now more than ever. She was
especially taken with the young volunteers who came from outside Mississippi.
Fannie Lou Hamer once commented, "I can hardly express what those students
and that summer meant to me — what it meant to the people who didn't dare
say anything."[2]

Fannie Lou never, for a moment, underestimated some racist whites who
were against her and went out of their way to do her harm. In this charged
atmosphere, Hamer stood out as a moral compass for the movement. Accordingly, "Each of the Freedom Riders was committed to nonviolence, but many
Southern whites were not."[3] Indeed, whites responded to black protest by
threatening the entire black community. White thugs used bottles, rocks,
bombs and bricks to attack blacks in plain sight, as well as torching their

homes. Many blacks were seriously injured in racially motivated attacks that went unchecked and unpunished. But it was a period of time that was not without precedent, as the "struggle brought about by the efforts of both the Federal Government and civil-rights organizations to banish discrimination in the area where it [had] been most militantly defended"[4] was a constant sign of a war of sorts, a seemingly never-ending battle. Journalist John Herbert writes:

> Although racial violence [was] not new to Mississippi, the conflict reached a new peak during the summer, when hundreds of civil rights workers, mostly student volunteers, poured into Mississippi communities from throughout the nation to help the state's 900,000 Negroes advance politically, socially and economically.[5]

Suffice it to say, the racial problem was more complex than ever. But the worst had yet to come for Fannie Lou Hamer. She never took foolish risks, but Hamer wasn't afraid of speaking up or doing things outside the box in racist Mississippi, like politically educating blacks and helping register them to vote, which was no small feat, considering the lack of participation and the immense scope of the racial problems in the South. Still, "the courage required" to face the evil actions of some white people who denied blacks such a basic constitutional right was "moral, rather than physical,"[6] especially in terms of fighting racism and discrimination. And the evilness was astonishing. Fannie Lou Hamer was continually baffled by the fact that there was so much animosity and deep-seated anger on the part of whites towards blacks. And the abuse of black people in Mississippi went on during Freedom Summer. What should have been one of the most basic things people in the state should have been able to do (such as voting) was a constant struggle for blacks in Mississippi. Indeed, "the conscious effort to create the Mississippi Summer with the involvement of hundreds of white students from the North was predicated upon the idea that the rest of the country had a responsibility for what was happening in Mississippi and the South."[7]

Fannie Lou Hamer once lamented, "We learned the hard way that even though we had all the law and all the righteousness on our side, that white man [was] not going to give up his power to us. We have to build our own power."[8] Such matters undoubtedly troubled Fannie Lou Hamer deeply. But in the end she absolutely believed that "you can kill a man, but you can't kill ideas." Hamer went on to say that ideas would eventually transfer "from one generation" to the next, until "after [a] while, if it's not too late for all of us, we'll be free."[9] Hamer, of course, knew the inherent dangers of involving herself in the civil rights movement, and the push to help blacks, especially in the Delta, escape their lives of poverty, but she didn't care. Hamer was particularly careful, however, not to get others involved in dangerous situations. She had to keep telling herself that anything was possible, but Hamer knew that it would take a great effort to change things in the state of Mississippi.

Hamer understood the risks, especially if members of the Ku Klux Klan became aware of what she and other black activists were attempting to do: namely, to educated the black population in Mississippi about voting and citizenship. So yes, Fannie Lou Hamer knew the terrible risks, but she took them anyway, as she worked hard "to overcome the bad schooling Delta Negroes [had] received when they receive[d] any at all."[10] Of course, it must be understood that "there were many threats" to Hamer after she fled the Marlow plantation and became an activist.[11] But before she was considered an expert civil rights field worker, Hamer received extra training for voter registration work and other civil rights activities, so that she developed a sophistication that wasn't always apparent beneath her plain exterior and down-home charisma. Fannie Lou Hamer would eventually teach citizenship classes; and at one time she "gathered names for a petition to obtain federal commodities for needy Negro families and attended various Southern Christian Leadership Conference (SCLC) and Student Nonviolent Coordinating Committee (SNCC) workshops throughout the South."[12]

True to form, Hamer attended a voter registration workshop and training program in South Carolina with five other field workers from the SNCC and SCLC. When returning to Mississippi on June 9, 1963, the Continental Trailways bus they traveled on stopped at the bus station in Winona, Mississippi. (Note: Some scholars have written that the voter-education workshop Hamer attended was actually in Tennessee, but this is not true.[13])

There they would become enmeshed in something they wouldn't readily be able to extract themselves from. Unfortunately, they had let their guard down. By her own account, Hamer had a sudden premonition that disaster might strike. She thought about the time when she first tried to register to vote, and the yellow bus that carried her and seventeen other plantation blacks to the court house in Indianola, Mississippi, was stopped by white law enforcement officials outside the city limits. The black bus driver was fined for driving "the wrong color bus."[14] Ridiculous. After paying $30 of an unfair $100 fine, they were released and allowed to return to their respective homes. Hamer would never forget that incident, and she contemplated what might happen to her and the rest of her small group if they got off that Continental Trailways bus in Winona, Mississippi. Colman described the subsequent incident in this way:

> When the bus stopped at the bus station in Winona, Mississippi, five of the people got off to get something to eat and use the bathroom. Fannie Lou

stayed on the bus. When she saw her friends rush out of the bus station, Hamer got off the bus. Annell Ponder told her that the police had ordered them out because the restaurant and bathroom were for white people only. Hamer got back on the bus. But when she saw the police shoving her friends into police cars, she got off again. "You're under arrest," a [white] police officer told Hamer and kicked her as she got into his car.[15]

It had been their extraordinary misfortune to be at the wrong place at the wrong time — the Winona bus terminal, where they mistakenly thought they could be served lunch like human beings. When Fannie Lou Hamer and the rest of the black civil rights workers were ordered off the bus, they were arrested almost immediately. Hamer noticed that the police chief had a dangerous look in his eyes. In hostile tones, with voices full of sarcasm and venom, the white policemen told them to shut up as they protested. Hamer and the others were threatened with death if they didn't stay quiet.[16] They had run out of luck. Later, Hamer realized that it had been a foolhardy thing to do to get off the bus. But Fannie Lou Hamer could only think of her friends and co-workers. It was a bracing moment when she left the Continental Trailways bus to find out what was keeping her brave friends and colleagues. It didn't matter to Hamer how dangerous it would be.

The situation broadly resembled what happened to any black person who defied white rule. Retribution. At first, Fannie Lou Hamer thought that these cowardly white men wouldn't have the temerity to touch a woman, even a black woman. But she was wrong. Hamer steeled herself for the worst.

Apparently, Hamer thought that it was her fault they had not been more cautious. Hamer and her companions were now at the mercy of violent white men, like John L. Bassinger. But what they would do to her and the others was not unprecedented. It was just another example of their cowardly deeds, these white racists and segregationists. Fannie Lou Hamer felt angry and ashamed. These savage white men would ultimately abuse and demoralize her. According to Dorsey, "They were taken to the jail and the last person brought in was June Johnson, who they began to interrogate."[17] The white policemen did not care about their discomfiture. Anyone would have been offended by the disrespect and discourtesy they showed these black women. Of course, these white men knew they could do pretty much what they wanted to any black person, without fear of punishment. Upon entering the Winona jail, Hamer understood what was about to happen to them. She felt it in her tired bones.

Indeed, Fannie Lou Hamer understood this quite clearly. They would be murdered, lynched or severely beaten, because Hamer knew that these armed white cowards would always raise bloody hands to the defenseless and innocent, even going so far as to attack women or even children. Fannie Lou's initial calm gave way to a wave of nausea when she heard the screams of fifteen-year-old June Johnson of Greenwood, Mississippi, who gasped and pleaded, asking why they were doing this to her. In a final act of defiance, June Johnson told the white men, "You all are supposed to protect and take care of us."[18] That was the wrong thing to say, because these evil white monsters were utterly brutal and heartless, as they savaged June Johnson. According to Fannie Lou Hamer, they "beat that child like she was an animal."[19] Then the beating and torture began for the others in earnest. Another scream rang out in some back room, rising above the wail of some of the others, as Miss Ponder was summarily beaten. There was also loud screaming coming from down the end of the corridor where Fannie Lou Hamer was being held in a separate cell. Hamer recalled the beating of Miss Ponder this way:

> I could hear these awful sounds and licks and screams, hear her body hit the concrete, and this man was yellin', "Can't you say yes sir, you nigger bitch?" But she never would say yes sir to 'em, and finally they passed my cell with her, and her mouth was all swollen and her clothes were torn to the waist and her eye looked like blood, it was horrible.[20]

After a while, there was total silence. Hamer somehow knew that she would be next. Fear seized her heart and mind, as she realized that she might be killed. It was hard for her to believe that someone would treat other human beings in such an abhorrent manner. Hamer racked her brain for a way to escape these evil men, but it was impossible. She nervously paced back and forth in her jail cell, as she waited for her turn to be savagely beaten. She knew what these white men were capable of doing to her, and would inevitably do to all of them, but it really scared her when she overheard the white law enforcement officials plotting to kill them and maybe throw their bodies in the Big Black River.[21]

The other women in their group cried out for someone to help them, to save them. But there was no one that would come to their rescue anytime soon. Hamer certainly wouldn't be able to save them. It was only when Hamer heard more screams and beatings, bangings and terrible scuffling sounds from another part of the jail house that she knew that her time had finally come. There was a dangerous note in white patrolman John L. Bassinger's voice when he commanded Fannie Lou Hamer to lie down (flat on her stomach) on the prison cot of her jail cell and stay down, as she was being severely beaten, almost half to death and without mercy. In a harsh Southern drawl, John L. Bassinger continued to tell Hamer to shut up, even though she was screaming in pain. Next, the white policemen artfully instructed some black prisoners where and how to hit the defenseless Fannie Lou Hamer. It was like beating a disobedient slave or animal. Hamer recalled:

They put me in this cell with these two Negro prisoners and threatened them if they didn't beat me. They gave one of the men a long blackjack and made him beat me till he was exhausted. Then, when he was tired, the second one sat on my feet and beat me some more. They beat me till my body was hard, till I couldn't bend my fingers or get up when they told me to. That's how I got this blood clot in my left eye — the sight's nearly gone now. And my kidney was injured from the blows they gave me in the back.[22]

Fannie Lou wept and wept and wept, hoping that God would hear her prayers and deliver her from such a ferocious beating. According to Hamer, these black men had already been brutally beaten themselves, and were further threatened; so she couldn't play on the racial solidarity of these black men or their chivalric notions, even though she tried. It was probably *do or die* for these black men. They didn't have much choice other than to expertly beat Fannie Lou Hamer. The pain was excruciating, as the impact of several blows took her breath away. Hamer never thought such pain was possible. Indeed, she was hit so hard and savagely that Hamer almost lost consciousness. It was sickening, and Hamer thought about dying. She, of course, did not want to die in isolation like this, like some animal that had to be put down. Out of fear, the black men, at the direction of the white policemen, continued to beat Fannie Lou.

Hamer felt self-conscious, embarrassed and ashamed when the men in the room pulled up her torn dress as they continued to beat her. According to Professor Chana Kai Lee, "Hamer readily acknowledged that the incident involved racial control, but in private [she] pondered the degree to which her [white] attackers might have experienced some degree of sexual gratification from the beatings."[23] It was more than a nightmare, Hamer thought, as she tried to hold back her cries and streaming tears. She cried out for them to stop, but they only hurt her more.

In a desperate attempt to obtain some relief from the beating, Hamer kicked out at her assailants, slapping, punching and squirming. Hamer struggled and fought them with all her might. She kicked at the men furiously, with a sort of hopeless determination — until she was finally warned to stop struggling, or face pain of a more severe nature. Hamer continued to scream and sob during her assault, as they hit her with "a long leather blackjack with lead or something in it."[24] Meanwhile, Hamer "tried to keep her dress down, but a white officer snatched it up [again], so that the blows fell on her unprotected flesh."[25] Hamer continued hearing the young black women bawling, screaming uncontrollably in horror and pain. She would *never* forget the piteous whimpering and sobs. Apparently, "the violence at Winona showed that their femininity did not necessarily protect [black] women from physical assault."[26] There was no one there to help her, no one to deliver her from her tormentors, as she begged for her life. The beating seemed to go on and on and on.

Then it was all over, and Hamer sat stunned in disbelief, bloody and badly bruised and aching from her terrible ordeal. The famous civil rights activist, and now Congressman, John Lewis summed up Fannie Lou Hamer's terrible experience by writing that Hamer "had been beaten by policemen who called her a 'nigger bitch,' and she would pay for that beating every day for the rest of her life with constant pain in her back and hips and a permanent limp."[27] After the beating, Fannie Lou Hamer sat hunched against the sticky, hot wall, on her crummy cot in the Winona jail, waiting.

12

The Rescue and Aftermath

We were taught something in Mississippi I'm not ashamed of today. We were
taught to love. We were taught to not hate. And we were taught to stand on
principle, stand on what we believe. I often remember my mother telling
me, "If you respect yourself, one day somebody else will respect you.[1]

— Fannie Lou Hamer

Hamer knew how dangerous things were, but she also knew she had to
get out of the Winona jail to survive. Much work still lay ahead for her. If
Fannie Lou Hamer could get away, she knew that she would no longer remain
behind the civil rights lines. At that time, the state of Mississippi was convulsed
with violence. The mutual hatred between blacks and whites had not subsided,
and there was little progress in terms of race relations. Indeed, there was an
intensification of violence against members of the civil rights movement. But
black people everywhere in Mississippi refused to be treated as second class
citizens, or viewed as less than human, anymore. It was a clear sign of things
to come. What started out as a political protest quickly turned into a viable,
growing, unstoppable movement. In this respect, Fannie Lou Hamer believed
that black people must take bold action to achieve the goals of justice and
freedom. According to Professor David Chalmers, "Black suffering was not
news, and in 1964, after three years of literally being beaten down to the
ground, they made the decision to bring in young, white volunteers in the
hope that this would draw media attention and protection by the national
government."[2] And this tactic would pay off in dividends, although some
activists, like Andrew Goodman, James Earl Chaney, and Michael Henry
Schwerner, would lose their lives because of their activism. About these matter,
Fannie Lou Hamer once stated:

We're tired of all this beatin', we're tired of takin' this. It's been a hundred
years and we're still being beaten and shot at, crosses are still being burned,
because we want to vote. But I'm goin' to stay in Mississippi and if they shoot
me down, I'll be buried here.[3]

In so many words, she was sick and tired and determined not to take it anymore. She fully understood the magnitude of what she was doing, always sacrificing for the cause. Of course, many blacks in the civil rights movement were ideologically and mentally committed to do whatever was necessary, but it had always been a challenge to get black people to come out and support the cause of freedom, because of fear of retribution from whites. Hamer, of course, "gave hundreds of hours to SNCC in 1964, working in voter education."[4] Fannie Lou Hamer liked that blacks were no longer falling on bended knee at the feet of whites.

But Jim Crow racism was a force to be reckoned with, one which had to be defeated. Some whites in Mississippi even believed that "black voting and the whole civil rights invasion was a 'Communist plot' directed by the Jews."[5] What rubbish. It was essentially about the fight between the oppressed black population and white Southern oppressors. As Paulo Freire has written, "The oppressors are the ones who act upon the [black] people to indoctrinate them and adjust them to a reality which must remain untouched."[6] Such an archaic, racist strategy had come and gone. And institutional racism would ultimately fall like a house of cards.

In the final analysis, black people in Mississippi, and elsewhere, were not content to live within the boundaries of the white power structure anymore. It should be noted here that "the majority of white Mississippians ... accepted institutional racism as a natural, even divine, social reality because their parents and grandparents, teachers, ministers, newspaper editors, and political leaders had drummed it into them from their birth."[7] Segregation had always struck Fannie Lou Hamer as odd. However, white racists and white "militants ... were willing to use violence to preserve segregation."[8] Violence against blacks had also been brewing, in the 1960s ever since James Meredith, a black man, made a bid to attend the University of Mississippi, or Ole Miss — a move resisted fiercely by whites. Meredith was academically qualified, but because he was black he was, at first, denied enrollment at the school. Ole Miss, of course, had been seen by blacks in Mississippi as a symbol of white privilege and wealth, as well as black repression and educational inequality. But in 1962 Meredith would become, much to the chagrin of the white community, and despite all the racist hoopla, the first black student to matriculate at Ole Miss.[9] In this sense, black people were not only willing to endure, they were also willing to fight and die for their rights. Hamer believed that everyone could do *something* to help black people that needed help. In fact, black and white activism was "symbolic of the very character of the civil rights movement itself."[10]

As Fannie Lou Hamer worked through what was happening to her, she reflected on other such adversities she had experienced. It was in this way that Hamer was able to survive and learn something from her current situation. Hamer actually wanted to achieve something more, to be part of history, to do something that maybe others were afraid or unwilling to do. When it was all said and done, Hamer was honored to be a part of something, a movement, that would help black people and the less fortunate. Nevertheless, separation from her family was hard for her. Indeed, being on the road all the time had definitely cut into her family life. Fannie Lou Hamer "spent much of the summer on the road, speaking at mass meetings in the state and fundraisers across the country in an effort to generate national support for federal intervention in Mississippi."[11] When Fannie Lou Hamer was away from home, spending more time in the field than with her husband and two adopted daughters, Pap Hamer remained patient. He accepted Fannie Lou just the way she was. Still, Pap could not help but worry about her being gone almost all of the time, especially as she was often on dangerous trips to help blacks attempt to register.

Obviously, a higher power had something planned for Fannie Lou Hamer, because for all intents and purposes she should have been dead after such a horrific beating. Hamer even made the sad comment, "And let me tell you, before they stopped beatin' me, I wish they would have hit me one lick that could have ended the misery that they had me in."[12] It made little difference to the Winona police officers, but Fannie Lou Hamer's tortured screams were real. She had fought back bravely, but it had not helped. Indeed, Hamer would be "permanently injured from the beating."[13] So severe and brutal was the whipping they gave her, Hamer "suffered kidney damage that didn't go away, and she developed a blood clot in her left eye that permanently limited her sight."[14] The white abusers had been unbothered by her gut-wrenching cries. Hamer recalled that when she continued to scream, one white man got up and began to beat her on the head while telling her to "hush."[15] These white assailants didn't worry about the consequences of the violent beating of Hamer and the other civil rights workers. It was as if they were accustomed to meting out their own sadistic brand of white Southern justice against black defendants. Hamer also noted that all the time during her assault, these white men made very rude comments about her body, calling her fatso and other awful epithets.

Later, the local, white law enforcement officers continued to beat her and the other activists until exhaustion. Hamer noted that "one of the plain-clothes fellows" got "so hot and worked up, he ran in there and started hitting me on the back of my head [too].... I was trying to guard some of the licks and they beat my hands 'til they turned blue."[16] But perseverance and faith pulled Hamer through.

When Lawrence Guyot, from the SNCC staff, showed up to bail out Fannie Lou Hamer and the other voter registration workers, he was treated no better.[17] Guyot, the young twenty-three-year-old black man who would later become the "chairman of the Mississippi Freedom Democratic Party,"[18] was beaten without mercy. And with sadistic glee, his white jailers burned his privates.[19] Lawrence Guyot feared for his life, as they charged him "with disturbing the peace and resisting arrest"[20] because he didn't say "sir" to Sheriff Earl Wayne Patridge.[21] They thought Lawrence Guyot wasn't being respectful or contrite enough. Guyot's white assailants later took him to nearby Carroll County where they allowed the Ku Klux Klan to beat him some more.[22] According to Lee, "Hamer was particularly disturbed by Guyot's appearance because he lacked his characteristic beaming grin."[23] Some might say that rushing to the rescue without a real plan was a foolhardy thing to do. But Lawrence Guyot survived. Equally remarkable, the black activists, consisting of Mrs. Fannie Lou Hamer, June Johnson, Euvester Simpson, James West and Rosemary Freeman, would all survive the dreadful ordeal — barely.

Obviously, this terrible incident and unjust beating took a toll on Hamer. It was probably the worst thing anyone could have done to her, but Hamer would overcome it. Though she would experience extreme emotional distress in the aftermath of the ordeal, she remained unbowed. She was still stunned to think that grown men would beat her in such an inhumane and vicious manner. And the memory of this heinous crime would rankle her for the rest of her life. In pain, Hamer was thoroughly exhausted and dazed, as she "was beaten even though she was in her fifties and obviously already in poor health."[24] It took an inordinately long time for someone else to finally come to Hamer's and the others rescue, as they had been at the Winona jail three days. According to the Reverend Andrew Young, "The sheriff at Winona would not [even] confirm that he had arrested the women, nor would he let them make phone calls."[25]

At first, Fannie Lou Hamer didn't want to leave the Winona jail; this was her way of protesting and showing her displeasure — a passive form of resistance. But when Andrew Young and James Bevel of the SCLC showed up to bail them out, the civil rights activists were delighted. They choked back tears of joy when they finally saw Andrew Young's angelic face. Throughout her detention, Hamer wasn't necessarily looking to be a *martyr*, but she no doubt thought that their lives had been on the line.

Andrew Young at first inventoried the situation, lest he be caught up in the same madness. Young's mind was racing, for he didn't want to piss off these racist whites and end up getting locked up and beaten himself. Of course, Andrew Young "was scared to death because in Mississippi, sheriffs had almost complete power; they were a law unto themselves."[26] So he tried to be smart about things, as the release of the civil rights activists seemed impossible at that moment. To Young's utter horror, he could see that the black activists had all been violated in some way. There was anguish in Andrew Young's bright face, as the pitiful sight of Hamer and the others was painful to look at. Everyone had tears on their haggard faces. Some of the civil rights workers sobbed uncontrollably. Terrified, tortured, bruised, and beaten on almost every part of their bodies, they continued to cry pitifully. Andrew Young tried to handle the wounded civil rights workers gingerly. Young was desperate to get them out of the Winona jail and away from the clutches of such unfeeling, brutish men.

Andrew Young, who would one day become a Congressman, U.N. ambassador, and mayor of Atlanta, Georgia, had to control his own incredible rage. Indeed, Young was confounded by the pure violence and disrespect that Fannie Lou Hamer and the rest of her companions had had to endure. He was aghast. The ugly frustration of Andrew Young not being able to strike back was apparent. Young wanted to do something to these evil white men, to get back at them, but to do so would have been foolish, insanity, given the situation. The white assailants acted as if nothing had happened. Fortunately, after demanding that the civil rights workers clean themselves up, the white sheriff finally released them to Andrew Young.[27] Significantly, "earlier that same day, NAACP field secretary Medgar Evers had been assassinated in his Mississippi driveway"[28] in Jackson by white racist De la Beckwith. Perhaps their lives were spared because "the federal government was paying close attention to the actions of the local [Mississippi] police"[29] after Evers' assassination. Andrew Young writes, "After the women were beaten they were forced to wash the blood from their own clothing and from their bruises as the deputies cruelly attempted to remove the visible evidence of their brutality."[30] Indeed, the condition of the civil rights workers brought angry tears to Andrew Young's eyes. He, of course, thought that the white assailants should have been punished, but he knew they would not be castigated in any way. Andrew Young described his compatriots' release in this way:

> The [black] women and Guyot were brought out, staggering and injured; the sheriff and the FBI agent watched impassively, as if nothing unusual was happening. We cooperated in the charade and concealed our shock at their condition so we could get them away from Winona without further trouble.[31]

Fannie Lou Hamer said nothing to her white attackers as she left the miserable place. But she slowly walked out of the Winona jail with her head held high. Young gasped when he saw Hamer. The humiliation was dreadful for them all, but Hamer was still able to maintain her dignity. Leaving the cursed Winona jail, she tried to control her emotions, and her spirits lifted. Through it all, Fannie Lou Hamer was extraordinarily brave. She fought back hot tears, a pained grimace on her face. It was a terrible moment, as Hamer gingerly walked to the waiting car, trying not to give in to the pain in her battered body. Fannie Lou Hamer appeared like a wounded soldier returning from a war-torn battlefield, the deep, dark, purplish bruises a badge of honor. The white law enforcement officials from Winona didn't seem to care, as they nonchalantly went about their day-to-day business. Eventually, she made it to the waiting car. With tears in his eyes, Young drove away with the miserable looking Fannie Lou Hamer and the others. Andrew Young saw the hurt and anger in Hamer's eyes, and he noticed that the damp clothes of the women hung in tatters, "as they had nothing else to wear."[32] There wasn't anything Young could do for the women immediately, other than take them to a hospital. Andrew Young's patience, loving concern and generosity meant a great deal to Fannie Lou Hamer. According to Rubel, "Hamer had received no medical attention while she was in jail, so Bevel and Young immediately carried her — half conscious and with a Justice Department escort — to a doctor in Greenwood, who stitched her wounds and bandaged her."[33]

Badly bruised, battered and sore, Fannie Lou Hamer was later taken "to some friends of the civil rights movement" in Atlanta, Georgia, "where she remained for a month, convalescing."[34] During this time of recuperation Hamer "refused to allow her husband to come to see how terrible she looked, until some of the scars were less livid and the swelling had gone down."[35] Fannie Lou Hamer recalled this period of time in the following way:

> After I got beat, I didn't hardly see my family in 'bout a month, 'cause I went on to Atlanta, from Atlanta to Washington, and from Washington to New York, because they didn't want my family to see me in the shape I was in. I had been beat 'til I was real hard, just hard like a piece of wood or somethin'. A person don't know what can happen to [their] body if they beat [you] with something like I was beat with.[36]

What happened to Fannie Lou Hamer makes for a grim story indeed, as it was a reprehensible act of unadulterated evil. She was psychologically wounded from being treated in such an undignified way. But what is so surprising is how Fannie Lou Hamer was able to cope with things after being beaten almost into oblivion. Hamer would continue to weather the coming racial storm. Pushing against the odds, Hamer hoped that she would come out on top in her grass-roots activism, as black people "refused to back down, and the situation grew ever more tense as the jails filled and the beatings continued."[37]

13

The Mississippi Freedom Democratic Party

Throughout much of recorded history, an assertion that adult human beings are entitled to be treated as political equals would have been widely viewed by many as self-evident nonsense, and by rulers as a dangerous and subversive claim that they must suppress.[1]

— Robert A. Dahl

Fannie Lou Hamer clearly understood what people were going to say about what had happened to her, as she continued to suffer in silence from her life-threatening injuries. She was still moving like the walking wounded, but she carried herself with what little dignity she could muster. Indeed, Hamer was gradually improving, health-wise; but because of the senseless, depraved conduct on the part of the Winona law enforcement officials, she still couldn't adequately get around as well as she would have liked. In fact, Hamer could barely sit down. As Hamer described it, "I just could hardly get up, and [back at the jail] they kept on telling me to get up. I finally could get up, but when I got back to my cell bed, I couldn't set down. I would scream. It hurt me to set down."[2]

There has never been a real explanation from the white culprits about what they had done to Hamer and the other black civil rights workers; but Andrew Young speculated that "they had been arrested because they tried to get coffee at 'white only' counters first in Columbus and then in the Winona bus stations."[3] But Hamer and her civil rights companions did not grovel in fear or wallow in self-pity. During her recovery, Fannie Lou Hamer had plenty of time to ponder what had happened. Should she have stayed on the bus that fateful day in Winona? Why didn't she take more sensible precautions? They should have been particularly careful because they were not completely oblivious to the dangers in Mississippi, especially as civil rights workers. Was she naïve not to see her impending assault. For a long period after the event in Winona, Hamer had recurring night sweats about the horrible incident. But she didn't feel sorry for herself. Fannie Lou Hamer knew that you had to put yourself in a position of danger in order to understand and overcome it.

Hamer was more than a little worse for wear. She still didn't want to see her worried family anytime soon. Hamer would never fully recover from her vicious attack, but she would bounce back in reasonably good shape. Hamer's concerned husband Pap had tried to warn her about her activities, but he believed in his wife Fannie Lou, especially in what she stood for and what she was trying to accomplish as a civil rights activist. He also loved and cared for her deeply. Perry "Pap" Hamer was also a good provider who worked extremely hard for his family, though he still had to make ends meet by making his own hard liquor and running "a little juke joint."[4]

Little did Fannie Lou Hamer know the impact that this unconscionable Winona incident would have on the state of Mississippi and the white community that continued to resist integration and desegregation. She was suddenly propelled into the limelight. In this regard, Hamer and other civil rights activists won a crucial test of political support because the beating and horrible crimes against Fannie Lou Hamer set a wave of indignation across the nation. The Winona incident sparked a national outcry after it was reported that Fannie Lou Hamer and other black activists were brutalized by white racists. It sparked nation-wide protests against "white rule" and so-called white justice in Mississippi. Many were stunned by the horrible incident. Black civil rights organizations and other groups like the NAACP were extremely angry upon learning how white law enforcement officers perpetrated such a heinous crime against innocent black people. For many, it was incomprehensible and unforgivable that *anyone* would do such a thing to human beings. Of course, it was something that should not have occurred, period.

The black community in Mississippi expressed great outrage about Fannie Lou Hamer's suffering and the complete failure of white law enforcement officials, especially as they were complicit in the beating of the black women. June Jordan recalled Fannie Lou Hamer begging for her life at the Winona jail, when she heard her cry out, "Don't beat me no more — don't beat me no more."[5] Jordan later testified that Hamer in her jail cell "cried at intervals during the night, saying that the leg afflicted with polio was hurting her terribly."[6] By all accounts, Hamer and the other civil rights workers might have died because of their beatings. Perhaps Fannie Lou Hamer still heard the angry voice of a white man who cursed, "Y'all just stirring up ... shit and making it stink." Y'all were doing a demonstration."[7] But they were not planning any demonstration. The civil rights workers were only tired and wanted to get something to eat.[8] Hamer and the others tried to explain this to the heartless white men, but it didn't matter to them.

The image of Hamer being seriously brutalized trumped almost everything else going on in Mississippi at that point in time. The Winona incident became an iconic moment for the civil rights movement. Fannie Lou Hamer emerged from the entire situation intact, mentally tougher, and transformed as a woman. The painful part was behind her. But Hamer would carry the terrible event with her for the rest of her life. When she rallied sufficiently from her horrendous wounds, Hamer was able to tell the world about the wicked white men in the state of Mississippi who would beat, maim and kill black women. Hamer just wanted people to know the truth about what she and her companions had to endure at the Winona jail in Mississippi.

Ultimately, this single event became a rallying cry for the black revolution in the state of Mississippi. From then on, it was not a matter of whether black people would receive their constitutional rights, but when. And Fannie Lou Hamer understood this better than almost anyone. Such a beating might have been too debilitating (both physically and emotionally) for some to continue, but Hamer would press on. Nothing would sap her will to fight on. She decided to keep moving as quickly as she could to get back on her feet. Indeed, Fannie Lou Hamer "remained tough-minded and determined to push for political change,"[9] even while recovering from her ordeal. She thought it important to continue with her job as a field worker for the SNCC, so she could focus on black people and their struggles. She wanted to be in the thick of things, to work on the political front lines. Besides, she didn't want to let her people down.

Hamer knew that she had to be extremely careful from then on around racist white people. But, surprisingly, her heart wasn't filled with hateful rage. According to Chris Myers Asch, Fannie Lou Hamer felt it took too much time and energy to hate the white man.[10] She didn't want to waste her precious time hating *anyone*.

Hamer had a fierce sense of purpose and was totally committed to the ideas and principles of black rights. She was always looking at the bigger picture. And the idea that she might make a difference excited her. Furthermore, Fannie Lou Hamer was "loving and open," and also "intellectually tough minded, quite capable of doing [her] own thinking,"[11] while canvassing black people to participate by voting. According to professor Charles M. Payne, black women like Fannie Lou Hamer "canvassed more than men, showed up more frequently at mass meetings and demonstrations and more frequently attempted to register to vote."[12] There was nothing predictable about the path that lay ahead for Fannie Lou Hamer. But co-founding the interracial Mississippi Freedom Democratic Party, "which challenged white supremacy"[13] in the state, put Hamer on the path to glory. She never really coveted leadership, but her unique abilities and place in the desegregation movement was born from conviction. According to professor of political science Mamie E. Locke, "the highlight" of Hamer's "political activism occurred, when she and several others set the wheels in motion for the formation of the Mississippi Freedom Democratic Party (MFDP)."[14] It was a gamble for Fannie Lou Hamer, "under the guidance of Ella Baker," and assisted by "SNCC members Annie Devine and Victoria Gray," to establish the MFDP, which would "contest the authority of the all-white Democratic Party in the state."[15] But they believed it had to be done if there was any hope of changing things for black people in Mississippi.

Indeed, creating the MFDP was a deeply unorthodox idea, but one whose time had come. The MFDP provided "an alternative to the racist Mississippi Democratic Party."[16] The fledgling organization was designed to allow the maximum participation of blacks in the political system of Mississippi. Fannie Lou Hamer sincerely believed that the MFDP was on the right track, as the organization needed to be relevant to potential black voters. Such a political idea was enormous, as Hamer and the others brought a lot to the table in terms of voter registration expertise. As Hamer's biographer, Susan Kling, has pointed out, "It was almost impossible to work for change within the all-white Democratic Party of Mississippi."[17] Consequently, the MFDP had to make their case without significant support from other white democrats in the state. To be sure, Fannie Lou Hamer "tried to work with the regular Mississippi Democratic Party by first attempting to go to work on the precinct level. [But] she had no luck at all." And when Hamer boldly "attended a [white] precinct meeting in Ruleville, her husband, recently hired on a new job, was fired."[18] It was a recent phenomenon for blacks to challenge the white political status quo. Many blacks applauded certain aspects of the MFDP, but some questioned whether forming the MFDP would create a conflict of interest, especially since it went against the wishes of the white establishment. The MFDP sent a strong political message, as "there were no blacks in the [all-white] Mississippi Democratic Party organization."[19]

Hamer thought that a long-term solution to white Mississippi politics was to form a "new political party, open to all."[20] It was an almost conspiratorial effort to break white politicians' stranglehold on politics in Mississippi and challenge the racist policies of the regular Democratic Party in the state.[21] The budding organization claimed new legitimacy from disenfranchised blacks in Mississippi. And members of the MFDP felt like they had the right to represent all registered voters in the state of Mississippi. Indeed, the MFDP was established to "hold meetings on every level within the state, from precinct on up, [and] to finally [choose] a delegation to the National Democratic Convention that [would] challenge the seating of the regular all-white Mississippi delegation."[22] Many were thinking: What if the MFDP could fundamentally change the way things were done politically in Mississippi? The goal of the burgeoning organization was to draw attention to the gulf between the white Democrats and blacks, who were denied a seat at the political table in Mississippi.

Fannie Lou Hamer, along with others, attempted "to go through the channel of voter registration, which ought to have been a very easy road, but they got all kinds of physical reprisals as a result of it."[23] Hamer and other blacks in the civil rights movement were directly challenging the dominant, repressive Mississippi government because "they were driven more and more into a realization that something had to take place."[24] It was fairly startling to discover that black activists had the smarts, courage, and wherewithal to fight back by forming its own political party. And the innocuously named group made a profound statement by providing a countervailing force against the white Democrats in the state. It was as if blacks and whites in Mississippi were permanently at odds, with their constant jockeying for power; white Democrats injected their conservatism and instinctive racism into the mix, while black activists fought them tooth and nail. Indeed, organizers of the MFDP saw their very existence as "an opportunity to keep the national spotlight on Mississippi and as a dramatic recruiting device to attract more local blacks into the movement."[25]

Annoyed white politicians and white Democrats were outraged by the actions of the upstart MFDP, which had the boldness to provide educational information on voting to black people, and to field and identify black candidates to run for political office throughout the state. Historians Jack Bass and Walter DeVries write:

> The Mississippi Freedom Democratic Party (MFDP) had been organized by a coalition of civil right organizations. After being excluded from the regular Democratic meetings, they developed a parallel political structure, selecting delegates, holding precinct meetings, running county conventions in 35 of the 82 counties, and holding a state convention attended by 2,300 people.[26]

Such an organization was unprecedented in the history of Mississippi politics, where political power had traditionally been *only* in the hands of whites. In fact, there were no active political parties that championed reconciliation between black Democrats and white Democrats, who had long ruled the political situation in Mississippi, other than the MFDP. And "the white leaders of the Mississippi Democrats gave ammunition to the MFDP by adopting a platform opposing civil rights and explicitly rejecting the platform of the national party."[27] The move to create the MFDP reflected the frustration felt by many blacks, who had formed an organization than would essentially castigate the white Democrats of Mississippi. After all, another major goal of the MFDP "was to unseat the [all-white] regulars and to gain official recognition as the legitimate Mississippi delegation."[28]

Apparently, Hamer and other members of the MFDP were claiming exclusivity for delegation representation for the upcoming Democratic National Convention, which would later have significant repercussions in Atlantic City in August. In this respect, the MFDP took the white power structure in the state of Mississippi by surprise. Hamer, as one of the leaders of the MFDP, also wanted to help stimulate a national discussion of racial problems in Mississippi. Of course, she was always looking ahead, moving forward; Hamer *never* wanted to look back. Therefore, "as early as May 1964 the MFDP opened an office in Washington, D.C., from which its representatives worked."[29] Historian Elton C. Fax tells us that members of the MFDP

> traveled about the nation, speaking at forums and conventions and informing all who would listen of conditions in Mississippi. Those who heard them were told that the terror characterizing life for Mississippi black people was being perpetuated by the very ones who had traditionally selected the regular delegates [at Presidential Conventions].[30]

Fannie Lou Hamer had great confidence in what the organization did for black people. Many in the MFDP felt that the voting responsibility of blacks was squarely in their hands. And the potential of the MFDP was obvious to most activists in Mississippi. But Hamer also knew that nothing would be handed to black people in the state on a silver platter. She provided the necessary focus and staying power needed to achieve some of the major goals of the organization. Hamer was particularly intrigued by the opportunity to engage the enemy. What was abundantly clear from the beginning was that the MFDP had a lot of work to do, and it would be a tough road ahead.

14

Preparing for the 1964 National Democratic Convention

The question for black people is not, when is the white man going to give us our rights, or when is he going to give us good education for our children, or when is he going to give us jobs. We have to take for ourselves.[1]
— Fannie Lou Hamer

In contemplating the possibility of making the MFDP a part of the mainstream political scene, Fannie Lou Hamer was willing to confront the white political machinery in the state of Mississippi. The MFDP had come under increasing criticism because of their unwillingness to give in to white Democratic control. And the white Democrats drastically underestimated the MFDP and their ability to do anything. MFDP workers worked in the open, without compartmentalization, which intensified the jockeying for who would represent the Democrats from the state of Mississippi at the upcoming National Democratic Convention in Atlantic City, New Jersey, in 1964. According to Hamer, the MFDP had "decided to challenge the white Mississippi Democratic Party at the National convention" simply because "the whites wouldn't even let us [blacks] register."[2] She continued:

> We followed all the laws that they made for [themselves]. So we were the ones that held the real precinct meetings. At all these meetings across the state we elected our representatives to go to the National Democratic Convention in Atlantic City.[3]

The MFDP expected some criticism, and they were prepared for it. White politicians in Mississippi howled that the MFDP had co-opted their authority. But it defied reason to think that blacks would always be satisfied with political impotence. Fannie Lou Hamer became the political representative of blacks in the organization, especially in its struggle against the racist tyranny of white supremacy in Mississippi. Indeed, she guided the MFDP, along with the assistance of Ella Baker and others, through its darkest days.

The grave site of Hamer at the Fannie Lou Hamer Memorial Garden, Ruleville, Mississippi, 2010.

Baker, of course, was fiercely loyal in her support of Hamer. And she and other members "in Washington [D.C.] continued to pressure delegations across the country for support."[4] Hamer was quite fortunate to be partnered with Ella Baker, a black woman and civil rights worker of some consequence who shared the same outlook on racial matters in the state. For example, Baker believed that "the Southern states functioned as an oligarchy and that the rest of the country went along with it."[5] In this respect, Baker and Hamer were together on things and understood each other. Fannie Lou Hamer found a friend in Ella Baker, a woman full of practical advice, intelligence and experience. Fannie Lou Hamer usually consulted with Ella Baker before she acted on anything important, and vice-versa. They worked extremely well together.

Ella Baker, who was the main leader of the MFDP, used Hamer as a sounding board on matters pertaining to the group. And Baker respected Hamer, even when Hamer essentially displaced her as the voice of the movement in Mississippi. Indeed, the MFDP became virtually synonymous with the name Fannie Lou Hamer. But Ella Baker was always there to share her expertise and understanding of political things, like the ramifications of challenging the white Democrats of Mississippi. Hamer relished working with Ella Baker. They both wanted to put a positive spin on the development of the MFDP. The collaboration between Ella Baker and Fannie Lou Hamer succeeded on many levels, but it was Hamer who made the biggest impact. Most members didn't have the name recognition, or inclination to work as hard for the cause, as Fannie Lou Hamer. For some members of the MFDP, the answer to desegregation wasn't as straightforward as it might have seemed.

But more sophisticated maneuvering made it easier. And with righteousness, humility and constant introspection, Fannie Lou Hamer was able to think deeply and make the right decisions about politics. She even became known for her brain-storming sessions with other members of the organization.

Fannie Lou Hamer wanted her team at the MFDP to focus on what the group was established for in the first place: to provide an alternative to the "white rule" of the all-white Democratic Party in Mississippi. Of course, the MFDP was "a collection mostly of rural Mississippi blacks with [almost] no political experience," which would later "challenge the state's all-white regular Democratic delegation."[6] In this respect, in Mississippi it was assumed "that massive [black] registration ... would create real power for black people."[7] Professor Mamie E. Locke writes: "Through the MFDP and grass roots efforts, Fannie Lou Hamer brought America one step closer to dismantling the barriers keeping African-Americans on the periphery of political involvement."[8] Fannie Lou Hamer and the others in the MFDP desperately tried to make sense of the bigger race-relations problems, as the cacophony of racial issues and separatist politics in Mississippi became almost deafening. But the political gains for blacks in the state would soon become self-evident, as the MFDP moved forward in the race for political justice. And Fannie Lou Hamer would, in essence, become the "spokesperson for the Mississippi Freedom Democratic Party."[9]

White politicians and Mississippi state leaders didn't like the attitudes of those who ran the infamous MFDP, as they believed you couldn't have two groups driving the same bus. But what the white Democrats would decide about the MFDP was disingenuous at best, particularly since they still wanted to exclude black people entirely from the political scene in Mississippi. Besides, it was too late to stop the momentum of the MFDP. Indeed, according to journalist Bill Minor, "This ragtag Mississippi 'freedom' delegation would rewrite the history of the national Democratic Party and [change] forever the relationship of Mississippi Democrats and other deep South Democrats to the national party."[10] Fannie Lou Hamer invited both blacks and whites to share their ideas, and to bring whatever they could to the table. But there was no appeasing the white Democratic Party of Mississippi, as they believed the MFDP organization was misguided. Many individuals in the civil rights movement, however, believed that the MFDP showed black people the way to solutions to intractable problems "that the other civil rights organizations [were] unwilling or simply unqualified to deal with."[11]

The MFDP was radical in the sense that it addressed the political disparities between blacks and whites. In this way, the MFDP became a watchdog organization of sorts, in terms of monitoring white hate groups like the White

Citizen Council, and even local white police authority. Indeed, it was perhaps "inconceivable that any politically aware person in the country could not know that a reign of terror existed in Mississippi, and that the regular delegation from Mississippi had been selected by the agents who perpetrated the terror."[12] Fannie Lou Hamer would come to understand that political power was what was absolutely necessary to fight the battles of injustice and discrimination. Some white critics called the decision to create the nontraditional MFDP an outrageous, ad hoc attempt to undermine the real political power in Mississippi. White members of the regular Democratic Party in the state even thought that the MFDP was shortsighted, parochial and exclusive to blacks. But this was not true. Former chairman of the Mississippi Freedom Democratic Party Laurence Guyot and Mike Thelwell, another founding member, wrote that the MFDP was summarily dismissed "as either an incongruous coalition of naïve idealists and unlettered sharecroppers without serious political intent or possibility — a kind of political oddity embodying simply a moral protest — or else [hinted] ominously as sinister, alien and, of course, unidentified influences, which [found] expression in an intransigent and unreasonable 'militance.'"[13] But such misperceptions were also untrue. The MFDP did not operate in private, or in some secret cabal; everything was done transparently. Still, the organization engendered a lot of resentment on the part of the white community, not to mention direct confrontation. The question was: Which political organization was going to have the most power and influence in the state of Mississippi, the white democrats or the inclusive MFDP? A fierce verbal battle erupted between blacks and whites regarding who would ultimately be seated at the 1964 Democratic National Convention. After all, the MFDP was an organization that was all about breaking the white supremacy rules of the day, as well as a way to keep the all-white Democratic Party off-balance. In this way, the MFDP was a serious counterbalance to white Democrats in Mississippi. According to professor Leslie Burl McLemore, in his seminal and groundbreaking work *The Mississippi Freedom Democratic Party: A Case Study of Grass-Roots Politics*, the MFDP "was developed for three basic reasons: (1) the long history of systematic exclusion of black citizen from equal participation in the political process in the state, (2) because the Mississippi Democratic Party had conclusively demonstrated its lack of loyalty to the National Democratic Party; and (3) the determination of the state's 'power structure' to maintain the status quo."[14]

Clearly, the MFDP's agenda was influenced by the way black people were being disenfranchised and oppressed in Mississippi. Indeed, sitting by and hoping against hope that things would change for blacks in Mississippi was unacceptable. And for a while, the MFDP emerged victorious. The organization was certainly a thorn in the side of white supremacy and those who supported segregation. It was hardly surprising that the MFDP would captivate the attention of the nation when it tried "to unseat and replace the fraudulently elected, all-white, regular delegation from Mississippi."[15] According to Elton C. Fax, "By its own admission the conventions in which its delegates were selected operated outside the framework of Mississippi law. Still, the MFDP did not consider itself a party of law-breakers because from their point of view [the] law, in the moral sense, did not and had not for years existed in Mississippi."[16] The MFDP had grandiose plans, but the organization, as we shall see, faced significant obstacles. Nevertheless, as historian John Dittmer writes, the MFDP's "challenge at Atlantic City [would serve] as the culmination of freedom summer and represented a turning point in the civil rights movement. It was the major story at the convention, played out before a television audience of millions of Americans."[17]

Fannie Lou Hamer consciously intended to make the MFDP a symbol of black disenfranchisement. As vice chairperson, she had every intention of making the MFDP just as important as the regular white Democrats in Mississippi. The organization would receive some powerful help. According to black congressman John Lewis, famous civil rights attorney, Joseph Rauh believed in what the MFDP was trying to accomplish; therefore, he traveled "to Mississippi to help guide the Freedom Democrats through the maze of precinct, county and state elections that marked the path to the national convention. The assumption was that the MFDP members would be excluded from each of these elections — which they were."[18] The discussions with Rauh and other members of the MFDP were aimed at strengthening the position of blacks politically in the state. Lewis goes on to tell us that Rauh and his staff prepared "carefully documented legal briefs" which became "the basis of the MFDP's claim that it should replace the regular [white] Mississippi Democratic Party in Atlantic City and fill the state's seats at the national convention with its delegates."[19]

Meanwhile, the MFDP's far-reaching goal of black participation in state and national elections was beginning to be realized with the registration of "63,000 black people from Mississippi into the Freedom Democratic Party,"[20] and the conducting of mock elections in unofficial Freedom Vote campaigns.[21] The MFDP would eventually "register eighty thousand people in its Freedom Ballot campaign,"[22] which made a difference in the final vote count when Fannie Lou Hamer became "the first black woman to run for Congress from the Second District of Mississippi."[23] Noted civil rights activist Aaron Henry from Mississippi discussed Hamer's run for political office this way: "By May 1964, four MFDP candidates had qualified to run in the Democratic congressional primary, including Fannie Lou Hamer, who later was one of the top drawing cards at the MFDP challenge in Atlantic City."[24] The fact that Fannie Lou Hamer was able to run for Congress was significant, but it became doubly so because, as a first-time voter, "the first ballot she cast was for herself, as a Mississippi Freedom Democratic Party candidate for the U.S. House of Representatives."[25] According to professor Susan Johnson, Fannie Lou Hamer "entered politics then to attain the necessary leverage to achieve particular goals for herself and the national black community."[26] So while the MFDP was dealing with social changes for blacks and human rights issues, Hamer was also focused on running a political campaign. When asked why she was running for Congress in 1964, she answered simply, "I'm showing people that a Negro can run for office."[27] "In the weeks just before the Democratic National Convention, emphasis was shifted from regular registration to gaining support for the Freedom Democratic Party."[28] Indeed, "voter registration workers spent most of their time explaining the [MFDP] to Negroes and getting those who supported it, and were without fear, to 'freedom register.'"[29] Later they focused on convincing blacks to vote for their respective candidates. In the end, under the banner of the MFDP "Freedom Ballot," Fannie Lou Hamer "received more votes than her white opponent, Congressman Jamie Whitten, but saw her election invalidated by the state."[30] Professor Linda Reed put it this way:

> Because the [all-white] regular Democratic Party disallowed her name on the ballot, the MFDP distributed a "Freedom Ballot" that included all of the candidates' names, black and white. Hamer defeated her white opponent, Congressman Jamie Whitten, on the alternative ballot, but the state refused to acknowledge the MFDP vote as valid.[31]

The results of the election surprised Fannie Lou Hamer. Although politically she could barely swim (literally, as well as she had never taken swimming lessons), Hamer had decided to wade into troubled political waters. And her unofficial win made Fannie Lou Hamer a successful black leader who showed that she could defeat a white opponent. The MFDP gave blacks a chance to vote for Fannie Lou Hamer and three other black candidates "running for national office in the 1964 elections" in Mississippi who did not "stand for political, social and economic exploitation and discrimination."[32] When all was said and done, the MFDP elected a delegation of 64 blacks and 4 whites to the 1964 Democratic Convention in Atlantic City, New Jersey. Accordingly, the MFDP attempted to unseat the all-white delegation, arguing that "it was the only Mississippi delegation that had been chosen in an election run according to the U.S. Constitution and the policies of the [National] Democratic Party."[33]

15

The Great Orator

Believe in yourself and your opponent will respect you.... People who believe
in themselves are worthier of love than people who doubt themselves.[1]

— J.M. Coetzee

It was hoped that through personal contact and dialogue, the MFDP
and the so-called "regular" white Democratic Party in Mississippi would take
credible moves to resolve their differences. But the white Democrats had no
intention of sharing power or allowing blacks to be a part of their exclusive,
separatist delegation. Nor did members of the MFDP have any face-to-face
meetings with their white counterparts. White politicians in Mississippi never
thought that the upstart MFDP would amount to anything. But they were
wrong. Some white leaders in Mississippi even said that Hamer wasn't savvy
enough to play the political game with the big boys. Denouncing her political
naiveté and righteous sermonizing, whites continued to verbally demean Fannie Lou Hamer and everyone else involved in the civil rights movement. They
also accused the group of inappropriately trying to grab political power. And
the MFDP *did* have power. In fact, "the MFDP experiment proved that blacks
could organize and work within the political system."[2] A major reason the
white Democrats disliked the MFDP was that this interracial group tried to
make things fair for both blacks *and* whites. Fannie Lou Hamer once commented, "We would have to have a change not only for the blacks in Mississippi but for the poor whites as well."[3] The MFDP tried to politically educate
whites as well as blacks.

The sheer gumption of establishing an opposition party like the MFDP
didn't sit well with the white community. White politicians in the state certainly did a fair amount of finger pointing for their inability to stop the MFDP.
It probably drove the white leadership crazy. They wanted to strike out at
anyone that dared question their authority. Fannie Lou Hamer's high profile
made her an easy target. Hamer had the kind of courage that could have
gotten her killed at any time. But Fannie Lou Hamer thought that her activism

was worth the risk. Still, her husband Pap didn't like the idea of Fannie Lou always putting her life in peril. In an interview before his death, Pap Hamer bitterly said, "I tried to warn my wife. I told her, 'You can't do everything.' But they still called on her. She would come in [from a trip] and as soon as she got in, they would call her again. They wore her down."[4]

Fannie Lou Hamer had become a maverick, and she would not slow down. Hamer was the epitome of the bold, fearless leader, as she became one of the principle architects of the MFDP. She was able to rebound from almost *any* adversity. Fannie Lou Hamer had come back from the brink of mental and physical disaster a bit stronger, smarter, and with renewed vigor. After all, Hamer was "a nonviolent soldier for a peoples' army engaged in a protracted conflict with the formal racism that ruled in Mississippi and across the South."[5]

Still it took Fannie Lou Hamer months of physical therapy to get fully back on her feet after the beatings at the Winona jail. During her seemingly endless speaking engagements, Hamer seemed frail and not quite her old self, but she struggled on. Regarding Winona, Hamer and the other black activists were intent on fighting the trumped-up charges brought against them there. Fannie Lou Hamer knew "that they should [not] be asked to give up so much to white racists after all they had suffered." Ultimately, Hamer would come to believe that whites "in power could not be compelled" to do the right thing toward them "by moral considerations."[6] At first, while she was locked up in the Winona jail, Hamer had thought that it would not be long before the FBI would come to rescue them, even though she never fully trusted the federal government. Indeed, Hamer once proclaimed, "I used to think the Justice Department was just what it said — justice." But in the end, she wanted to know if we had "a Justice Department or an Injustice Department."[7] She ultimately came to believe that the FBI was complicit in what happened to her and the others in Winona, because the agents were "too intimidating, too friendly with the other side, and above all too late."[8]

Apparently, the FBI was indeed on the side of sheriff Earl W. Patridge and his men, as they did not take the issue of what had happened to Hamer and her five companions seriously enough. Andrew Young of the Southern Christian Leadership Conference remembered how the FBI matter-of-factly told him and James Bevel that "a federal brutality complaint had been filed in the case, and he [an unknown FBI agent] had come over to investigate whether the sheriff and his deputies had been brutal."[9] So even though the FBI had learned that Hamer and the rest of her companions were locked up in the Winona jail, were intermittently beaten and tortured, were held without food for a period of time (and *never* provided access to a phone, clean clothes or even an attorney), they did nothing. As far as Fannie Lou Hamer was concerned, "They [the FBI] didn't investigate what happened to us — they investigated us."[10] The FBI inquiry concluded that there was insufficient evidence to make a definitive judgment about the guilt or innocence of her white attackers, despite the overwhelming evidence to the contrary, which clearly indicated assault and bodily harm. In other words, the FBI halfheartedly investigated the case of Hamer and the other black civil rights workers; but as far as Fannie Lou Hamer was concerned, the FBI "had done nothing of consequence" except "file a perfunctory report with the Justice Department after her assault in Winona."[11]

Perhaps sheriff Earl W. Patridge and Winona police chief Thomas Herod chalked it up to being the price you pay for going against the established white order. In fact, many white officials at that time in Mississippi made light of Fannie Lou Hamer's brutal beating because they believed "white authority" took precedence over everything else. The white men thought their cruelty was somehow justified. They tried to turn black people into something less than them; so these white lawmen felt they had the right to do exactly what they wanted to black people they arrested. The white lawmen had certainly overstepped their authority and "violated Hamer's civil rights."[12] But the white law enforcement officials acted like they didn't care about what they were doing to Hamer and the others. In so many words, it appeared no one cared about the magnitude of their terrible crimes. These white brutes didn't think they had to explain their actions to anyone. Indeed, the white lawmen were as nonchalant as they could be, as if they knew nothing would happen to them. Hamer had carefully and surreptitiously studied her white assailants. She had looked squarely at these white men, remembering their hateful faces and most of their names.

Still the white law enforcement officials indignantly stood by their story of innocence during the FBI investigation. They tried to raise doubts about what had actually happened at the Winona jail. The white lawmen even testified that Hamer and her companions were perfectly fine after their experience of being locked up. Later, it was revealed that the white lawmen got a thrill out of beating Hamer and the other black women. The pain and suffering these monsters inflicted upon Fannie Lou Hamer and her companions was unconscionable. However, such misdeeds by the white Mississippi lawmen would ultimately go unpunished.

Indeed, when the Winona law enforcement officials "were finally brought to trial in federal court," for the unlawful beatings, "they were acquitted of all charges by an all-white jury."[13] The white defendants were found *not guilty*, which begged the question: Why was there a trial in the first place? Indeed, what difference did it make, when "the same white policeman who was responsible for Ms. Hamer's beating served on the jury at her trial?"[14] Hamer and the other civil rights workers felt a profound sense of sadness and humiliation after their experience at the trial. The white lawmen never apologized to Fannie Lou Hamer and the other black women; they were cowards without any remorse. This so-called trial served to further enrage many of Hamer's supporters.

Although they lost this particular battle, Fannie Lou Hamer hoped that they (members of the MFDP) would be more successful in August 1964 in challenging "the regular state organization for seating at the Democratic National Convention in Atlantic City."[15] But it wouldn't be easy. Ella Baker kept Hamer informed about the intricacies of national political conventions, as Fannie Lou Hamer's knowledge of what to expect in New Jersey was somewhat limited. It would be her first National Convention. About attending the 1964 Democratic Convention, Fannie Lou Hamer commented:

> When we went to Atlantic City, we went there because we believed that America was what it said it was, "the land of the free." And I thought with all of my heart that the [white] people would have been unseated in Atlantic City. And I believed that, because if the Constitution of this United States means something to all of us, then I knew they would unseat them. So we went to Atlantic City with all of this hope.[16]

According to Hamer, the MFDP was serious about seating all of their sixty-eight delegates. She wanted everyone to know the whole scope of what the organization represented. But the trip to New Jersey to attend the 1964 Democratic Convention was a major undertaking indeed. Fannie Lou Hamer would come to believe that black people elsewhere were treated just as badly as they were in Mississippi, because they had to stay at a hot, segregated un-air-conditioned flea bag place called the Gem Motel. Most of the MFDP delegation arrived by bus. Hamer, however, arrived on August 22, 1964, from New York, "where she had made a speech before the parents of Freedom Summer volunteers a few days before the convention."[17] Those MFDP members who arrived by bus missed Hamer's camaraderie, as she would sing gospel and freedom songs on long bus trips. Indeed, many would feel comforted when Fannie Lou Hamer would belt out a powerfully emotional song of the civil rights movement in a "voice that moved all who heard her."[18] Hamer felt honored and humbled by all of the attention she and the MFDP was getting from the media. It wasn't necessarily her cup of tea to be in the mix of things, but Fannie Lou Hamer would do what she could all the same.

When Hamer and other MFDP leaders showed up at the Democratic Convention headquarters in Atlantic City, the regular, all-white Democratic

Party from the state of Mississippi "openly professed their disloyalty to the national party,"[19] because it had been "ruled that all convention delegates would be required to make a pledge of party loyalty."[20] Although many might have considered what the regular Democrats from Mississippi were doing as so much posturing, they still thumbed "their noses at the party's national leaders and [made] it difficult for the president [Lyndon B. Johnson] to continue to back them."[21] According to political historian John Dittmer, "To challenge successfully the legitimacy of the [all-white] Democratic Party in Mississippi, [the MFDP] needed to prove that blacks were systematically excluded from participating in the regular party's selection of delegates to the national convention."[22] This was all Hamer and the other delegates of the MFDP needed to hear, as they were capable, ready and enthusiastic about doing anything and everything for their cause. Therefore, they set out to lobby other delegations.[23] Professor Jack Minnis wrote:

> Every delegate from every likely state was provided with a copy of the brief to the credentials committee. Every request for information and justification was filled. MFDP, with the help of SNCC, produced brochures, mimeographed biographies of the MFDP delegates, histories of the MFDP, legal arguments, historical arguments, and distributed them to the delegates. In short, no avenue of political persuasion was left unraveled.[24]

In addition, at least "twenty five Democratic congressmen were also backing" the MFDP.[25] The "regular" white delegation from Mississippi, of course, thought that President Lyndon B. Johnson would back them up, so they "found it unnecessary to mount such an effort."[26] The MFDP went all out to be seated at the 1964 Democratic Convention. The unrelenting pace of Hamer and other MFDP members would continue for the duration of their time in Atlantic City, New Jersey. In the end, the "regular" white democrats would come to hate President Johnson as "a traitor to the South; as they categorically opposed civil rights, and they had no intention of supporting the national ticket."[27] The regular Democrats certainly made matters worse by criticizing the efforts of the MFDP. Personally, Fannie Lou Hamer was convinced that the white delegates from Mississippi didn't care at all about them, because they simply couldn't "see the error of their ways and seat the MFDP."[28]

Fannie Lou Hamer and the MFDP faced a daunting challenge. For Hamer and the others, it was a revelatory experience. There were few periods during Hamer's life when she didn't think about change and justice for black people. As events unfolded, Fannie Lou Hamer felt that she had nothing to lose by throwing herself headlong into the political fray, especially when she "took the cause of black political representation to the floor of the Democratic

National Convention to demand seating of [the] popularly chosen black delegates."[29] But this was not to be.

The credentials committee began the hearing of the MFDP's challenge by listening to the testimony of Aaron Henry, a black man and one of the leaders of the black delegation, as well as Fannie Lou Hamer and the Reverend Edwin King, a white man and another MFDP leader.[30] When Hamer finally addressed the convention, her heart was pounding as she made her important delivery. But she relaxed herself and went on as if she were having a conversation with a next door neighbor. Hamer unhurriedly talked about her dark and sad experiences. Though unaccustomed to the national spotlight, Hamer's voice had a measured quality to it, as she spoke very clearly about their group's intention. It was a pivotal moment. Hamer paused to compose herself during her testimony, and her voice dropped almost to a conversational whisper. That day, "with a bloody eye from the [Winona] assault still visible,"[31] Hamer's eyes were fixed as she recalled the horrors of her life, and the punishing blows that rained down upon her at the Winona jail. The eloquence of her sad recollections and the intensity of her voice got everyone's attention. It was the speech of her life, and it resonated with the crowd of attendees. The atmosphere was electric. It was as if America had been struck silent for the short time Fannie Lou Hamer spoke.

This was definitely an eye opener for many who didn't know what was going on in Mississippi: the harsh episodes of racism and discrimination against the descendants of African slaves. How could anyone ignore that? Hamer told them how the civil rights activists, herself included, shrieked in excruciating agony while they were being abused. She remembered momentarily blacking out, but still being beaten when she came to. It was extremely hard for her to talk about such matters, but she forced herself to do it. Her unprepared, impromptu statement sent a devastating message to the nation about the plight of blacks in the state of Mississippi.

Hamer had a powerful voice. By describing what was really going on in Mississippi, Fannie Lou Hamer had hoped to make people aware of the pain and suffering of blacks in the state. She went through a terrible period of remembering what she probably wanted to forget: that she suffered a severe beating at the hands of evil white men, not unlike an African slave being whipped unmercifully by an overseer. Prior to this time, Fannie Lou Hamer wasn't ready to fully discuss what happened. But on that day she talked bravely to the American people. It wasn't a particularly brilliant speech; the brilliance came from *how* she said it. Her words sent shock waves nationwide. Fannie Lou Hamer "stunned the convention when she described how Mississippi police had repeatedly beaten her in jail after her first attempt at voter registration."[32]

This was Hamer's opportunity to capture a national audience that wanted, perhaps, to hear the truth. So with determination in her voice, uttering arguably her most famous phrase, Fannie Lou Hamer ended her testimony by stating, "If the Freedom Democratic Party is not seated now, I question America."[33] Showing an expression of pain, Fannie Lou went on to ask, "Is this America, the land of the free and the home of the brave, where we have to sleep with our telephone off the hooks because our lives [are] threatened daily because we want to live as decent human beings in America?"[34] Her words and appeal unquestionably carried the day. Hamer's testimony at the 1964 Democratic Convention was nothing short of a triumph. She had hitherto been known as a stern fighter in the background of the movement. But Hamer captivated the nation with her simple talk, her grace and modesty. She certainly sparked debate after her glorious moment of fame. Many white Southerners, however, saw Hamer's testimony as nothing more than a melodramatic mess. Fannie Lou Hamer had tried to retain her composure during the entire time of her testimony, but according to Sanford Wexler, Hamer finally "broke down and wept before network television cameras that were providing live national coverage of the testimony."[35] It was very emotional and difficult to watch. Fortunately, Hamer was able to get her point across. After delivering her statement, Fannie Lou Hamer was seen by some of her fellow civil rights activists as the black *Joan of Arc*. Her speech was probably one of the most important things she had every done in her life. And Hamer was shrewd enough to understand the political impact of her little talk. Hamer "gained national attention when she testified as an MFDP representative before the convention's credentials committee."[36] Everyone took note of this plump black woman. And after hearing her story, almost everyone interested knew what motivated Fannie Lou Hamer. The 1964 Democratic Convention made Fannie Lou Hamer a national celebrity, a national hero.

16

Continuation of a Political Struggle

Certainly for many the late 1960s seemed like the dawn of a new era, one
during which the wrongs of so many centuries could finally be righted. In
that sense, the leaders of its movements saw themselves as the heirs to the
revolutionaries who founded the nation, the abolitionists and suffragettes
who fought to realize the promise of liberty for all citizens, and the labor
leaders who fought for equity and dignity.[1]

— Ronald V. Dellums

Fannie Lou Hamer continued to maintain a dim view of white politicians
and the white Democratic delegates from Mississippi. Indeed, she expressed
disapproval of their uncouth decision not to include black Democratic delegates. Therefore, the MFDP, in no uncertain terms, "asked to represent the
state of Mississippi."[2] Hamer, of course, never remotely believed that a white
politician in the state of Mississippi would "speak for them [black people]."[3]
Therefore, she and others had to do things outside the expected political
norm. But the fundamental differences between the two groups were not
enough to distract Fannie Lou Hamer and other MFDP leaders from their
calculated plan to unseat the delegates of the all-white Mississippi Democratic
Party. The MFDP's technique of *direct action* was profoundly reactionary and
profoundly revolutionary. Additionally, the impasse between the segregated
Mississippi Democratic Party delegation and the Freedom Democratic Party
represented a major challenge for the National Democratic Party in Atlantic
City. Nevertheless, the main focus of the MFDP was to do whatever it took
to seat the integrated delegation, no matter how impossible it might seem.
Consequently, the all-white Mississippi Democratic party delegation, along
with other "delegations from five other Southern states, boldly threatened to
walk out of the convention if the Mississippi segregationists were not seated."[4]

The MFDP ambitiously attempted to change the way things were done
at the Democratic Convention, and how people viewed the regular white
Democratic Party from Mississippi. It was a bold move, but it seemed to have

gone a long way toward forcing the National Democratic Party to make a decision about who would be seated. "The Democratic Party had to decide which delegation represented Mississippi."[5] Indeed, members of the MFDP wanted swift recognition of their delegation, which would have decreased the importance of the segregationists. The MFDP also believed that they were the more legitimate of the two rival Mississippi delegations. In this regard, the MFDP "argued that an all-white delegation could not [possibly] represent the whole state."[6] The situation came to a head at the 1964 Democratic Convention. And the American people were definitely watching, with the focus resting on the larger-than-life persona of Fannie Lou Hamer. According to black writer June Jordan, when the American people "heard [Hamer] speak, all good people were shocked by her suffering." And when all was said and done, "Thousands and thousands of people wanted to help her [Hamer] on to a freedom victory."[7]

It was a spellbinding, big-stage moment, and an electrifying day to be remembered. People watched and listened in disbelief as this poor black woman "in an inexpensive cotton dress"[8] spoke passionately about her awful experiences. In the end, people throughout the nation "were amazed at how brave she was. Thousands of people across the country wrote letters of support for Fannie Lou and her [Freedom Democratic] party."[9] But not all interested parties were pleased by Hamer's speech. In his award winning book *Bearing the Cross*, David J. Garrow writes: "Mrs. Hamer's powerful testimony—a vivid account of the brutalities she had suffered as a grassroots activist in Mississippi—shocked a nationwide television audience until coverage was suddenly shifted to a quickly called presidential press conference."[10] This press conference was a deliberate effort to remove the spotlight from what was being said by the MFDP and other black activists.

This particular time at the 1964 Democratic Convention was certainly an awkward, even embarrassing moment for President Lyndon B. Johnson and many in the audience Fannie Lou Hamer had spoken to that day. Indeed, watching this drama unfold in front of a national broadcast audience was a disturbing thing for President Johnson to witness. After all, as Dittmer related:

> The Democratic National Convention of 1964 ... was to be a coronation of sorts for President Lyndon B. Johnson. No other names would be placed in nomination; there would be no major platform fights. A week before the convention the only item of suspense was Johnson's choice of a running mate. But the sixty-four blacks and four whites who constituted the Mississippi Freedom Democratic Party delegation threw a monkey wrench into the President's plan for an orchestrated convention. For four days the FDP challenge of the Mississippi regulars was the major event in Atlantic City.[11]

When President Johnson got wind of the messy development, he tried to stop the MFDP from gaining any real traction because "he feared that if the convention officially booted out the Mississippi regulars and replaced them with the mostly black MFDP delegation, other Southern delegations would walk out in protest too."[12] In this respect, things were not going as planned, as the MFDP played the spoiler to the Mississippi segregationists. Ultimately, it was this noncommittal attitude on the part of President Johnson and his advisors that was the straw that broke the camel's back. Johnson didn't like the idea of this Fannie Lou Hamer woman and other MFDP members waltzing into the place — essentially *his* Convention — and telling the National Democratic Party leaders about the racial injustices going on in Mississippi. Hamer's damning comments made some leaders of the National Democratic Party nervous. In explaining her beliefs, Fannie Lou Hamer tried to make people understand that blacks had come too far to turn their backs on their hard-fought civil rights work. In her own indelicate words, Hamer once stated: "We're getting sick of this [giving in to whites]. We want somebody that's going to say, 'Well, now this is wrong, let's talk about doing something.' And that's what we been fussing about."[13]

In explaining President Lyndon B. Johnson's unorthodox efforts to divert attention away from Fannie Lou Hamer's testimony — because she was diverting attention from *him*— political historians Frances Fox, Lorraine C. Minnite and Margaret Groarke write:

> Most but not all of Fannie Lou Hamer's story of her beating in a Winona, Mississippi, jail cell was aired live. Worried about the impact any testimony from MFDP delegates could have on public opinion, President Johnson conducted a hastily organized diversion campaign by alerting the media to a planned meeting at the White House with thirty Democratic governors. Johnson deliberately misled the press into assuming that an announcement of his vice presidential choice was imminent. As Mrs. Hamer neared the end of her statement, NBC broke away to cover the president's press conference. Johnson used up as much time as he could without making any announcements or revealing any news....[14]

But the plan didn't quite work. According to Kotz, President Johnson's "ploy [indeed] knocked the latter part of Hamer's testimony off the air. [However], that evening ... the television networks replayed Hamer's graphic account in prime time."[15] Fannie Lou Hamer had previously been treated mostly with indifference by whites from Mississippi, but "it took [her] stirring testimony ... to trigger events that would later doom forever the Democrats' domination of Mississippi politics."[16] Some white Southerners felt that too much was being made of Hamer's singular voice. Journalist Bill Minor has pointed out that Hamer's "words that day ignited the emergence of the Republican Party to become in the next 25 years a dominant political force in Mississippi."[17] President Johnson thought that it would be a good idea to negotiate an end to the Mississippi delegation debate. Indeed, Johnson wanted a quick resolution to the impasse and relief of tension that was bubbling to the surface in Atlantic City. According to Laura Baskes Litwin, President Lyndon B. Johnson "assigned Hubert Humphrey, one of the U.S. Senators from Minnesota, to handle the situation."[18] Johnson and Humphrey, of course, wanted to control how the media handled the story of the 1964 Democratic Convention and the ramifications of two opposing delegations from Mississippi.

Ultimately, via some complex political maneuvering, a compromise was suggested for all involved. The "lobbying efforts" of the MFDP "were clearly effective, and when it appeared that sufficient support existed in the Credentials Committee to bring the challenge on the convention floor, administrative forces led by Senator Hubert Humphrey (who was eager to become the vice-presidential nominee) proposed a series of compromises."[19] Some individuals at the 1964 Democratic National thought that it would be an impossible task for the two Mississippi delegations to agree on anything. And the MFDP was facing an uphill battle. During this entire time, Fannie Lou Hamer kept her wits about her. She wasn't seeking some kind of scorched-earth battle; but she wasn't willing to make any concessions either. She was hurt and upset. The National Democratic Party officials essentially offered "to seat the white delegation if they would take a loyalty oath and ... give delegate-at-large status to two individuals [delegates Aaron Henry, a black man, and Ed King, a white man] from the MFDP."[20] The proffered compromise to the MFDP appeared to be quite straightforward, but it would never do. Fannie Lou Hamer believed that to accept such a paltry offering would have been an ignoble, humiliating departure from what the MFDP wanted to do. Accordingly, "the MFDP promptly rejected the compromise and with that their hopes of replacing the Mississippi regulars withered and died."[21]

It angered Fannie Lou Hamer to have the MFDP's efforts devalued. Hamer felt that any compromise would be an admission of defeat. She didn't want to squander the opportunity to challenge the regular white Democrats from Mississippi. Hamer decided that she wouldn't be forced to accept any compromise or unreasonable terms — from anybody — even though a political deal was anticipated and expected. Fannie Lou Hamer and other MFDP leaders "felt the Johnson offer was little more than an insult, and found it particularly offensive that the President's forces had specified the two MFDP delegates who should assume the seats."[22]

After lengthy discussions, and under the aegis of Ella Baker and others, like Dr. Martin Luther King, Jr., Hamer was not persuaded. Some felt the compromise was fair and accommodating, but Fannie Lou Hamer remained unyielding. The compromise didn't seem like a very good bargain to her, as she thought it was disingenuous. Indeed, "The two at-large seats were not enough for the MFDP." More importantly, "The at-large label meant that the convention [would not recognize] the MFDP's right to represent Mississippians."[23]

Fannie Lou Hamer felt that the weight of the world was on her shoulders. Ultimately, she was just as frustrated and angry as anyone else. All Hamer wanted from the other MFDP delegates was for them to think twice, while listening to their conscience, before accepting the compromise or any concessions. Hamer tried to remind them of why they were there at the convention in the first place. She finally wanted them to act in their own best interests, reminding them that it was not over unless everyone believed that it was over. Fannie Lou Hamer remained hopeful, tempering her expectations for getting *anything* for her efforts with pragmatic realism. But many MFDP members were worried that their endeavors would prove counter-productive. Seating the MFDP was their top priority. It was hard finding a middle ground. Therefore, the compromise received caustic criticism from the predominantly black Mississippi delegation of the MFDP. Their harsh reaction was unexpected. And things unraveled as everything happened very fast. Many were particularly incensed by Senator Hubert Humphrey's patronizing and energetic efforts to broker the compromise.

It was a cantankerous affair filled with anger and recriminations and disturbing implications. In the end, "The MFDP delegates and other civil rights leaders believed that the white liberals had sold them out."[24] Hamer voiced her frustrations in blunt terms:

> A few of the Mississippi delegation favored the compromise and wanted me to convince the others, but I said, "I'm not making a decision for the 68 delegates. I won't do it." So, you see, after they talked to these people and we didn't know nothing about it, then they had the press outside waiting [to write] that they was going to accept the compromise.[25]

It was not only Hamer and the MFDP who rejected the proposed compromise. It also caused an instant backlash from the white "regular" Democrats from Mississippi. The unrepentant Mississippi segregationists became extremely upset because of Senator Hubert Humphrey's optimism about the compromise and pitch for racial reconciliation. It also didn't take long to understand that the National Democratic Party, in defiance of the all-white regulars, would permit blacks to be seated in two at-large seats. The white delegation thought this was outrageous. Hence, "The regulars denounced this compromise and all but three of them walked out of the convention."[26]

For the famously outspoken Hamer, it was an exhausting time. Hamer had become a symbol for what the MFDP stood for. Over the course of the 1964 Democratic Convention, she became deeply involved in the business of the MFDP, making key decisions. And Hamer pulled things off at the Convention magnificently. She never wanted to bow down to members of the National Democratic Party, as she stuck to her high ideals regarding the fight to seat the MFDP. Political expediency was not a principle she embraced. And she would never compromise her principles. Some believed that the two Democratic groups from Mississippi would cancel each other out, but Hamer firmly believed that the MFDP should be chosen over the regular white Democrats. Garrow described the situation:

> By late Tuesday afternoon it was clear that the MFDP and its supporters faced an unpalatable choice: surrender their pride and accept the two token at-large votes, or reject the Johnson offer and condemn the blatant hypocrisy of a president and a party that professed a commitment to civil rights but refused to seat an integrated group of delegates fully supportive of the policies that president and party claimed to advocate.[27]

When the MFDP refused to accept the two-seat compromise, they were summarily excluded. Hamer had put everything on the table, but the MFDP had not been voted in or seated. The rejection came as a devastating blow to Hamer and the rest of the MFDP delegates, as all thoughts of replacing the all-white Mississippi Democratic Party delegation vanished with a swift vote by the National Democratic Party to seat the regulars. In other words, "the Democratic Party let the all-white delegation represent Mississippi,"[28] in 1964. While the fears of the regular Democrats were assuaged, members of the MFDP delegation were extremely upset. And to show their displeasure by not being seated at the Democratic Convention, nine MFDP delegates "infiltrated the [convention] hall and unfolded signs during the nominating speeches."[29] Although they would ultimately leave the convention hall later, the MFDP delegates took some satisfaction from the protest. While Fannie Lou Hamer lamented such a bad result, according to Asante, "The rejection of the MFDP's delegation did not prevent Hamer from condemning racism in Mississippi and hypocrisy in its democratic process."[30] Undaunted, Fannie Lou Hamer continued to voice her opinions about political injustices at the 1964 Democratic Convention.

Fannie Lou Hamer was not pleased with Senator Humphrey's role in the debacle, as she thought he was in some way complicit in the decision not to seat the MFDP. Hamer later told Humphrey that she would pray for him for his transgression. "In tears," according to Taylor Branch, "Humphrey protested that his commitment to civil rights was long-standing. Hamer cried, too, saying she was going to pray further over him."[31] Hamer had other things on her mind as well, because "for two days [Hamer] tried to walk into the convention and take a seat. Each time, guards stopped her. But she made her point."[32] Meanwhile, Hamer was having a hard time coping with the Democratic Party's rejection. To soothe her nerves, Hamer began singing, to keep everyone feeling like they were still in it together. Indeed, "the political delegation became an impromptu choir," as Hamer "led the MFDP delegation in singing gospel songs,"[33] like "Go Tell It on the Mountain," "Ain't Gonna Turn Me Round," and her famous rendition of "This Little Light of Mine." Fannie Lou Hamer was able to take solace from her music, which "permeated her whole life."[34]

17

Racism, the White Citizens' Council, and the FBI

On the surface at least, the beginning and the end of Mississippi politics is the Negro. He has no hand in the voting, no part in factional maneuvers, no seats in legislature; nevertheless, he fixes the tone — so far as the outside world is concerned — of Mississippi politics.[1]

— V.O. Key, Jr.

Although President Lyndon B. Johnson "had deployed his considerable forces to counter every MFDP move,"[2] Hamer and other leaders of the group were able to accomplish much of what they set out to do at the 1964 Democratic Convention — to challenge the conventional wisdom of depraved "white rule" in Mississippi without fear of death or other repercussions. The MFDP had effectively undermined the entire "regular" white Democrats in the state, while reforming the entire political system.[3] Additionally, one day these hardened white Democrats would eventually become staunch Republicans — the party of Lincoln — which white Southerners generally despised at one time. "The switch of Southern whites to overwhelming support of Republicans"[4] can be traced to Hamer and the MFDP and their machinations to change the dominant white political structure in the South. Public opinion about racial matters in the South would drastically shift after Fannie Lou Hamer's famous words at the 1964 Democratic Convention. Indeed, Hamer captured the public's imagination with her elegant speech. Former president of the Southern Christian Leadership Conference, the Rev. Ralph D. Abernathy, once commented that Fannie Lou Hamer "touched the lives of countless numbers of individuals, and her message of hope and steadfast determination [stayed] in our hearts."[5]

Some members of the civil rights movement believed that although they lost the delegation battle at the convention, it was still a moral victory, especially for those who cared about racial equality and voting rights. In fact, the rejected offer to seat at least some of the MFDP delegates was a major triumph. Some even saw it as the turning point of Democratic politics. But it was not a victory for Fannie Lou Hamer, certainly not a *moral* one. Hamer stated:

> What do you mean, moral victory, we ain't getting nothing. What kind of moral victory was that we'd [sat] up there, and they'd seen us on television? We come on back home and go right up on the first tree that we get to because, you know, that's what they were going to do to us. What had we gained?[6]

Despite the turmoil and hard feelings, Fannie Lou Hamer's presence at the convention had a calming affect on the other activists, as she engendered a feeling of well-being and cockiness that rubbed off on some people. And the nation began to pay even closer attention to her. Some people even sought her autograph, others wanted Hamer to speak at certain progressive functions. The MFDP workers left the convention in New Jersey figuring they had at least been heard. But it was not enough. For some black activists and organizers, "fresh from the deadly struggle in Mississippi, such a rationalization was unacceptable, even incomprehensible."[7]

Returning home on chartered buses, the MFDP delegates and Hamer tried to put some kind of perspective on everything that had happened in Atlantic City, as they sang wonderful "songs about Jesus, freedom songs, southern black work songs, [and] protest songs learned from Southern black religion"[8] on the long, sad trip back to Mississippi. The most important thing Fannie Lou Hamer took away from the 1964 Democratic Convention was that it helped her realize that white Democrats from Mississippi would never willingly give in when it came to racial issues and equality; they would have to be *coerced* and pushed hard into doing the right thing. Indeed, her valiant refusal to give in to the National Democratic Party's compromise, and her famous stance at the convention, prepared her for even greater challenges as a civil rights activist. Due to her positive frame of mind, Hamer had no doubt that the MFDP could still do great things and succeed in the state. Hamer was decidedly more optimistic than some of the other MFDP members. But Fannie Lou Hamer and her allies would discover "the emptiness of traditional American liberalism." In addition, she "quickly came to understand that the opposition to freedom of some in this country was a political expediency." Therefore, Hamer believed that whites wanted the MFDP "to be destroyed, not just as a black people's movement, but as a symbol of rising grassroots democracy."[9] Although sophisticated whites did not elaborate in public about what hateful measures they might take against the MFDP, Fannie Lou Hamer's "name was in the little black book of the White Citizens Council."[10]

As she thought about her next move, Fannie Lou Hamer didn't want to show the MFDP's cards, or radical white groups might try to get the upper hand against them. Hamer's overwhelming priority as one of the leaders of the MFDP was to get back and start quickly registering black people to vote again. With an abundance of energy, Hamer knew that the MFDP faced a formidable task. But she and other black activists would not be sidetracked by white hate groups. In contemplating what should be done, Fannie Lou Hamer was always a voice of reason. She had a positive perspective and outlook on life. But Hamer was also "a radical in the deepest sense of the word, seeking to understand, expose, and destroy the root causes of oppression."[11]

Blacks were proud of their expanded role in Mississippi politics. Indeed, according to Lawrence Guyot and Mike Thelwell, the television coverage at the week-long Democratic Convention "did more than a month of mass meetings in showing people that there was nothing necessary and eternal about white political supremacy, and that they — who had been told by the system that they were nothing — could from the strength of organization affect the system."[12] Fannie Lou Hamer had generated a groundswell of hope and good will, but she could not erase the fact that the MFDP had returned from the 1964 Democratic Convention defeated and powerless. Some success was inevitable, Hamer believed. And things would be different. For example, the credentials committee of the National Democratic Party proclaimed that, "the Mississippi delegation must integrate its forces before the next convention — or be disqualified."[13] So in other words, the national party changed its convention rules to state that "in the future no state would be seated if blacks were barred from the selection process and none were in their delegation."[14] This important development was a good thing because it meant that the "regular" Democrats from Mississippi "could no longer play by their own rules if they were going to participate in the national party."[15] Fannie Lou Hamer was no doubt pleased about this decision from the National Democratic Party, while whites in Mississippi took offense. And in the end, the MFDP "forced the attention of the nation from President Johnson on down."[16] Johnson, of course, had been so upset by the electrifying Fannie Lou Hamer that he said, "She must never be allowed to speak again at a Democratic Convention,"[17] which would essentially keep her out of the political spotlight. Such was the power and influence of Fannie Lou Hamer. She knew that something substantial had happened at the convention, which could have a profound effect on black politics in Mississippi. This is important to understand, because as far back as 1963, civil rights activists in the state had been searching "for new ways to crack the closed [Mississippi] society."[18] Journalist Elliot Jaspin cogently explained it this way: "The mark of citizenship is the right to vote, and that right was largely denied to blacks. Worse still, segregation widened the gulf between blacks and the community they lived in."[19]

As previously mentioned, Fannie Lou Hamer had run for Congress but lost, and even contemplated a run for Ruleville mayor.[20] When asked why she thought blacks should actively run for political office, Hamer indicated that "she wanted to show people that a black person *could* run for public office."[21] Many blacks in Mississippi were still afraid to challenge the establish order. Therefore, many kept their opinions to themselves. But this was the time when almost everything started to crumble for white Democrats in the state, as unregistered black voters continued "to dramatize the flagrant totalitarianism of Southern politics," and the white power structure began to take black activists more seriously.[22] Whites in Mississippi were troubled by the new spirit of political activism in blacks, because white racism was still the main frame of reference for black people during the 1960s, and segregation was the dominant style.[23]

Many whites believed that it was *heresy* for blacks to fight for changing their positions in life. And these whites would attack anyone, other whites included, who spoke out against them and their brand of white power and racism.

Consequently, many thought that Mississippi would never overcome its image of racial intolerance and injustices because of the terrible behavior of some whites. Meanwhile, "Nightriders [white men] poured volleys of shots into the homes of [blacks] active in civil rights work. Gasoline and dynamite bombs were tossed at homes from passing cars. Crosses burned as fiery symbols of opposition to integration — and a challenge to the [black] invaders."[24] Nonetheless, blacks like Fannie Lou Hamer in Mississippi continued to risk their lives for the right to vote and to be accommodated at restaurants and other public and private establishments. Hamer paid almost no attention to the hateful words and criticism from whites, as she had a job to do. For example, Hamer "helped distribute clothing sent down from the North"[25] for needy black families in the Mississippi Delta, as well as passing out surplus commodities from the Federal government, like powdered milk and processed American cheese.[26] A profoundly intelligent person, who could confound you with her keen understanding of social and political matters, Fannie Lou Hamer believed that she could change things for blacks everywhere by direct confrontation, although she didn't believe in making a mountain out of a molehill. For these reasons, whites in Mississippi were quick in trying to defame and humiliate Hamer for going against the traditional powers of "white rule." Indeed, she remained a thorn in the side of white politicians in the state as they tried to keep a tight grip on power.

Groups like the White Citizens' Council were "dedicated to the preservation of Jim Crow."[27] The White Citizens' Council wanted to keep blacks and whites separated at all cost. They also wanted whites in Mississippi to turn a deaf ear to the complaints of black people in the state. Their immediate challenge was to stop the momentum and keep blacks in their so-called place, while slowing down the spread of the civil rights movement. They wanted to undermine the successful efforts of the MFDP and other black activist groups. According to Whitehead, "the convulsion" of the White Citizens' Council "was triggered in part by angry reaction to COFO's voter-registration drive and its organization ... of the Mississippi Freedom Democratic Party (MFDP)."[28] Disgruntled white people in the state who had racist and white supremacist agendas didn't like the idea that there were black groups forming alliances against them, ready to boycott or demonstrate at the drop of a hat. Indeed, some whites in Mississippi decried the new attitudes of blacks. Fannie Lou Hamer, however, wouldn't take a back seat to anyone in her commitment to helping blacks in Mississippi. In other words, Fannie Lou Hamer was resolute in refusing to be stopped by threats of any kind. In many ways, the White Citizens' Council conspired directly against Hamer, ratcheting up their opposition to the civil rights movement. Fannie Lou Hamer was challenging the authority of "white rule" and the old guard. Indeed, many whites had trouble digesting the fact that things were going to eventually change for black people in Mississippi, especially regarding voting rights and race relations. Needless to say, some white racists believed that "black people should always remain subordinate to white people or be *exterminated* [my emphasis], for all time."[29] Fannie Lou Hamer famously found herself again at the center of controversy, as she seemed willing to violate the white *status quo*, regardless of the consequences. She knew her purpose in life was to fight vigorously the terrible forces of racism. Hamer didn't hesitate to write:

> The sickness in Mississippi is not a Mississippi sickness. This is America's sickness. We talk about democracy, we talk about the land of the free, but it's not true. We talk about freedom of speech, but in every corner of this United States men who try to speak the truth are crushed.[30]

Many whites in Mississippi thought that it was unrealistic for Hamer and other black activists to expect change immediately. As it was, white politicians were not concerned about lifting black people from their ugly poverty and terrible existence. Indeed, the White Citizens Council "managed to divert the antipathy of most white Mississippians for integration into a mold which [included] the total rejection of any deviation from the status quo."[31] Black people in the state were still being ignored by whites, especially in regards to politics. White participants of the Citizens Council, fighting the new Supreme

Court ban on segregation, especially in public schools, "looked upon them-selves as nonviolent [white] men, seeking to forestall [black] hotheads." They organized "to bring economic pressures upon" blacks, thinking they could discourage activists from any "political activity in the state."[32] They were wrong. Equally important, the White Citizens Council in Mississippi used "economic pressure against dissenting whites" and blacks as a "main weapon" to isolate "moderate and liberal whites from the rest of the white community," completely destroying any notion of "interracial communication."[33] In essence, groups like the White Citizens' Council discouraged cooperation with blacks in Mississippi, and condemned any kind of racial reconciliation, because their ultimate goal was to deny the socio-political equality of black people.[34] After all, Mississippi during the late 1950s and early 1960s had the highest black population in the nation but the lowest percentage of registered black vot-ers.[35]

But the day of reckoning for white racist groups like the Citizens' Council appeared imminent, as far as Fannie Lou Hamer was concerned. She felt that things would eventually become clearer for whites who resisted change. How-ever, the White Citizens' Council "was dedicated to preserving white supremacy," and even "politicized religion in defense of segregation."[36] His-torian Frank Lambert writes: "Recognizing that segregation had widespread appeal among [white] Mississippians ... the Council published a series of pam-phlets arguing that segregation was not only the Mississippi way but also that of [supposedly] orthodox Christianity."[37] What rubbish. All in all, the White Citizens Council helped "to create the attitude of violence" that was so evident at that time; and white segregationists in Mississippi and "throughout the South ... resorted to claiming that their social heritage and mores were vio-lated" by the Supreme Court's decision in favor of integration.[38] Even the late President Ronald Reagan described such integration measures, as well as the Voting Rights Act of 1965, as "humiliating to the South."[39] Furthermore, as Phillip Abbott Luce has pointed out, many white leaders in the South "cried daily tears over the fact" that they wouldn't be able to deny "the Negro his vote and his place in society."[40]

During this time, many believed that Fannie Lou Hamer was under peri-odic surveillance by the FBI for her involvement in the civil rights movement in Mississippi. Indeed, this was ultimately confirmed by the FBI. But they were spying on Hamer, not protecting her. In fact, "The FBI spied on anyone interested in the state of race relations in the United States, including Hamer and her Mississippi Freedom Democratic Party."[41] According to Kenneth O'Reilly, FBI "agents stood by, to all appearances allied through their own studied neutrality with the [white] enemies of black people rather than with those who risked their lives to demand justice, dignity, and a fair share of the democracy that white America always seemed" to celebrate.[42] Nevertheless, Hamer was a pugnacious and seasoned activist by this time, and she took no prisoners when it came to voter registration and involving herself in Mississippi politics. And although Fannie Lou Hamer had been quickly thrust onto center stage in the civil rights movement, she expressed little more than pessimism when considering the FBI, because white law enforcement officials *never* did anything to make her life easier or safer. Regardless, Hamer at this time began in earnest to make herself better known by her speaking engagements, where she spoke out forcefully against racial intolerance and injustice. Fannie Lou Hamer felt her life's mission would always be concerned with the civil rights movement in some way or another.

18

The Mississippi State Sovereignty Commission and a Trip to Africa

True freedom requires both knowledge of the good and the will to choose the good when known. The denial of either is a denial of freedom, and the denial of freedom is the rejection of that moral agency in [humankind] which characterizes [our] humanity.[1]

— John H. Hallowell

To her credit, Fannie Lou Hamer tried to maintain a positive frame of mind, as unknown whites in the state of Mississippi continued to taunt and make disparaging comments about her, usually via the telephone.[2] Hamer wasn't easily frightened, but she once stated: "There's times when it gets a little scary, but don't kid yourself about these [white] crackers. They respect you when you stand up for yourself."[3] Some hateful whites in Mississippi wanted Hamer to disappear, but regardless of their vile threats, Hamer insisted, "I ain't going no place. I have a right to stay here. With all my parents and grandparents gave to Mississippi, I have a right to stay here and fight for what they *didn't* get."[4] Still, many white leaders felt that blacks like Hamer had overstepped their bounds.

Some white leaders in Mississippi did almost *anything* to cast aspersions and doubt on Fannie Lou Hamer and other black activists. And without any consequences for their violent behavior, some whites in Mississippi continued to harass and threaten blacks with acts of terrorism. Some white Southerners also found it difficult to believe that anyone would put much weight in Hamer's words or deeds. Indeed, they thought that blacks like Hamer were inconsequential at best. Hamer was something of a black joke among some whites, who spoke of her dismissively. Also, many whites in Mississippi didn't think Hamer was too bright. But they were wrong. Whites tried to ignore Fannie Lou Hamer, but it was impossible to do so.

Some whites even refused to believe that racial and political things would change in their lifetime. But everything whites believed about their racial superiority was being stood on its head. According to Jaspin, "Whites worried that armies of blacks were forming in the night waiting for the right moment to pounce."[5] What nonsense. It was also a sad but well known fact that whites didn't have much use for blacks in Mississippi, except perhaps to exploit them. Many whites believed that "the only reason for risking the presence of blacks in a [white] community was economic necessity."[6]

Some whites in the state even believed that blacks did not have a right to speak out against their racist government and other segregated institutions. Their basic ideological and political beliefs dictated that white people should be in charge, no matter what. But it was absurd to think that blacks would accept this forever. Nevertheless, whites expected to continue their dominance in the face of what was going on with the civil rights movement.

Naturally, Fannie Lou Hamer didn't expect whites to fall over themselves about providing equal treatment to blacks. She felt that whites would never consider how their behavior affected the lives of black people in general. And Hamer gained the acrimony of whites in the South everywhere. White political leaders believed that Hamer's very ideas were a source of revolution and radicalism. There was significant resentment toward the civil rights movement in general, and Fannie Lou Hamer in particular, as she had become public enemy number one. And the confrontational rhetoric of whites went on, unabated. In this particular climate, black people in Mississippi "were living each day under the threat of violence and death."[7]

Any criticism of the white power structure would have been unthinkable just a few years before, in the 1950s, when black people lived in total fear and isolation. White leaders believed that the less black people knew about politics and government, the better they could be controlled. Some black activists, especially black militants, were considered a threat that must be eliminated at all cost, as white segregationists seethed at the possibility of sharing political power. Some whites in Mississippi didn't like outsiders, as they were considered dangerous free thinkers and communists who stirred up their so-called good Negroes. White politicians believed that outsiders were politically destabilizing Mississippi. It was as if white segregationists in Mississippi were offended by the actions of Fannie Lou Hamer and other black activists in the state. Even so, Hamer tried to stay "committed to the political process."[8] Fannie Lou Hamer wanted to open the eyes of white Mississippians to the simple fact that what they were perpetuating and perpetrating against black people was wrong, inhumane, and nonsensical. Hamer once commented: "What would

I look like fighting for equality with the white man? I don't want to go down that low. I want the true democracy that'll raise me and that white man up ... raise America up."[9] Fannie Lou Hamer disliked the self-righteousness and irrationality of white Southerners who refused to listen or bend on issues of race. She knew that full integration was the right thing to do. Hamer clearly understood sanctimonious talk from whites when it was spoken to her, as she didn't believe there was liberty and justice for *all*. How could there be, when blacks were being threatened daily for demanding what was rightfully theirs?

White racists continued to harp on the idea that they were superior to black people. These staunch segregationists often strategized about how to stop integration and racial equality between blacks and whites. Groups like the Mississippi State Sovereignty Commission wanted to push such matters to the periphery of Mississippi politics. Indeed, the Commission "embodied the mind-set of most white Mississippians, who were determined to resist any meaningful change in the state's racial status quo."[10] In so many words, the Mississippi State Sovereignty Commission was a devious organization secretly and carefully orchestrated by white officials who wanted to maintain the white power structure while locking out blacks from participating in the political system, even voting. In essence, the Commission "was a product of Mississippi society of the 1950s and the 1960s — a society where the fears, angers, and sometimes unreasonable reactions of the white citizenry in pursuit of their dogmatic cause of white supremacy dominated the course of the state's politics."[11] Whites resisted change, the notion of giving blacks *any* concessions, because it would have gone against the norm — their perverse, white Southern way of life.

The Mississippi State Sovereignty Commission did its racist work mostly in secret, under their warped umbrella of "confidentiality." The Commission didn't want the general public to know what was going on in regards to keeping tabs on white supporters, black activists, and who they deemed communist radicals. The Commission used tax payers' dollars to fund their activities. Professor Yasuhiro Katagiri writes, "The Mississippi State Sovereignty Commission [was] the result of an abominable and unsavory segregationist enterprise staged by leading Mississippi white officials, and the very tragedy of its existence was that the agency used the constitutional mantle of 'state sovereignty' to try to perpetuate white Mississippi's inhumane treatment of the state's black citizens."[12]

Whites in Mississippi, in the 1950s and 1960s, certainly had a sense of entitlement. Moreover, many white racists, some even thugs and murderous criminals, felt themselves exempt from state laws — that is, when they concerned black people. One thing was clear, whites wouldn't give up their sense of privilege easily in Mississippi. The exposure of the Mississippi State Sovereignty Commission sparked an outcry in the black community, which suspected such a clandestine organization all along. But white officials certainly didn't mind undermining the public trust of black citizens in Mississippi. In other words, whites on the Commission thought that white authority should be a lot tougher on black people, especially in keeping "its watchful eyes on Mississippi's civil rights activists"[13] to maintain order and control. But white leaders thoroughly misled and lied to the average white person in Mississippi, as they distracted and misdirected everyone from the *real* racial evils perpetrated against its black population. The Commission was totally against any movement which might enhance the lives of blacks, as they firmly believed they had some moral imperative in championing the welfare of white people in Mississippi.

Fannie Lou Hamer was of great interest to groups like the Mississippi State Sovereignty Commission because she posed a persistent threat to their way of life, especially as she tried to persuade whites in Mississippi to loosen their grip on political power. White leaders in the state considered Fannie Lou Hamer a dangerous person. Whites criticized and blamed black activists like Hamer for supposedly being tools of outside agitators. Hamer wanted to discuss racial issues that would help blacks and whites understand one another. She believed that there should be a meeting of the minds between blacks and whites in Mississippi, especially in terms of discussing race relations. Furthermore, she wanted to freely discuss the racial matters of the day, criticize white politicians and argue against complete "white rule" in segregated and racist Mississippi. Hamer felt she had a better chance of convincing whites than any other black activist in the state. Hamer's true intentions had nothing to do with how whites reacted to her, but she knew she had the power to influence black people. And she never hesitated to follow her intuitive hunches. Fannie Lou Hamer wanted to increase the public discourse about the nefarious activities of white racists and other pressing race-relations problems.

Unfortunately, whites in Mississippi could not provide a coherent explanation as to why black people were treated in such abhorrent ways. They thought of what they were doing as somehow noble, a way to protect their so-called Southern Heritage, which did not include black culture. Even more important, some whites in the state just couldn't understand why black people began to challenge the political legitimacy of whites. Essentially, the white Democrats from Mississippi had a bad case of "groupthink" because they were quick to claim that blacks had no rights when it came to politics or social issues. According to professor Irving L. Janis, "Groupthink refers to a deterioration of mental efficiency, reality testing, and moral judgment that results from in-group pressures."[14] White hate groups and strict segregationists were victims of "groupthink." This is to say, some white Southerners and Mississippians followed well-known racists by jumping on the hatred bandwagon without thinking. And little did white Southerners know it would be a mistake of historic proportions to fight against the civil rights movement. Indeed, whites who resisted integration and human rights for black people came out on the wrong side of history.

Many were realizing that their political power was not absolute. This was probably a frightening thought for many white leaders in Mississippi. And this was serious cause for concern for white segregationists, especially if things got too far out of hand. Many members of the Mississippi State Sovereignty Commission believed that equality and integration were closer to being accepted in Mississippi because of Fannie Lou Hamer, and that would never do.

It was during this time that Fannie Lou Hamer was asked by Harry Belafonte, the black civil rights activist and famous American singer, to join him in the autumn of 1964, along with eleven SNCC members and MFDP delegates, to travel to Guinea, Africa. Hamer didn't hesitate. Indeed, she was extremely pleased. And although she suffered a bit from claustrophobia, Hamer was absolutely thrilled to take the long plane trip to Africa. According to Litwin, Harry Belafonte was friends with Sekou Toure, "the president of Guinea, a [predominantly black] country in western Africa that had fought and won its independence from France just six years earlier."[15] Hamer was surprised and impressed when President Sekou Toure met with Belafonte and the others at their hotel. Later, however, Hamer and the other delegates would be invited to the presidential palace as special guests.[16] Fannie Lou Hamer thought that many of the black people she met in Guinea were worth meeting. And many of the horrible indignities of her life were worth living through because she had survived to take this picturesque adventure to West Africa.

With typical aplomb and candor, Hamer recalled "the irony of having to go thousands of miles" to Guinea, Africa, "to be personally greeted and made welcome by the head of a foreign nation."[17] She considered herself fortunate. In the end, Fannie Lou Hamer "sat at tables with the great and shook hands with the mighty,"[18] such as with the amiable President Sekou Toure. It was an opportunity of a lifetime, as Hamer had come a long way from a shack in the Mississippi Delta to becoming a world traveler. The trip to Africa gave Hamer a chance to collect herself and be alone with her thoughts. Professor of history at the University of Georgia, Chana Kai Lee described Fannie Lou Hamer's trip to Africa in this way:

> In fall 1964 Hamer accompanied a SNCC delegation to West Africa at the invitation of Guinea's president, Sekou Toure. Coming on the heels of the disappointing defeat in Atlantic City, the trip was like a balm to Hamer's wounded and dismayed soul. The visit fed her emotional reserve and deepened her commitment to political change.[19]

19

Speaking Out Loud and the 1968 Democratic Convention

Our lives begin to end the day we become silent about things that matter.[1]
— The Rev. Dr. Martin Luther King, Jr.

Fannie Lou Hamer made no bones about discussing the problems black people faced in attaining their rights. Blacks in Mississippi were still being subjected to great pain, suffering and indignities in the 1960s. The black community was plagued by problems, as whites in the state continued to place barriers for their social, economic, political, and educational development. At the time, Mississippi was a "closed society," and what kept it closed was "the prejudice of white Mississippians who [were] prevented from learning the truth and dispelling their misbeliefs about Negroes."[2] Hamer was able to raise the consciousness of the public about these contentious things with her strong voice and opinions about racial matters. Indeed, Hamer would become the most effective communicator "to northern white audiences, describing the desperation of blacks' situation in Mississippi and their determination to change it."[3] Hamer went almost anywhere to talk to black people. According to Penny Colman, "She went to their shacks and their houses and churches." In addition, Hamer "spoke at mass meetings and led voter registration workshops."[4] Fannie Lou Hamer knew that change would be incredibly hard, but her main purpose in the civil rights movement was still "to encourage black people to register to vote."[5] It was important for Hamer to let people know about what was going on in Mississippi. Hamer also "traveled to northern states to raise money for SNCC's programs,"[6] the MFDP, the civil rights movement in general, and to help poor black people in the Delta.

Fannie Lou Hamer, moreover, wanted to tell white Americans that blacks and whites needed each other. Although she found effective communication with some whites difficult, Hamer believed that she could have a real conversation with white people. Furthermore, Hamer didn't hate whites, because it took too much energy; and she believed that very often black people were their own worst enemies. In an imaginative play entitled *Fannie Lou Hamer: This Little Light*, by black poet and writer Billie Jean Young, Hamer states:

> Let's face it, what's hurting black folk that's without is hurting white folk that's without! If the white folks fight for theyself, and the black folk fight for theyself, we gone crumble apart. These are things we gone have to fight together. We got to fight in America for all the people, and I'm perfectly willing to help make my country what it have to be.[7]

This awkward but powerful passage from Young's play lets us know that Fannie Lou Hamer knew that the only way our nation could survive was together — both blacks and whites — not polarized. Hamer irked the sensibilities of some whites, as many did not express any desire to hear the truth as Hamer presented it. Some whites were especially disrespectful to those blacks, like Fannie Lou Hamer, who were semi-illiterate. Indeed, the fact that Hamer's grammar "was often poor caused some people to question her intelligence."[8] The amount of hatred and vitriol from white leaders was surprising, as well as frightening. Hamer believed that whites throughout the nation would have to come to terms with their hateful feelings toward blacks, as a day of reckoning was in the cards in the near future. But many whites were hell-bent on getting their way, no matter the circumstances, which reflected the hypocrisy of those who only *talked* about justice, equality, and the rule of law. And unfortunately, some whites in Mississippi even tried to reconsolidate their political positions through threats of violence.

Fannie Lou Hamer was never silent about these matters. The famous black writer Maya Angelou notes: "Fannie Lou Hamer and the Mississippi Democratic Freedom Party were standing on the shoulders of history when they acted to unseat evil from its presumed safe perch on the backs of the American people."[9] And make no mistake, things would eventually change in a real, tangible way, despite the efforts of some whites to prevent the integration of blacks in Mississippi. Fannie Lou Hamer often felt threatened by whites, but nothing would weaken her resolve. Hamer refused to wilt in the face of adversity. And no one was able to destroy her credibility. Some might have worried that now, in her fifties, Hamer wasn't up to the task anymore, but she never gave up, especially in difficult circumstances. Fortunately, "She could reflect with an abundance of understanding and a tiny amount of satisfaction upon the earlier years of her life."[10]

But some of her critics thought that Fannie Lou Hamer had bitten off more than she could chew when she accepted the mantle of leadership. Hamer disagreed, as she had a profound influence on people, blacks in particular. More importantly, as Fannie Lou Hamer stated, "You can pray until you faint, but if you don't get up and try to do something, God is not gonna put it in your lap."[11] Hamer meant that blacks would not be given their rights on a silver platter; they would have to fight to achieve anything. And naturally, the notion that whites would give in without a fight was ridiculous. There were knee-jerk reactions from most white Southerners against any black person who had the temerity to question white supremacy. Whites in the state of Mississippi wanted things to stay the same, as they vigorously tried to enforce their policies of "white rule," creating laws that restricted blacks. Professor Joseph Crespino explained:

> By 1963, membership in extremist groups like the Ku Klux Klan and Americans for the Preservation of the White Race was on the rise. White elites feared that violence by these groups would draw unwanted outside attention, possibly leading to declarations of martial law and destroying the economic prospect of towns struggling to recruit outside industries. [Consequently], the potential for extremist violence made white leaders more willing to grant some concessions to political opponents.[12]

Whites were under enormous pressure to change their segregationist ways. But whites failed to deliver any meaningful reconciliation. Indeed, pervasive white racism continued to make things bad for blacks in Mississippi. Nonetheless, blacks in Mississippi during the mid–1960s were losing their fear of white people and their vile threats. Fannie Lou Hamer believed that the only path to truth and reconciliation for whites was for them to take responsibility for their actions, without complaint or indignation. Still, some whites were hard pressed to accept the truth, especially when the truth wasn't flattering to them. For some, it was a shocking turn of events. Some white Mississippians believed that blacks had gone too far. But whites in Mississippi had no right to be angry with blacks for demanding their constitutional rights. Inexplicably, for many whites the idea of blacks demanding their rights was an annoyance. Moreover, for some white Mississippians it didn't matter that the infamous Fannie Lou Hamer spoke her mind, because they were clearly not interested. However, Hamer's civil rights work created controversies among whites in the state; and then they paid attention. Fannie Lou Hamer believed that the truth was the best way to negotiate with white folks, but many didn't really want to hear the truth. According to Tom Hayden, discrimination and "white rule" was "barbarism — pernicious, sophisticated, subtly concealed from public view, [and] massively protected from political attack."[13]

Consequently, some black activists believed that Hamer was "speaking truth to power"[14] as she dealt with the seeds of racism. To be sure, white "power's traditional answer to such [brutal] honesty," especially from Fannie Lou Hamer, was "to avoid or silence the truth."[15] But Hamer would not be kept silent. She always kept her poise, never asking anyone to speak for her. Sometimes Hamer looked like a young woman, especially when she smiled her famously huge smile. Hamer was able to command attention with her penetrating eyes and physical presence. And even with a bad hip, Fannie Lou Hamer had a sort of swagger that you responded to. She didn't even realize it. Hamer had such a cockiness about herself. You could tell immediately that she was made of sterner stuff. But Hamer stood out early on by dint of her curiosity and work ethic. You might have been roused by Hamer's philosophy about life, because "she saw oppression of black people in Mississippi as the responsibility of all America."[16] In terms of her speeches, Hamer believed that less was more. She didn't know a lot of fancy words, but the simple things she said were often most important. Hamer's ability to speak the truth validated her sometimes harsh remarks, as she made a great deal of common sense. But her blunt public comments sometimes rubbed people the wrong way, especially her detractors. Furthermore, Hamer wouldn't hesitate to criticize white Mississippians on human rights violations, something that ordinarily would have been ignored. Toward this end, Hamer was never worried about sending the wrong message about what she thought should be done, because in her heart she felt that God was on her side. According to L.C. Dorsey, Fannie Lou Hamer "was the prophet feeding the people the truth. And she really was the fearless person going forth not on her own power but with the power of God."[17]

A supremely confident orator, Fannie Lou Hamer focused particularly on the issues of equality, human and voting rights, and social justice. Sometimes her moving words made her audiences cry, and then think critically about the fight to come. Many said she was at her most infectious when she gave her extemporaneous speeches before a large crowd. Often Hamer didn't give speeches; instead, she told little stories, anecdotes grounded in wisdom and experience. And she often scolded her audiences outright; the fact that they accepted this, and even applauded, is a remarkable testimony to her legacy in the civil rights movement. With precise words Hamer could condense a big idea into easily understandable language. She also tried to keep her message positive, especially when speaking to young people. Fannie Lou Hamer spoke with an unvarnished Southern accent, but not the nasal twang that a lot of white Southerners talked with. Her words and sentences were "riddled with grammatical imperfections," but she told her stories "with an earthy eloquence that [had] been sharpened by suffering."[18] In front of any podium, Hamer seemed most at ease. Her ability to talk to anyone made a strong and indelible impression, which made her words, her voice, hard to resist. Hamer spoke to the hearts of people and she had a knack for a speaking the way people wanted. What Hamer said was jarringly true, and her relationship to the truth and plain speaking was perhaps the salve that soothed the open wounds of racial hatred and injustices inflicted upon blacks in Mississippi. Ultimately, people were willing to listen to Fannie Lou Hamer's philosophical and political thinking.

Many were drawn to Hamer and the prospect of what she could deliver to the movement. When listening to Fannie Lou Hamer, you had no choice but to understand the folly of cultural differences between whites and blacks in the state. With Solomonic wisdom, Hamer voiced her concerns. She got people to talk and listen to her. Her powerful oratory, including her little gospel songs at the beginning of her speeches, rhapsodized about overcoming disenfranchisement and discrimination. Authenticity oozed from her as she spoke out against injustice. Still, many whites in Mississippi derided Fannie Lou Hamer for her crude speaking voice, as she would often split English verbs with some facility.[19] Nonetheless, Hamer always seemed to be moving forward, making speeches or pronouncements about racial matters. In a way, she became the mouth piece for the black community in Mississippi. And her words gave black people and others ample food for thought. You could not deny Hamer's stage presence and oratory skills, but it was her compassion, crude eloquence, and clarity of thought that made her famous.

But in 1967, all her fame couldn't help save her oldest daughter, Dorothy Jean, who "had recently given birth to her second child and was weakened by complications from the delivery."[20] In the end, Dorothy Jean would die of "a cerebral hemorrhage ... because no well-equipped white hospital nearby would admit them."[21] Hamer would angrily accuse the white hospital that turned them away because of their race. If Hamer didn't have "to drive to Memphis, Tennessee — more than one hundred miles away to find a hospital that would treat her daughter,"[22] Dorothy Jean might have lived instead of hemorrhaging to death. Although Fannie Lou Hamer had an indefatigable determination, her daughter's unexpected death was devastating. And she felt powerless to do anything. Perhaps Hamer had "endured too many hardships."[23] An exhausted Fannie Lou Hamer tried to put on a brave face after Dorothy Jean's death, but her heart was breaking. Her family life had been turned upside down. Her days were now tinged with sadness, as Hamer had to grapple with her daughter's absence. Dorothy Jean had been very serious, trying always to do her best to please her mother, who was a big influence on her. A short time later, another daughter would die "from chronic malnutrition."[24] Fannie Lou Hamer would struggle with private grief over the death of her two daughters. She mourned them every day. It was particularly challenging for her during the holidays. But Fannie Lou Hamer did not begrudge the fact that her husband Pap and she were grandparents to two small girls,

Lenora Aretha and Jacqueline Denise. Therefore, in her fifties, Fannie Lou and Pap Hamer "adopted their two grandchildren."[25]

Fannie Lou Hamer had to remain strong not only for herself, but for the rest of her family too. Indeed, none of her terrible experiences had "shattered her faith or weakened her indomitable courage."[26] So when the 1968 Democratic Convention rolled around, Hamer was ready. Of course, "the 1968 presidential campaign encapsulated the strains of cultural politics and violence of the mid–1960s, and raised profound concern over the viability of the American political system."[27] For a while, especially outside the main event in Chicago, there was pandemonium. It became a sort of no-holds-barred battle for attention. Fannie Lou Hamer had worked extremely hard to form a "coalition of her Freedom party with other black and liberal white groups," which would be known as "the Loyal Democrats of Mississippi."[28] This group attended the convention, as well as the white delegation. Fannie Lou Hamer arrived "as a member of the Mississippi Loyalist Democratic Party (MLDP)." And this time she would win the battle.[29]

When all was said and done, the Loyalist Democrats of Mississippi "successfully challenged the state's all-white delegation."[30] This is to say, "the Credentials Committee of the Loyalist convention voted to seat" the Loyal Democrats from Mississippi,[31] while expelling "the all-white delegation."[32] Professor William Simpson explained: "The Loyalist democrats easily won full recognition over the regulars at the 1968 Democratic National convention in Chicago, a convention remembered more for the violence outside the Amphitheatre than for the pious and boastful harangues of candidates and campaign managers within."[33]

It was a personal triumph for Fannie Lou Hamer, because she had never been in this type of situation before. Hamer "and her [MLDP] colleagues were finally to have a legitimate place in the convention hall."[34] Although she didn't speak specifically about all the horrible things that were still happening in Mississippi, she spoke out forthrightly for civil rights. And her brief remarks at the 1968 Democratic Convention represented the highest ideals of hope and reconciliation. Members of the Democratic hierarchy did something totally unexpected. They gave Fannie Lou Hamer "a standing ovation" when she finally took her seat at the 1968 Convention as a delegate.[35] In the end, members of the Mississippi Loyalist Democrats realized that the goal of ending political repression involved stewardship and patience. Fannie Lou Hamer, however, was still pessimistic about the future for black people; at the Chicago convention in 1968 she stated, "We're still powerless, and the Loyalists haven't done nothin'."[36] Hamer would have mixed emotions about the success of the MLDP, as this group would not survive the test of time.

20

The End of Activism

Before white Americans can even begin to uncover the deep links between class exploitation, disempowerment, and racial privilege ... they would have to face the reality of "the South" ... All of us, white and black, northern and southern, would have to think of "the South," the "race problem," and the "burden of history," not as the weight of some other, of a dark and distant place and time, but as a burden that we still carry and as a history that we have not agreed to face or acknowledge as a source of our subjectivities.[1]
— Grace Elizabeth Hale

Fannie Lou Hamer was always able to find suitable words to express the frustration and ordeal of poor blacks. And her remarkable voice aided her ability to get her point across. Hamer's "ability to capture the essence of the struggle in compelling language that all could understand made her a favored speaker."[2] And she had acquired knowledge that she wisely imparted to others. Hamer was quite nuanced in the racial situation, especially in Mississippi. She also had the ability to recognize opportunities where they existed. Hamer had a relaxed, down-home, earthy style that won her acclaim as a speaker. Some might say it was a pragmatic or realistic style. And she often spoke with passionate determination. Eleanor Holmes Norton once commented that Hamer "was an orator without equal."[3] Indeed, her plain speaking often saved the day, as she "put together a mosaic of coherent thought about freedom and justice, so that when it was all through, you knew what you had heard because it held together with wonderful cohesion."[4] And Hamer never shied away from telling the truth, which had become her trademark. Hamer could charm people into submission with her words and graciousness, as her message was one of confidence and pride. But Hamer was sometimes frustrated with her inability to use certain words properly. Her English never quite lost its slang and slow cadence. But her particular speaking style became noteworthy as she continued to take center stage in the civil rights movement. What was most celebrated, even with her limited vocabulary, was her remarkable emotional impact on people.

Hamer had no vanity about herself, and she was very much straightforward in her conversation. Her speeches were designed to keep the race-relations dialogue going between blacks and whites in Mississippi. Fannie Lou Hamer had no special powers other than her ability to connect with people. Hamer's frank words about economic fairness and social justice won people over. This was especially evident when she voiced her concerns about black people everywhere. Inherent in Hamer's message was that justice and freedom wasn't just for white Americans. Despite the discomfort her speeches brought to the white population, it highlighted what was going on in Mississippi against blacks. And the media loved her for that very reason. However, many whites in the state took umbrage and protested how white Southerners were being negatively portrayed in the media. Fannie Lou Hamer was called many names by angry white people in the state, but she had the kind of fortitude to ignore their hateful verbal attacks. Some whites in Mississippi thought of her speeches as so much rambling about things they thought Hamer knew very little about. With her colorful personality and thick Southern accent, Hamer's forcefulness and accusatory rhetoric was a reflection of the times and her temperament. She looked a little like Hattie McDaniels, who was the first black American actor to receive an Oscar (as Best Supporting Actress for her convincing role as a house slave called Mammy in *Gone with the Wind*).

Fannie Lou Hamer often spoke from first-hand experience. And usually her remarks were evocative and provocative at the same time. Her enthusiasm and optimism was infectious, and she would frequently enthrall her audiences. Hamer had an intense presence that made you stand up and pay close attention. Indeed, there was something exhilarating about watching Fannie Lou Hamer. Always with her characteristic stride and noticeable limp, Hamer would slowly approach a stage. Sometimes, depending on the time of the year, when Hamer finally reached a particular podium, sweat would stream down her shiny forehead. Then she would raise both her hands in a sort of deprecatory salute, with her palms turned downward before the crowd as if saying, please calm down. Clearly she could rile people up, then put them at ease. Sometimes her eyes were bloodshot, but always her eyes would blaze with warmth and intelligence. Often, before beginning her little talks, Fannie Lou Hamer would take a deep breath. "Hallelujah," she would sometimes say, evoking God. Or she would start her speeches with a quick gospel song to settle her nerves.

Hamer's signature refrain was "This Little Light of Mine." Some might even say that this particular song was her *shtick*. When she stopped singing, Hamer was ready to deliver inspiring words, which soared across the audience. Her face at that point would often be furrowed in concentration, with a severe look. Hamer was an imposing presence, and you could see real emotions on her face. Her audience — sometimes intimate groups, sometimes large gatherings — would look up at her expectantly. Hamer spoke calmly, and would answer questions put to her reflectively, frequently quoting parables or passages from the Bible. It was particularly important for Hamer to highlight God in all her speechmaking and civil rights activities, because she believed that some people were certainly not good Christians. As she spoke, Hamer would sometimes gesture grandly to emphasize her point. She spoke in a matter-of-fact voice. One could appreciate Hamer's simple but precise words. Many listened to what Fannie Lou Hamer had to say. And what she said was concise and useful, and right on point. Sometimes a sort of frenzy would descend upon her audiences — right at the moment Hamer reached the podium. They knew what to expect. Fannie Lou Hamer, of course, "was a woman of action as well as words."[5]

Hamer's words often left you in awe of the courage it took for her to reveal the truth about racism before a crowd, as she emphatically detailed how blacks in Mississippi were being mistreated. Hamer "warned of automatically equating black voting rights with real power," while describing "the new political issue of the late 1960s and 1970s as not whether blacks would vote but who would control that vote."[6] Hamer's voice was exceptionally clear when talking about such matters. You were compelled to listen to her, maybe even learning something about the political situation in Mississippi. As Hamer spoke, her expressive face, her convincing body language — everything — suggested that she was in control, talking directly to the people. Sometimes you could hear genuine fury in her voice because she knew black people had been through so much. And as you listened to what she had to say about the poor, downtrodden and oppressed people, you knew she was authentic. Hamer wanted to be upfront and absolutely straight about what she had to say. And for this, Hamer usually received a boisterous response and loud applause. Hamer was known for speaking bluntly. Indeed, she would forcefully tell blacks that they should take responsibility for their own lives, because "she worried about too much dependency being created by handouts, and wanted [black] people to stand up for themselves."[7] Hamer also made the point that "if the white man gives you anything, just remember when he get ready he will take it right back."[8] Some might call these extreme statements, but Hamer knew that self-determination was the key for black survival. So it was true that Hamer used her speaking platform as a sort of bully pulpit to get her message across. Hamer also spoke "out against the involuntary sterilization of African-American women," of which "she had been a victim herself."[9] Hamer never put her own personal concerns above others. She was interested in having everyone understand what she was saying, hammering this home by leaning forward with enthusiasm from the podium. And sometimes her voice would trail off for a moment, as if she was worried about something, as if she wanted to have a long heart-to-heart talk with you while she revealed some amazing truths.

Fannie Lou Hamer's passionate and authoritative words about the disparities of life between blacks and whites in Mississippi shamed a lot of people. Hamer spoke enthusiastically about sensitive racial issues, as there was always urgency in her voice. Hamer was extremely confident in what she stated, especially in her brutal analysis of the racial situation. She often made sweeping condemnations of what was still happening in Mississippi. Apparently, Hamer never really understood "this kind of hatred, but fighting it gave her courage."[10]

Hamer had an open mind and powerful desire to speak the truth. But she was never bombastic about things. Hamer's words were never forced or contrived. Her speeches were never convoluted. Though Fannie Lou Hamer always tried to hold herself proudly, she presented herself without affectations. Hamer had infused excitement into the civil rights movement. She believed that you had to fight — to be proactive rather than passive. And Fannie Lou Hamer was convinced of this notion almost every day while living in the state of Mississippi.

Fannie Lou Hamer would disagree with you without being disagreeable. And she never tried to state things in an inflammatory way. Hamer's speechmaking was a significant part of her character. She took up the grassroots and intellectual battles regarding race relations when she gave keynote addresses and speeches throughout the nation. In fact, Hamer would give "numerous speeches across the country into the 1970s."[11] Professor Jane Rhodes asserts that Fannie Lou Hamer understood that "gender and religious conventions prevented [her] from functioning as [a] visible leader."[12] But nothing could be further from the truth, because Hamer was at the forefront of the fight against racial injustices and oppression, especially in Mississippi. She was well known, a visible opponent against "white rule" and racism. Fannie Lou Hamer was not only outspoken, but she was more visible, perhaps, than anyone in the civil rights movement in Mississippi. Reed points out that Hamer's "frankness, determination, courage and leadership abilities made her a memorable figure in the 1960s civil rights struggle."[13] Rhodes goes on to write that Fannie Lou Hamer actually "performed '*bridge leadership*' activities by providing crucial links between formal organizations and black communities."[14] Clearly, Hamer provided this bridge leadership in Mississippi in spades, as her name resonated throughout the state and the nation. She became a powerful spokesperson, and Hamer would receive "wide recognition for her part in bringing about a major political transformation in the Democratic Party and raising significant questions that addressed basic human needs."[15]

Fannie Lou Hamer would be one of the original signers of the "Black Manifesto" in 1969, where the demands for black reparations were presented by civil rights activist James Forman and others to white churches of America.[16] But Hamer knew that the issue of compensation for blacks for the free labor of their slave ancestors would probably never be resolved. Fannie Lou Hamer also agreed, "from the perspective of her own eminently practical experience," that blacks were "a dependent people," living in "some quarters of Mississippi" under what political scientist James W. Prothro chose to call "a totalitarian local system" in "a land of unremitting white supremacy."[17] However, according to professor Neil R. McMillan, by 1970 "the percentage of the state's eligible blacks registered to vote (67.7) exceeded the regional average (66.9) for the first time" in the twentieth century.[18] Equally important, Fannie Lou Hamer "ran unsuccessfully for the legislature in 1972"[19] in Mississippi because she felt it was the right thing to do. In fact, Hamer "continued to be active in political campaigns" as time went by, especially in her efforts "to elect black officials once the Voting Rights Act became law."[20] But Hamer was becoming exhausted by her civil rights work and speaking commitments. Many people from all walks of life wanted to make her acquaintance.

Hamer was just tired, intellectually exhausted. Some supporters thought that Fannie Lou Hamer was pushing herself too hard, even later from her hospital bed. Many commented that Hamer now appeared noticeably tired. Hamer needed a break from the daily grind. Equally important, Hamer regretted not always being there for her husband Pap and their two granddaughters. Fannie Lou Hamer had not turned out to be the wife she thought she should be — that is, Hamer felt like she could have been a better wife to Pap and mother to her two grandchildren. Therefore, feeling emotionally torn and physically tired, Hamer decided to quit the SNCC. After all, two hard-core activists whom she greatly admired had already resigned in 1966 because of the radical new direction of the organization. John Lewis "resigned soon after Stokely Carmichael was elected to replace him as SNCC chairman," and Julian Bond "resigned soon after the election" as the SNCC's public information officer.[21] Essentially, Lewis and Bond quit the SNCC organization because they were "critical of black power."[22] Black power means a show of force and authority over the lives of black people in an institutionalized racist society. According to Joyce Ladner, black power was "viewed as a means of combining Negroes into a bond of solidarity. It was [also] seen as a rallying cry, a symbol of identification, and a very concrete tool for action."[23] Hamer seemed puzzled by the "black power" movement. The rhetoric and actions of black radicals disturbed her. Indeed, "most of the nation's top civil-rights leaders denounced the [black power] slogan — or vigorously embraced it."[24] To be sure, black activists "in Mississippi had immediately embraced the black-power slogan — because of the already widely-held belief that power was an effective tool for obtaining demands from the ruling elite in Mississippi."[25] Fannie Lou Hamer, of course, embraced what Martin Luther King, Jr., said about the matter of "black power." In essence, they both "advocated the acquisition of 'power for all people.'"[26] So it was power to the people.

Fannie Lou Hamer thought that it was a mistake on the part of the SNCC organization to involve itself with radical black extremist groups like the Black Panthers and the Nation of Islam. It was an internal political crisis. Hamer just couldn't come to terms with the reality of the radical changes taking place within the SNCC. She thought she would never disassociate herself from the SNCC, the group that basically made her, but Hamer was unwilling to entertain the notion that black radicals and non-violent members could work together collectively. Some black activists in the movement were extremely impatient, often becoming frustrated with the white power structure, even through "things were beginning to change for the good."[27] Many black radicals in the civil rights movement thought that violence was the answer. It was not. And these radicals undermined the progress made toward moving the SNCC into the mainstream of society. The SNCC was now divided by controversy. The young black radicals thought that white civil rights workers in the movement had divided loyalties; therefore, they wanted whites expelled from all black organizations. According to Ladner, "Black activists in addition constantly complained about the focus of the mass media on white 'all–American' volunteers who had come south to work in the movement."[28] Hamer, however, felt that the new black leaders in the movement should show restraint in throwing whites out of the SNCC and other black organizations because it would have "negative effects" in maintaining such groups.[29] Complications between the old guard in the movement and new black militants, especially in the SNCC, developed rapidly. As Aaron Henry writes, "The SNCC leaders represented the first concrete evidence of the ideological conflict between the more moderate NAACP leaders and the radical SNCC cadre."[30] Fannie Lou Hamer would come to regard the young black leaders with ambivalence, but she never saw them as monsters.

Hamer was willing to give the new black leaders a chance to run the movement. She never wanted to say anything bad about the young people in the SNCC. Fannie Lou Hamer didn't want to make things harder for herself and others. She was ready to pass the torch on to a new generation. But to

Hamer's surprise, she found out that she too was being asked to move on. For as much as the new black leadership was beholden to Hamer, they held different opinions about what was best for the organization and movement. This was a distressing period for Hamer, and a real turning point for her. Some of the young black radicals in the movement thought that Hamer wasn't quite up to their standards. Perhaps some of the college-educated blacks in the movement thought that Hamer's lack of education was a hindrance. She had always regretted never finishing her schooling. The young black turks in the movement "were considered rebellious youth who wanted only to act out their rebellion in the most unconventional ways."[31] And for these young radicals, Hamer seemed a stern and outdated figure from a bygone time. But many black radicals tried to point out to Fannie Lou Hamer that it wasn't so much a rejection as a desire to go in a different direction. Moreover, some young black radicals insisted that they never got the respect they thought they deserved. But Hamer was never tolerant of others who tried to impose themselves on poor black people through some misguided ideology. Fannie Lou Hamer was one who cared about things, especially young, black, educated people. Nevertheless, Hamer was displeased with what was going on in certain black groups like the SNCC, as more concerns were being raised about the older activists in the civil rights movement. A generational divide had developed between the young and old members of the movement. And such schisms would be the downfall of many black organizations during the 1970s.

At this point Fannie Lou Hamer realized that the time had come for her to retire from a full-time role in the movement. The young black radicals in the movement were constantly harping that the older black activists should step aside for the younger blacks and their leadership. So the road-weary female warrior Fannie Lou Hamer decided to walk away from her active role in the civil rights movement.

21

Creation of a Freedom Farm

Love makes growth possible, it has economic value, not to mention that the
happiness it gives us is the elusive purpose of all our economic and political
activities.[1]

— Koigi Wa Wamwere

Many were devastated by Fannie Lou Hamer's departure from the movement. Hamer, admittedly, was conflicted about leaving the SNCC. But she
felt no guilt for turning her back on the young black turks like H. Rap Brown
and Stokely Carmichael (Kwame Toure). She was dismayed by the direction
the civil rights movement was going, especially toward militancy. Indeed, it
was argued that some of the young black radicals "had appropriately found
their place in the midstream of a violence-prone culture."[2] Fannie Lou Hamer
couldn't see eye-to-eye with either conservative whites *or* black militants. Nor
did she believe in bad-mouthing anyone, even if they spoke ill about *her*. It
was with a heavy heart that Hamer resigned. But, all through this period
Hamer was treated with deference and respect, and so had no hard feelings.
Plus there was still enormous popular support for Fannie Lou Hamer. The
immediate question was: What would happen to the civil rights movement
in Mississippi if she left for good? Hamer had been an important presence for
many years. Now who would symbolize the continuing struggle in the state?
Hamer had been an unparalleled chronicler of the racism in Mississippi, and
many were used to her prophetic and intuitive words. Who would take her
place?

Hamer tried to be optimistic about the movement. But she found herself
at a crossroads. It was a good time to leave the scene. Hamer turned her attention to raising "enough money to buy another 640 acres" to add to the forty
acres she had already bought in 1969 in order "to start her Freedom Farm
Cooperative (FFC)."[3]

Fannie Lou Hamer had worked her butt off for many years, and she had
"used her position to influence [Democratic] party policies, representing in

particular the point of view of blacks."[4] Eventually, because of Hamer and her good works, the civil rights movement attracted new black registered voters, more than ever before in the history of the state. She made the case forcefully for the voting rights of blacks, demanding that whites follow the inherent democratic principals in the national Constitution.

Fannie Lou Hamer told the world about the oppression still happening in Mississippi and elsewhere against black people, although many whites in the South didn't want to hear. "Many white Mississippians were uncomfortable with the state's image as a lawless home of Negrophobic vigilantes."[5] Moreover, white leaders talked about "a new Mississippi, still proudly segregated but dedicated to the peaceful coexistence and well-being of all of its citizens."[6] Of course, Fannie Lou Hamer never believed in such divisive segregation nonsense, as she wanted to emphasize that there was more to black people than met the eyes. It took very little provocation for Hamer to battle against white supremacy and discrimination. Furthermore, Hamer's very words prompted a more serious look at what was actually occurring in Mississippi. Unfortunately, many blacks still lived in the same type of eyesore homes they had occupied since the time of slavery.[7] According to journalist Walter Rugaber, "A visitor stopping at random" at such homes, found "gloomy interiors, empty windows, leaking roofs, and substantial cracks in the walls and floors."[8] Rugaber goes on to say that "most observers believe that poverty in the [Mississippi] Delta — and in other areas of the South as well — [could not] be easily attributed to any single factor."[9] But Hamer didn't believe in such random speculation about black poverty. She knew it was because of the dominant group's lack of interaction and unwillingness to help poor black people. And it was only these matters that made Hamer feel bad about leaving the movement, especially with what was happening with the young black turks in charge.

Hamer had wanted to leave the movement on a positive note, but it wasn't meant to be. Many assumed that Hamer's activist days were over. Some of the younger members of the movement respected her less than others because they felt that Hamer was undereducated. Other black supporters felt like there wasn't anything they could do. And still other activists convinced Hamer that she shouldn't overreact. Fannie Lou Hamer believed things happened for a reason, by the grace of God. And she never walked around with a chip on her shoulder. Some of the young activists in the movement explained that it wasn't that they wanted to take anything away from what the great Fannie Lou Hamer had done for the movement, it was just that many felt she should give herself a break and not work so hard anymore. Many, however, underestimated her worth. Hamer wanted to retain a measure of respectability by leaving her position as a full-time field worker on her own terms.

As mentioned, the new black radicals in the SNCC came up with an audacious plan to get rid of white members, circumventing real integration and fairness. They felt that the relationship with whites was too conventional for them. Some white members in the civil rights movement thought that the new black leaders' call for the expulsion of whites originated with outside forces, radical influences that might have affected their better judgment. But to her credit, the understanding and compassionate Hamer felt completely at ease with whites in the SNCC, especially those who cared strongly about racial and humane matters. Hamer was extremely mindful about treating everyone in the movement the same. In the end, Hamer hoped that members of the SNCC could concentrate on the positive things the organization was trying to do while going forward without her.

Though Fannie Lou Hamer loved working with others in the movement, resigning was perhaps a relief because Hamer could finally spend more time with her family — her husband Pap and two adopted granddaughters. There is this remarkable quote from Fannie Lou Hamer: "My family have suffered greatly since I started working with the movement. Although we've suffered greatly, we have not suffered in vain."[10]

Hamer was hailed as an organizing genius until it became apparent (to black radicals anyway) that she was perhaps too old to continue. It was something that was very painful for her. But there was the possibility that Hamer could do something else worthwhile with her professional life, like establish her Freedom Farm Cooperative or "provide low-cost day-care centers and housing for poor people."[11] Hamer would leave with a clear conscience, as she believed she had done her part. But she wouldn't leave the civil rights struggle behind entirely. Indeed, Hamer followed the dictates of her own conscience while remaining committed to political activism. Rubel cogently put it this way:

> Hamer would remain active in Democratic Party politics for the rest of her life. She served on the party's ruling body, the Democratic National committee, from 1968 until 1971. [And] as late as 1976, when her health began failing, she was still working tirelessly to unite the blacks and whites of Mississippi into one integrated party.[12]

It was still a real "David and Goliath" struggle," a racial crisis of the first magnitude. And although the SNCC and the civil rights movement were wobbling,[13] Fannie Lou Hamer hoped that the lives of blacks would eventually change for the better. Though Hamer thought that these new leaders of the SNCC, who had "entered a brief, ill-fated merger with the Black Panther Party,"[14] were misguided and unmindful of all the sacrifices she and others had made, she had passed the baton to this more radical group of black activists. Hamer knew in her heart of hearts that this would mean the beginning of the end for the SNCC. And she was right. She had hoped that the political struggle would continue, as "some questioned whether desegregation and voting rights would in themselves transform the lives of rural black southerners."[15]

Hamer found herself in Ruleville, Mississippi, again, after being away for long periods of time. It was her life now — and a relief from the bickering with the younger radicals of the SNCC. And Hamer "went right back to her earlier work as a farmhand,"[16] though now she was setting up and working the remarkable Freedom Farm, which was "a throwback to the populist movement of the latter part of the nineteenth century."[17] For Hamer, it was a very good feeling creating such a place. The decision to establish the Freedom Farm Cooperative took the form of a vow to herself. Hamer wanted to do something that was relevant to all poor people — blacks and whites — who lived in the Mississippi Delta. Exhausted by years of round-the-clock responsibilities in the civil rights movement, this was a new endeavor — and perhaps the right thing for Hamer to do. Indeed, establishing her Freedom Farm Cooperative proved to be one of the best things she ever did.

It did seem implausible for Fannie Lou Hamer to start a farm cooperative. But it was a worthy endeavor. Starting the Freedom Farm awakened once again the ingenuity and resourcefulness of Hamer. And she wasn't afraid to fail or initiate a bold plan for the survival of black people in the Delta. Equally important, working on her Freedom Farm gave Hamer another perspective on life. Hamer, of course, recognized that she had a lot of hard work ahead of her to make the farm a success. Hamer wanted to grow enough food so that they could give some of it to the needy. "She wanted to make sure that poor people [both whites and blacks] would have enough to eat." Of course, Hamer "remembered too many times in her own life when she went hungry."[18] Therefore, she was not averse to again working the good red dirt of Mississippi. The place became a sort of food bank, where they would distribute crops to those who couldn't afford it. The Freedom Farm gave Hamer control over her own destiny; it gave her the flexibility to be her own woman — and, to do the things *she* wanted to do.

Fannie Lou Hamer wanted "to offer scholarships and to help poor families raise food and livestock."[19] Hamer believed strongly in the vision of helping black people feed themselves and reach their full potential. Hamer wanted poor blacks and whites to have enough to eat without scrounging, begging or stealing. Hamer, however, was also well aware that black youngsters in the Delta at that time did not like the idea of working on a farm with their hands anymore. It was the new way of things. But Hamer didn't hesitate to take direct control over the Freedom Farm Cooperative. Of course, Fannie Lou Hamer never expected more out of anybody than what she expected from herself. The establishment of the Freedom Farm was very satisfying to Hamer because there she could expend her energies somewhere other than with the movement.

Though Fannie Lou Hamer didn't feel bad staying home in Ruleville, Mississippi, and didn't feel the need to go out and do something immediate for any civil rights organization, she did go on limited speaking engagements. According to Professor Linda Reed, Hamer "gave numerous speeches across the country into the 1970s," accepting "invitations to speak about the issue most dear to her, basic human rights for all Americans."[20] And Hamer continued to cajole and persuade "Northerners to send food, clothing, and money to black Mississippians who were struggling to resist the retaliation visited upon them by plantation bosses"[21] and white night riders or white hate groups, like the Ku Klux Klan.

Fannie Lou Hamer thought that her Freedom Farm would give her a worthy alternative to all her civil rights activities. Indeed, she wanted to turn over a new leaf, while continuing "the fight to transform" Mississippi and "the South into a safe and just place for African-Americans to live."[22] Her immediate challenge would be to feed hungry people, because as a child Hamer never had enough to eat. In growing food to eat, many black farmers who worked at the Freedom Farm were assigned various tasks to get the planting and harvesting jobs done. It was a labor of love for Hamer, and she was able "to feed over 5,000 people."[23] The Freedom Farm was by no means an ostentatious place, but Fannie Lou Hamer was very happy being directly involved in this Freedom Farm. The place demanded her attention each and everyday. Hamer was of the opinion that you had to sweat a little in order to get the food you wanted. Hamer thought that the world did not exist to spoon feed people; therefore, hard work, especially when tilling the soil, was very important.

Fannie Lou Hamer knew that you couldn't get blood from a turnip. Therefore, figuring out how best to run an effective farm cooperative was another challenge for her. Hamer quickly made herself busy with the place. Though by no means well-off herself, she was determined *never* to turn away needy people. For many, attempting such an ambitious project as the Freedom Farm would have seemed impossible, but Hamer was more than willing to give the place a chance to succeed. To accomplish this, Fannie Lou and Pap Hamer needed enormous amounts of funds, as much as her supporters could possibly spare. Hamer wanted the Freedom Farm to eventually become self-sustaining, possibly through some kind of cooperation with other farmers in the surrounding Mississippi Delta. It would give people in the Delta the opportunity to work with others, as well as forge connections for the future. Fannie Lou Hamer wanted people to feel like they could pitch in without hesitation. In many ways, working on the Freedom Farm was an unexpected gift for many. In essence, Hamer's Freedom Farm "gave people the opportunity to grow their own food."[24] It was a momentous endeavor that helped a great many people. Both blacks and whites were able to substantially improve their lives and those of others by working on the Freedom Farm and participating in the cooperative. Hamer was noted for saying, "You can give a man some food and he'll eat it. Then he'll be hungry again. But give a man some ground [or land] and he'll never be hungry no more."[25]

This bit of sage wisdom would carry her far, along with her hard work, as Hamer's Freedom Farm was very much like a micro-enterprise farming operation. Though they would operate the place by the seat of their pants, selling some of the excess food to the local community allowed them to raise funds for the upkeep and survival of many Delta families. Her intention was to give what she couldn't use to other poor black families, especially those in serious need.

Fannie Lou Hamer didn't have any real experience running a business, but she became the bread and butter for her cherished Freedom Farm, as she was the face of, and spokesperson for, the fledgling operation. Hamer was economically resourceful, and was able to raise needed funds at critical times to keep the place going, even at a time when people in the United States didn't really have a lot of resources. And these funds were usually given to Hamer with few strings attached. Hamer was able to obtain donations from her "speaking trips around the country," where she would talk up her Freedom Farm.[26]

Financial matters certainly demanded Hamer's attention at the Freedom Farm. She was brilliant in the art of scrimping and saving. Hamer often felt overworked and exhausted, but she would give what she could to people in need. Fannie Lou and Pap Hamer would put a lot of hard work, time and labor into the Freedom Farm. The two of them got a lot of gratification from working with, and being helpful to, others.

Hamer wanted to spend the remainder of her life doing something positive and productive for people. Indeed, Hamer believed that if she remained positive, she would get positive results; but her incredible Freedom Farm would eventually fail.[27] She had quietly accomplished her goal of creating the Freedom Farm Cooperative, a feat that was a testament to her fame, but she would never realize the total completeness of her vision. When all was said and done, Hamer cherished every single day she was able to manage things at the farm. In the end, Fannie Lou Hamer believed that the endeavor was totally justified.

22

The Death of Fannie Lou Hamer

Her religion gave meaning to death and gave an ethical basis facing death with courage, just as it had provided the ethics of courage for confronting county voter registration officers, hostile plantation bosses, harassing sheriffs, and compromising government officials.[1]

— Gayle Graham Yates

One of the greatest things Fannie Lou Hamer did was look for opportunities to help poor people. She wanted to do something that would give black people in the Mississippi Delta a ray of hope. The Freedom Farm Cooperative taught black families a lot about individual responsibility and teamwork, especially when it came to producing food for the poor black and white communities. Fannie Lou Hamer wanted to foster a sustainable way to lift people up from poverty. She had thrown herself into making the Freedom Farm Cooperative a success. Her goal had been to raise a contingent of poor farmers who would do most of the work on the place. Meanwhile, she would raise money for the farm, manage the operations, and grow the business. Hamer's political connections and her ability to raise money for this farm cooperative was definitely a plus, but it was still a stretch. Hamer "asked friends, all around America, to give her money enough to open [and operate] such a farm."[2] One thing that Hamer *never* tried to do was rest on her laurels. At the farm, Hamer was finally in charge of her own destiny. Upon returning to Sunflower County, she took her idea of a Freedom Farm Cooperative to the next level. Throughout her life Fannie Lou Hamer worried about getting enough to eat, because of the austerity of her childhood and her family's poverty. Therefore, Fannie Lou and Pap threw caution to the wind and decided to buy as much land as they possibly could afford to establish her Freedom Farm. Fannie Lou Hamer had the entrepreneurial spirit, and it drove her from 1969 to 1974.[3] Moreover, Hamer's hope was to pursue a simple life in Sunflower County on a bit of land that could be worked by *anyone* interested. Sewell explained:

[Hamer] devised a practical plan for feeding Sunflower County's poor blacks and whites and feeding them with dignity through "Freedom Farms." The plan [owned] several acres of black delta land; provide[d] plots so the occupants [could] produce their own cotton, can their vegetables, raise hogs and cattle; first to feed themselves well and then, if there [was] a surplus, to offer it for sale. Many individuals and organizations helped her establish this project.[4]

Hamer would often smile while going about her important work on the Freedom Farm, but she was becoming unduly fatigued because of an ailment. Yet Hamer still had a great appreciation for hard work. And things for a while were unquestionably better for some poor people. The work at the farm seemed very much a part of her activism and vision. Many were particularly struck by her astute method of doing things. Fannie Lou Hamer had always been taught to earn an honest living through hard work. Though often sick and exhausted, Hamer was satisfied with what she was doing at the place. And she knew how to balance responsibilities, as she was properly organized. According to Sewell, Hamer's "initial goal was three thousand members each paying three dollars a year."[5] But this inexpensive payment plan for those workers on the farm never fully materialized because poor black people couldn't pay the required three dollars. Furthermore, Fannie Lou Hamer would let others run the day-to-day operations of the Freedom Farm during her extended hospital stays or when she went on speaking engagements. Fannie Lou Hamer "kept busy as a lecturer, traveling throughout the nation, preaching her unique gospel of freedom and human dignity."[6] When the Freedom Farm finally failed, Hamer thought it a very disappointing thing, because the place did some wonderful things, like providing jobs and food to the black community in the Mississippi Delta. However, Hamer's "Freedom Farms Cooperative and the other economic and political stirrings of Sunflower County's black citizens [were] a long way from freedom."[7] Hamer had hoped to turn the corner with her Freedom Farm Cooperative, but it was probably never in the cards because she was so giving to those who had less than she did. And this was no way to run such an ambitious operation. Without profits, any business will fail in the end. According to Chana Kai Lee, Hamer's biographer, the Freedom Farm "owed taxes, and land payments [that] were always delinquent."[8] Therefore, the farm cooperative "failed in part because of poor management." In addition, "individuals were often loaned money and could not pay it back."[9] But Hamer was not particularly concerned. Nor did Hamer place any kind of contractual obligation on the people who owed her money. In other words, she would help others at her own expense.

When you stopped by her house, Hamer would try to make you feel at home.[10] Indeed, Hamer was big on "Black Southern hospitality," in that she always inquired whether you wanted something, or if she could fix you something to eat, no matter who you were.[11] Even with the many financial setbacks and problems at her Freedom Farm, you could at times find the welcoming Hamer sitting in her favorite rocking chair on the front porch of their rustic home, sipping on ice water from a quart mason jar and reminiscing with her husband Pap. No doubt Hamer had some fond recollections of friendships made during her days as a field worker and organizer for the SNCC, and as a member of the Mississippi Freedom Democratic Party (MFDP) and the COFO (the Council of Federated Organizations, a coalition of civil rights groups in Mississippi, such as the NAACP, CORE, the SCLC and other local organizations,[12] which helped with the rights of poor and middle-class folk). Hamer had also enjoyed her association with Aaron Henry, from Mississippi, who became the president of the Council of Federated Organizations (COFO). Moreover, "31-year-old Harlem-born, Harvard-educated Robert Moses" was named COFO's first director.[13] Or perhaps Hamer recalled the time when she left Shirley MacLaine, the white movie actress, best-selling author and sister to U.S. film actor Warren Beatty, "at her stove stirring a pot of beans while she went to a Freedom Democratic Party meeting one day."[14] What MacLaine thought about Fannie Lou Hamer at that time might be interesting thing to know, as she certainly believed in what Hamer stood for. It was perhaps Hamer's unmistakable human touch which solidified her reputation as a humanitarian. Fannie Lou Hamer never lost her gentleness or concern for others.[15] Of course, it was the twilight of her activism, as she thought back over the years with pride and gratitude. Hamer often felt that she was fortunate that she had survived the times.

It had certainly been very rewarding to be able to work with other civil rights activists and leaders, and now Fannie Lou Hamer looked to enjoy her golden years with her beloved Pap. She had settled down to wait and see what would happen. She didn't wait long, as Hamer was soon instrumental in helping "bring the Head Start program to the Mississippi countryside," as well as helping start "a child-care center" where black "children would be taken care of while [the parents] worked."[16] Hamer's ability to accomplish all these remarkable things, even while ill, was a feat in itself. Hamer also wanted to stay in the mix of political things and remain socially engaged while supporting the rights of blacks and other minorities everywhere. Even the issue of women's rights did not escape Hamer's attention and involvement. One might say that she was a quasi-feminist before it was fashionable. Professor Bernice Johnson Reagon writes, "As a leader in the movement and in her community, [Hamer] did not hesitate to criticize men who wanted to lead but were unable to confront their fears. She believed that leadership came from actual work and commitment and was not preordained by sex."[17]

At this particular time, the Vietnam War was still in full swing and "absorbing much of the nation's attention." Therefore, "the government had little money to spend on new programs"[18] to help poor people. According to historian Michael Weber, the war in Vietnam also divided the nation and civil rights movement.[19] Indeed, most activists in the civil rights movement were against the Vietnam War. About the Vietnam War, Fannie Lou Hamer said, "It's wrong to fight [in Vietnam] — I don't just say only the black man, I just don't think nobody with any decency should go to a racist war like that."[20] Hamer was a pacifist who abhorred using violence to settle conflicts or political disputes. Fannie Lou Hamer also supported the Freedom Schools in Mississippi for many years, which gave poor students a political education and a means "to learn about society's rules,"[21] good or bad.

Hamer realized that each day was a blessing, and she tried to live her life to the fullest, given the often bleak circumstances. Not surprisingly, in her late fifties she was now a profoundly different woman. And she suffered from breast cancer. The breast cancer had taken its toll on Hamer, as she was a mere shell of her former robust self. But in many ways Fannie Lou Hamer still had an undiminished zest for life. Seriously ailing, Hamer was still a solid woman, though now somewhat fragile. But fragility actually made her strong. When Hamer was finally able to have a medical screening for cancer and other health problems, it was discovered that she had indeed malignant breast cancer. And "even when a cancerous growth meant her breast had to be removed, [Hamer] was not self-concerned."[22] Despite her illness, Fannie Lou Hamer continued to work extremely hard "on into 1976 to unite the black and the white factions of the Mississippi Democratic Party so that a single integrated delegation could represent the state at the 1976 Democratic Convention in New York."[23] After all, she had been thoroughly disgusted by what happened at the 1972 Democratic National Convention, held in Miami Beach, Florida, when black delegates, such as herself, didn't even have a voice.[24]

Fannie Lou Hamer didn't have to prove anything to anyone anymore. Nor did she have to prove she was some kind of hero. Hamer had become everything she had ever hoped to become: "a champion of her people."[25] Yet she was deeply weary at times. The breast cancer and the failure of her Freedom Farm had been blows to both her mind and body. Hamer suffered a nervous breakdown in the 1970s. Lee writes, "By January 1977, Hamer was in a deep depression, a paralyzing gloom that occasionally left her listless."[26]

Ultimately, however, a deep sense of peace came over her, even as she "was frustrated because friends were not responding to calls for help, and Pap was spending [too much] time away from home."[27] And she was hospitalized on several occasions, for diabetes, hypertension and heart disease. Hamer was also having trouble with her polio-afflicted legs. Some of her female family members and friends stayed by her side as her condition worsened. Her prognosis was grim. Unable to work because of her frail health, Hamer was able to reflect upon her life and whether it had any meaning. She felt appropriately proud of what she had accomplished, especially since she and other black activists had upset the old equilibrium of "white rule." Hamer felt she had made a significant difference in the lives of some black people. Her exuberance hadn't dulled either, even though she suffered from obesity, high blood pressure and breast cancer. Hamer wasn't bitter, nor did she take it personally. Even after all the bad things that had happened to her in life, Hamer was not angry about the way things turned out. She still continued to live her faith. Indeed, Hamer was comforted by her faith in God.

Fannie Lou Hamer was worried about what might happen to black people in the future. She knew how far blacks in Mississippi and the United States had come in the 1970s, but they still had a long way to go. In some ways, she didn't believe that it was getting much better for black people. For instance, some whites in the state of Mississippi, and elsewhere in the South, tried to stop the progress of blacks by political hook or crook. Professor Mark Newman put it this way: "To reduce the impact of black votes, Southern white officials and legislators switched from district to at-large elections, made elective offices appointive, redrew electoral boundaries, adopted multimember legislative districts, and annexed areas with large white populations."[28] Fortunately, "enforcement of the pre-clearance requirement of the Voting Rights Act eliminated some of these discriminatory devices and acted as a deterrent,"[29] but white leaders did everything they could to impede black participation in electoral politics. The way Fannie Lou saw it, not much had changed in white people's attitudes. Some white segregationists, she knew, would never change their minds about blacks and whether they should have the same rights as whites in Mississippi. But Hamer also believed that the future in the state was certainly going to be very different from the racist past. She knew that blacks and whites must continue to work together to eradicate racism and discrimination, to genuinely cooperate to change the racial status quo. People, of course, were baffled by Hamer's devotion to the civil rights cause in the face of her poor health. For a while, Hamer did seem to regain strength and energy — in fits and spurts. To the bitter end, Fannie Lou Hamer kept fighting, rallying against injustice as the dreaded cancer was getting the better of her. Her speaking engagements — to help pay the bills — were sapping her energy and strength. Hamer held up as long as she could; but her health continued to deteriorate.

Although Hamer was not happy about the fact that she was going to die, she had accepted it. And even though Hamer didn't know how long she had, or if the new chemotherapy would hold the advancing cancer at bay, she was very much at peace with herself. Hamer no longer wanted to be a burden on anyone.

When Fannie Lou Hamer was hospitalized for the final time for cancer in 1977, at the Mound Bayou Community Hospital in Mississippi, her oval face looked strangely lopsided. But her deep-set, blood-shot eyes showed a burning spirit. Hamer was as compelling as ever, but you could see the wear and tear on her, as she often cried because of the intense pain. Gone was her garrulous presence, as she talked to visitors in motherly, measured phrases, with a comforting cadence. Hamer's voice, however, still had an edge, as if indicating that what she had to say was more than important. The breast cancer had spread, but Hamer did not want to undergo any more invasive surgery, because of her experiences over the years with doctors. She was now fighting the toughest battle of her life, one even harder than scrimmaging with hard-core racists. Ultimately, Hamer became too sick and tired for anything. At one point she was too weak to even get up from her hospital bed. Indeed, Hamer had nothing left to spare. She had no more strength in her, despite having weathered so many storms over the course of her life. Fannie Lou Hamer let go finally, ready for her next adventure in death. Previously, Hamer had put her life in order. She didn't worry about leaving any worldly goods to anyone at the end, because she didn't have very much to begin with. Indeed, there wouldn't be any substantial assets left behind. She had stayed in a simple house on their farm in Ruleville, with Pap and her two granddaughters, where she had lived a simple life during her last years. Hamer thought God was compassionate, and she wasn't afraid to die if He called her home. Her belief in God never wavered.

Upon her death bed, Hamer reserved judgment about the state of black America. She remained upbeat and optimistic that some things would change, and blacks in Mississippi would be okay. Hamer had worked feverishly, almost to the end and in considerable pain, with "a selfless concern about other people."[30] But on March 14, 1977, because of the advanced stages of breast cancer and a weak heart, Fannie Lou Hamer died. Perry "Pap" Hamer firmly believed that some of the things that contributed to his wife's death were "the fact that she never took care of herself physically, that she never got the proper rest and sometimes didn't even take time to eat property."[31] But Fannie Lou Hamer had died with grace and dignity.

Conclusions

Fannie Lou Hamer knew that she was one woman and only one woman. However, she knew she was an American, and as an American she had a light to shine on the darkness of racism. It was a little light, but she aimed it directly at the gloom of ignorance.[1]

— Maya Angelou

When Fannie Lou Hamer died in 1977, at sixty years old, "in the hospital at Mound Bayou, Mississippi, a black-governed town thirty miles north of her home in Ruleville,"[2] many were saddened by her death. Many didn't even know she had been sick with cancer. Hamer had been born into grinding poverty and raised in segregated Mississippi. She lived a hard life, but her later life as a civil rights activist was deeply satisfying. Hamer was able to effectively voice the frustration and concerns of poor blacks living in the state. And she never stopped believing that things would change for the betterment of black people and poor whites. Indeed, Fannie Lou Hamer lived her adult life "for all people without reference to gender, ethnic grouping, or creed."[3] She hoped that one day all human beings could embrace a time when everyone was valued and treated with respect. Hamer didn't have any regrets about what she did during her activist days in the civil rights movement. She also strove to be politically relevant throughout her adult life. In the end, Hamer would become more than some brief phenomenon because she always inspired people by her exuberance and participation. She was a dynamic, huge personality. Hamer's ebullience and generous spirit was enough to make her triumphant in many ways, even with a limited education.

Fannie Lou Hamer had always wanted to be associated with something bigger than herself, and she found this association by becoming part of the civil rights movement. Hamer made an indelible impact on many black people in the state of Mississippi through this important movement. The interesting thing about Fannie Lou Hamer's political proclivities was that she always told you the truth. Hamer was exceptionally earnest, with an energetic disposition.

As we have seen, Hamer accomplished a number of praise-worthy things, but she never tried to toot her own horn. Moreover, Hamer demonstrated gargantuan moral courage in the face of "white rule" and political repression. Blacks in Mississippi simply wanted to freely participate in state and local politics while being protected from violence and hate groups like the racist Ku Klux Klan. Hamer was able to assist with transforming the social and political landscape in Mississippi in terms of eliminating segregation. She went against the white racism grain to essentially chart the course for black political participation. Hamer had to be tenacious and consistent. Hamer once stated, "I'm determined to give my part. Not for what the movement can do for me, but what I can do for the movement to bring about a change in the state of Mississippi."[4] She provided the civil rights movement with something new and different in terms of organizaing. Hamer was certainly one of the more impressive and strong-willed black leaders. Former Mississippi NAACP director Aaron Henry stated that Fannie Lou Hamer was "one of the truly dedicated and gifted persons with the intense desire to make sure that human relations for all people become reality."[5]

The road for Fannie Lou Hamer wasn't an easy one. To say the least, there was political upheaval and turmoil galore. But even at an early age, Hamer had the wisdom of a very old soul. And she had an extraordinary ability to connect with people. Without a doubt, Fannie Lou Hamer "lived on the edge of tragedy and oppression." Still, in the end, "she never permitted her misfortunes to dictate the way she lived her life."[6] Hamer gave everything she had to give during her days as a civil rights worker. She was able to deconstruct the hateful ramblings of white supremacists by turning what they stood for on its head. Hamer argued that some whites in Mississippi just didn't see the big racial picture.

Hamer often got worked up about racism and the injustices perpetrated against poor black people, sometimes becoming beside herself. She certainly ruffled a lot of feathers, especially among whites who despised her. Fannie Lou Hamer frequently reminded white Southerners of the democratic principles upon which the nation was founded. But many dismissed or ignored her. In other words, Hamer told the truth that white leaders and politicians in Mississippi needed to accept but often ignored, especially the fact that black people were human beings too. Her aim was to move beyond the lies and deceit of white segregationists.

Inspired by many black activists, like Rosa Parks, Ella Baker, Robert Moses and James Forman, Fannie Lou Hamer always tried to do what she thought was right, especially when it came to making political decisions about what to do in Mississippi.[7] And Hamer risked everything, even her mental and physical health, to change things in the state, to get political things done. Essentially, Fannie Lou Hamer helped blacks achieve their voting rights in Mississippi. In point of fact, "the denial of the franchise to Mississippi blacks helped lead to the Voting Rights Act of 1965, which brought in federal registrars and suspended literacy requirements,"[8] and other devices to limit or deny black people their right to vote. Hamer would later conduct citizenship classes to help newly-minted black voters learn about the voting process in the state of Mississippi — to the chagrin of white political leaders and politicians. She never lacked courage in her public life, especially during the early skirmishes of the civil rights movement. Indeed, Hamer tried to incite righteous fervor in the apathetic black people of the Delta, who had almost given up and accepted their second-class status. She was also a pioneering advocates for women's rights. In the 1970s, Hamer worked with "the National Council of Negro Women" and other women's groups, as well as helped "to convene the National Women's Political Caucus."[9] Hamer was equally well-known for her outreach work. With her big heart driving her, Fannie Lou Hamer touched the lives of countless blacks in Mississippi, as she was "deeply committed to improving life for poor minorities."[10] And Hamer's commitment to the black community became more passionate and intense the longer she was involved with the civil rights movement, though she was highly motivated by her own life experiences. Unfortunately, many blacks in the Mississippi Delta were doomed to spend the rest of their days working at the back-breaking job of picking cotton, or working the dusty fields under the hot Mississippi sun. But Hamer refused to be limited to such a sad life.

Fannie Lou Hamer was a woman of great character and integrity, one who worked tirelessly for the betterment of blacks in Mississippi and throughout the nation. Hamer was politically confrontational, which served her well as a civil rights activist. She worked hard to make things less complicated for poor black people. And she did everything humanly possible to impart her intuitive understanding of the racial situation. Inevitably, Fannie Lou Hamer would come to define the governmental parameters, as she had "a tremendous impact in the black political arena of Ruleville,"[11] Mississippi. She remained passionate about inspiring young black people to fight for their rights, as Hamer embodied the soul of blacks in the Mississippi Delta. Hamer's character was defined by strength, courage, optimism, and unwavering dedication to the cause of freedom and human rights. Hence, Hamer was more than a witness and participant in the civil rights movement, she was an *icon* of the cause. According to Professor Susan Johnson, "all of these personal qualities ... endeared Ms. Hamer to her brothers and sisters in Ruleville" and elsewhere. But while "some [admired] her courage, others [envied] her strength and success."[12]

Hamer helped make American civil rights history, adding a new dimension to a multi-dimensional grassroots movement. What happened in Mississippi during its legal segregation years reflected the great racial dilemma. One of the greatest misconception some whites had about black people in the South (and in Mississippi) was they were satisfied with their lives. Nothing could have been further from the truth. Being able to speak forcefully and convincingly about such racial issues was a skill that Fannie Lou Hamer developed and used throughout her adult life. But she did not live a fairy-tale existence, as she got in trouble for condemning racist people. Hamer weathered horrendous personal storms and survived them without missing a beat. Even more important, Hamer believed that if people had more compassion and common sense, they might be able to build a bridge to racial understanding. Toward this end, wrote Rachel Davis DuBois and Mew-Soong Li, the "work of developing harmonious relationships must be done by millions of *little people*, not only in day-to-day contacts but in small groups." They go on to say, "Life is one organic whole, and that not to give to and receive from people who have come from different parts of that whole is to live less than completely."[13] Fannie Lou Hamer, of course, used a similar group conversation method in resolving conflicts and social tensions in her own field work and while teaching voting rights classes. It seemed that many civil rights activists used some form of Rachel DuBois's techniques in conflict situations. A very thoughtful, spiritual and thought-provoking person, Fannie Lou Hamer was not thinking about grabbing media attention — even as she was catapulted to fame. She was never interested in being a celebrity. But eventually Hamer came to understand the power of her personality and how she could use it to her own advantage. According to historian Melba J. Duncan:

> Fannie Lou Hamer's most widely celebrated moment was her stinging rebuke of the 1964 Democratic National Convention's Credentials Committee. The committee ultimately denied her upstart Mississippi delegation the right to be seated at the convention, but she won the media war when network news shows aired her remarks. [14]

Although Hamer mostly hated the limelight, her notoriety after the 1964 Democratic Convention in Atlantic City, New Jersey, turned national attention to the plight of the Mississippi Freedom Democratic Party and black people from the Delta. In her own inimitable style, Hamer stressed tolerance and the importance of the movement. Hamer had an almost mystical ability to make people listen to her. Fannie Lou Hamer was legendary for her speaking ferocity. Hamer's words made people feel good — or they made people cry. Indeed, she was almost always able to rouse an audience and rally them around a common purpose or concern. Hamer developed "an immediate rapport with

[her] audience," while exhibiting "political sophistication."[15] Her powerful speeches were designed mostly to inform by presenting the absolute truth. Hamer often provided eloquent insight into the racial problems of Mississippi. She talked about the many challenges that faced poor black people. Hamer announced to the world the sad status of blacks in the Delta, and how some whites in Mississippi had been mistreating blacks for generations. Hardly anyone knew or cared about such racial matters — until Hamer started talking about them. Some whites were even intimidated by the indomitable Fannie Lou Hamer. Through her words, she almost single-handedly inspired blacks and other poor minorities to stand up to "white rule" and the sheer arrogance of some white racists and segregationists. Hamer was indeed a heroine of some repute and significance. In so many words, she gave hope to those who had no hope.

Often Hamer was buoyed by the crowds that would come out to hear her speak, because she was also a voice of conscience. And Hamer made important, grandiose comments and pronouncements. Her voice was strikingly reminiscent of Dr. Martin L. King, Jr., as she often interspersed her speeches "with Biblical quotations."[16] Furthermore, her words were uncommonly sophisticated, given her lack of knowledge about the bigger world. But Hamer was always able to hold her head up high, no matter what. "Courageous and frank," she was able to take white segregationists to task for their racist actions, which took on a broader resonance. Hamer often spoke of "freedom and struggle at mass meetings,"[17] because she wanted to change the racist political system in Mississippi, no matter what.

Still, Fannie Lou Hamer was not indoctrinated with the fiery rhetoric of the Black Power Revolution going on in the United States at the same time. In hindsight, perhaps Fannie Lou Hamer was a very unlikely person to become the voice of the civil rights movement in Mississippi because of her lack of higher education. But Hamer had the combination of political insight, charisma, organizing brilliance and national recognition that made her an incredible and credible black leader.

Hamer's fierce drive and commitment to the civil rights movement may have been because of her hard life and childhood. Hamer was always concerned about the homeless, so she "joined a group called the Young World Developers"[18] (a precursor to today's Habitat for Humanity) because this organization helped "build houses for both African Americans and white families in need."[19] Hamer would come to believe that if you really wanted something, all you needed to do was ask God — while persistently pursuing your goal. Even in the late stages of breast cancer, for instance, Hamer ran for state senator.[20] And Hamer never regretted throwing her hat into that ring in the 1970s. Nonetheless, she lost to the incumbent, Robert Crook, a white man.[21]

According to professor Sharon Bramlett-Solomon, Hamer received "little recognition of her achievements, until the end of her life."[22] To this day, many people fail to appreciate the importance of Fannie Lou Hamer's contributions. She still doesn't receive the awareness or adulation enjoyed by most civil rights icons. Even during the civil rights movement, Hamer was given less than her due. But Hamer had more gumption and character than most people. As it turned out, Fannie Lou Hamer was an unapologetic freedom warrior. And the role of Hamer in Mississippi politics and history cannot be ignored. Bramlett-Solomon writes that Hamer, "like other under-recognized [black] women — played many roles in the civil rights movement. Night visitors riddled her house with bullets; [and] she suffered other dangers and indignities. But she persevered; [and] her comments on national television galvanized many."[23] Clearly, some white Southerners today would like to forget the ugly history of Mississippi. But Fannie Lou Hamer should never be dismissed or forgotten. Fannie Lou Hamer, along with Rosa Parks, should be considered the "gold standard" in terms of the civil rights movement, especially regarding black women activists. But Hamer has remained in obscurity, almost unknown to some in the United States. Many poor minorities benefited from the commitment and generosity of Fannie Lou Hamer, as she was a sort of social and political prophet, and giver of things. What Hamer was able to do for blacks in the Mississippi Delta was an impressive achievement. If nothing else, she helped change how white people viewed black people. Fannie Lou Hamer made a lot of white people come to grips with their prejudices. Moreover, we owe Hamer a debt of gratitude for leading the way for black politicians in Mississippi. She paved the way for blacks to vote and run for political office. Indeed, because of Fannie Lou Hamer, there is "greater ease in registering to vote [in the state]," and remarkably "fewer obstacles in actually casting one's ballot." Additionally, blacks can now impact election outcomes, and succeed as office seekers.[24] According to historian E. C. Foster, by 1971, 60 percent of eligible black voters "were registered to vote in Mississippi elections,"[25] which has significantly changed the political landscape in the state.

Before Fannie Lou Hamer died on March 14, 1977, she truly believed that the time had come when, as a nation, blacks and whites had no choice but to rally around the civil rights and freedom causes. Had she not lived, perhaps the politics in the state would have taken longer to change. Or Mississippians might have encountered more racial violence and chaos. Hamer believed in what she was doing as a civil rights worker; and her insight and wisdom were second to none. Hamer's quiet strength, combined with her ability to speak out on the issues that no one else would, certainly raised awareness. Furthermore, she was a brave spirit who overcame almost intractable racial problems. What Fannie Lou Hamer did will have lasting significance. Her life was a true testament to her devotion to the cause of justice and the rights of people. And Hamer can be looked upon as an important reminder that racism, violence, and bigotry should be eliminated. Her almost mythical life is something to praise, emulate and celebrate, especially when one considers the magnitude of her accomplishments. No one can say that she didn't personify the civil rights movement in the state of Mississippi. Indeed, Hamer was responsible for organizing the grassroots support necessary to undermine the various injustices perpetrated against many blacks by white Southerners.

There will never be another person like the great Fannie Lou Hamer. Her death triggered a wave of mourning in the state. Many showed up at her funeral to pay their last respects; it was standing-room-only. Although it wasn't the biggest of funerals in the history of Mississippi, it was one of the most publicized. Indeed, white and black people together drove in cars, or flew in planes from neighboring states, to join the ranks of those who had already lined up to say their final farewell to Fannie Lou Hamer at the Williams Chapel Church and sing her favorite church and freedom songs. According to Kay Mills, "Mrs. Hamer loved wearing white, and she was buried in a white dress." Mills goes on to write that Fannie Lou Hamer "also loved flowers, so her open casket at the front of the tiny church was surrounded by bouquets."[26] She was not forgotten by her colleagues in the cause that day. George Sewell described the event and funeral services this way:

> Hundreds of black and white mourners came to Ruleville to pay final respects to the gallant gladiator for human freedom. Among them, U.S. Ambassador Andrew Young, Stokely Carmichael, Ralph Abernathy, Dick Gregory and [many] others. [And] ironically, perhaps, the Mississippi House of Representatives passed a formal resolution praising Mrs. Hamer.[27]

Many effusively praised Fannie Lou Hamer at her funeral services. Joyce A. Ladner writes that "much was said at her funeral that made us look at who Fannie Lou Hamer was. But in the end, it was her wisdom that told us the most."[28] It was incongruous that so many who had criticized and ridiculed Hamer at the end of her activism days were now eulogizing this champion of the civil rights movement at her funeral. Indeed, for some, it was a rather sad state of affairs. Charles M. Payne explains:

> For some in SNCC-COFO her funeral ceremony was an embarrassment, a media event with dignitaries from around the country competing with one another to be seen on camera, pushing her neighbors into the background. It seemed the perfect contradiction of the values [Hamer] tried to live by.[29]

Nonetheless, many felt that Fannie Lou Hamer's funeral service was a fitting memorial. After the services at Williams Chapel Church, a slow procession headed to her final resting place. Fannie Lou Hamer was later buried at a somewhat private burial site, because she knew that Ruleville was where she belonged. Her gravestone bears an epitaph that cites Hamer's famous dictum — a testimony to this great black woman: "I'm sick and tired of being sick and tired."

Epilogue

When pride cometh, then cometh shame: but with the lowly is wisdom.
— the Book of Proverbs, chapter II, verse 2

Without a doubt, Fannie Lou Hamer is still considered a distinguished African-American icon and woman activist.[1] Hamer, of course, was no stranger to hardship, as she endured so much, but she proved that she was her own woman. Indeed, Fannie Lou Hamer was a righteous individual who cared deeply about people in general. Furthermore, she maintained a level of humility that was unmatched by other civil rights activists. Sometimes she tried to take on more than she could ultimately manage; but Hamer regretted nothing. As a civil rights activist, Fannie Lou Hamer taught "us how to shift public sentiment, challenge entrenched institutional power and find the strength to persevere despite all odds."[2] Hamer had bad things happen to her almost her entire life, but she never held a grudge.

Fannie Lou Hamer was one of the titans of the civil rights movement. And she was able to speak the loudest on social, political and racial issues. Hamer was a bulwark against the spread of white supremacy. White rule in Mississippi violated black people's civil rights and liberties, because for a long time there were no restrictions against white terrorism and political dominance. Black people in the state were told that they didn't have to participate in politics or concern themselves with any political matters. But Fannie Lou Hamer focused on political matters, like ensuring blacks obtained their voting rights. She was equally focused on continuing her teaching efforts in the civil rights movement. In the end, many whites in the state of Mississippi begrudgingly acknowledged that because of Hamer they were fighting a losing battle in terms of maintaining segregation.

When Fannie Lou Hamer decided to give up her active position in the SNCC, she turned to running her Freedom Farm Cooperative. It went a long way toward alleviating the depression she had been suffering from in 1972.

Hamer wanted to find something different that would address the needs of black and white people living in the Delta. Although some political progress had been made by this time in the 1970s, there were still food shortages in the black community. Hamer firmly believed that her Freedom Farm would address this issue; but ultimately the farm did not succeed. The place failed "in part because of Mrs. Hamer's tendency to trust people who did not necessarily deserve it."[3] Still, for a good while Hamer made a real difference for black and white families in need through her Freedom Farm Cooperative. Hamer's Freedom Farm has since gone completely out of business, mostly because of her death. Hamer had obviously held things together at the cooperative — until she could work no more. Hamer had found solace in the daily work on the farm. And before she was hospitalized for the final time, Hamer had reengaged herself in the hard work at the Freedom Farm Cooperative, and was still trying to make the place work out in the end.

When Fannie Lou Hamer discovered that she had inoperable cancer, she still wanted to help people. Hamer had always been motivated to take action. But her breast cancer became an incapacitating burden. As with many blacks in Mississippi who could not afford health insurance, her spreading cancer went undetected for too long. But Fannie Lou Hamer's energy level was remarkable. Some who visited her near the end were surprised, as Hamer was frenetically trying to get things done, even as her health continued to deteriorate. Perry "Pap" Hamer was often by her side at the hospital when Fannie Lou became increasingly ill. He was always there for her. But Pap Hamer was also upset; he once angrily complained that Fannie Lou "raised lots of money and she would come back and give it to the people. And when she died, she didn't have a dime."[4]

Although Fannie Lou Hamer was not highly educated nor well read (with the possible exception of her knowledge of the Bible), she was particularly impressive when it came to talking about the trials and tribulations of poor blacks in Mississippi. She was a woman of great determination and old-school wisdom. She was also considered a saintly person. Indeed, Hamer's deeds were just as important as her words. Fannie Lou Hamer ultimately wanted to help create an environment where people in the world could come together. She couldn't avoid reminding us, while she lived, that both blacks and whites should be tolerant and respectful of each other. In this respect, Hamer was abundantly successful, as she became a sort of catalyst that brought people together.

As we have seen, Hamer was one of the most influential black feminist activists in Mississippi during her life and times. Perhaps Fannie Lou Hamer should have received the prestigious Horatio Alger Award, as she certainly struggled against poverty and adversity. This award is given to leaders who give back to their respective communities while building a significant life after starting out with very little. Fannie Lou Hamer certainly fit this profile. Hamer earned our respect and admiration. Some even see her as a heroic martyr for the cause of black civil rights. Eventually, Hamer would become the talk of the town in Ruleville, and even throughout the state of Mississippi. She will always be a larger than life historical figure.

Many showed the appropriate deference to Fannie Lou Hamer. The mourners at her funeral laughed and sang. They also cried, but they mainly praised Fannie Lou Hamer. There were endless tributes. She was considered more than a great lady; she was a warrior in the cause of freedom. Her death elicited condolences from people throughout the world.

Fortunately, some accolades were given to Fannie Lou Hamer even before she died. And she happily accepted the honors, and other awards and compliments bestowed upon her, although in her humility Hamer wasn't sure that she was worthy to receive them. Still, the recognition and attention deeply moved her. And she was more than appreciative. While she lived, Hamer received numerous honorary degrees, mostly from black colleges and universities, such as Morehouse College, Howard University, Tougaloo College in Mississippi, and Shaw University. Additionally, according to Sandy Donovan,

The burial site of Fannie Lou Hamer and her husband, Perry "Pap" Hamer, Rulesville, Mississippi, 2010.

"in 1969 Hamer was invited to the White House for a conference on health and nutrition."[5]

Since Fannie Lou Hamer's death, many individuals and organizations, such as the "Fannie Lou Hamer Flame Keepers,"[6] have kept her legacy alive, celebrating her many accomplishments. A "Fannie Lou Hamer Memorial Garden" has been established at her gravesite in Ruleville, Mississippi. (Upon his death on May 19, 1992, Fannie Lou's husband, Perry "Pap" Hamer, the great love of her life, was buried right next to her.) Currently, the former chairperson of the MFDP and Hamer's one-time campaign manager, Charles McLaurin, directs a project to build a statue of Fannie Lou Hamer, to be located at the Memorial Garden site.[7]

In 1997, "at a National Endowment for the Humanities Summer Seminar for College Teachers," a group headed by Dr. Leslie B. McLemore, emeritus professor of political science at Jackson State University, founded the Fannie

Lou Hamer Institute, which "conducts seminars and workshops for K–12 teachers and students that feature the role played by the Civil Rights Movement in expanding the meaning, scope, and practice of citizenship and democracy in America."[8] In February 2006, the Fannie Lou Hamer Institute was named Mississippi Humanities Educator of the Year for 2005[9] for (as the mission of the organization states) promoting "positive change by examining the tools and experiences of those who [struggled] to create, expand, and sustain civil rights, social justice, and citizenship."[10] In this way, the institute dedicated to Hamer has carried on her great legacy. Additionally the Fannie Lou Hamer Project has been established in Kalamazoo, Michigan. There is also a celebration day each year in Ruleville, Mississippi, aptly named "Fannie Lou Hamer Day." Finally, Fannie Lou Hamer has been inducted into the National Women's Hall of Fame in Seneca Falls,

Fannie Lou Hamer testifying before the Democratic National Convention in Atlantic City, New Jersey, representing the Mississippi Freedom Democratic Party, 1964. Library of Congress.

New York. Although Hamer's story in the national civil rights discussion has sometimes been overlooked, her role in American history and the civil rights movement should never be dismissed as an accident of history.

Fannie Lou Hamer, however, always thought her contributions were insignificant compared to those of, say, Rosa Parks or Ella Baker; but she made a big, positive sound with her voice, which made a difference to many people. Her actions certainly made conditions for black people in Mississippi better, especially in terms of politics, as Fannie Lou Hamer made it possible for young black Mississippians to achieve great things. We should remember that Hamer was responsible for nominating the former NAACP director in the state, Charles Evers, a black man and activist, for governor of Mississippi,[11] but he lost that election. She also ran for governor herself, but lost that election too.[12] However, because of Hamer's work, "Mississippi has more African American elected officials than any [other] state in the union."[13] Perhaps our world is less of a place without Fannie Lou Hamer. But Fannie Lou Hamer's legacy of accomplishments will live on, and the bright radiance of her life will continue to captivate people, even though Fannie Lou Hamer died in 1977. What she did for humankind will endure.

Chapter Notes

Preface

1. Jabari Asim, *The N Word: Who Can Say It, Who Shouldn't, and Why* (New York: Houghton Mifflin, 2007), p. 232.
2. Erik H. Erikson, *Gandhi's Truth: On the Origins of Militant Nonviolence* (New York: Norton, 1969), p. 10.
3. *Ibid.*
4. Susan Kling, *Fannie Lou Hamer: A Biography* (Chicago: Women for Racial and Economic Equality, 1979), p. 42.
5. Michael J. Klarman, *Unfinished Business: Racial Equality in American History* (New York: Oxford University Press, 2007), p. 221.

Introduction

1. Mary Beth Rogers, *Barbara Jordan: American Hero* (New York: Bantam, 2000), p. xiv.
2. Molefi Kete Asante, "Fannie Lou Hamer, 1917–1977," in *100 Greatest African Americans: A Biographical Encyclopedia* (New York: Prometheus, 2002), p. 148.
3. Whitney M. Young, Jr., "A Vanishing Era," *Harper's Magazine* (April 1965), p. 172.
4. Laura Baskes Litwin, *Fannie Lou Hamer: Fighting for the Right to Vote* (Berkeley Heights, NJ: Enslow, 2002), p. 46.
5. Juan Williams, *Eyes on the Prize: America's Civil Rights Years, 1954–1965* (New York: Penguin, 1987), p. 246.
6. Kay Mills, *This Little Light of Mine: The Life of Fannie Lou Hamer* (New York: Dutton, 1993), p. 93.
7. Alice Walker, Review of June Jordan, *Fannie Lou Hamer* (New York: Thomas Y. Crowell, 1972) in *The New York Times Book Review* (April 29, 1973), p. 8.
8. Litwin, *Fannie Lou Hamer: Fighting for the Right to Vote*, p. 54.
9. June Jordan, *Fannie Lou Hamer* (New York: Thomas Y. Crowell, 1972), p. 2.
10. Fannie Lou Hamer, Foreword to Tracy Sugarman, *Stranger at the Gates: A Summer in Mississippi* (New York: Hill and Wang, 1966), p. ix.

11. Walker Percy, "Mississippi: The Fallen Paradise," *Harper's Magazine* (April 1965), p. 169.
12. Washington, "Medical Apartheid," p. 190.

Chapter 1

1. John Oliver Killens, *'Sippi* (New York: Thunder's Mouth, 1967), p. xv.
2. Rochelle Sharpe. "More Money, More Kids," *USA Weekend* (April 4–6, 2008), p. 25.
3. Linda Reed, "Hamer, Fannie Lou," in Darlene Clark Hine, Elsa Barkley Brown, and Rosalyn Terborg-Penn, *Black Women in America: A Historical Encyclopedia* (Indianapolis: Indiana University Press, 1993), p. 518. Faith and religion were extremely important in the Townsend family. Fannie Lou Hamer joined the church at a very early age, drawn there by her mother.
4. Stephen Yafa, *Big Cotton: How a Humble Fiber Created Fortunes, Wrecked Civilization, and Put America on the Map* (New York: Viking, 2005), p. 177. Yafa also speculated that "whites and blacks alike were ... both slaves to cotton."
5. J.H. O'Dell, "Life in Mississippi: An Interview with Fannie Lou Hamer," *Freedomways*, 2nd Quarter (Spring, 1965), p. 240.
6. Reed, "Hamer, Fannie Lou," p. 518.
7. John Egerton. *A Mind to Stay Here: Profiles from the South* (New York: MacMillan, 1970), p. 96. Fannie Lou Townsend didn't mind picking cotton at first. But she never liked the hours — from perhaps 5 A.M. until late into the night. Often it was sixteen-hour days.
8. Molefi Kete Asante, "Fannie Lou Hamer, 1917–1977," *Greatest African Americans: A Biographical Encyclopedia* (New York: Prometheus, 2002), p. 146.
9. Mary Beth Rogers and Barbara Jordan, *American Hero* (New York: Bantam, 2000), p. 39.
10. Asante, "Fannie Lou Hamer," p. 146.1.
11. Penny Colman, *Fannie Lou Hamer and the Fight for the Vote* (Brookfield, CT: Millbrook, 1993), p. 12.
12. Kay Mills, *This Little Light of Mine: The Life of Fannie Lou Hamer* (New York: Dutton, 1993). See also J.H. O'Dell, "Life in Mississippi:

An Interview with Fannie Lou Hamer," pp. 231–232.

13. *Ibid.*

Chapter 2

1. Harriet A. Washington, *Medical Apartheid: The Dark History of Medical Experimentation on Black Americans from Colonial Times to the Present* (New York: Doubleday, 2006), p. 189.

2. Annelise Orleck, *Storming Caesars Palace: How Black Mothers Fought Their Own War on Poverty* (Boston: Beacon, 2007), p. 9.

3. Valerie Grim, "The Impact of Mechanized Farming on Black Farm Families in the Rural South: A Study of Farm Life in the Brooks Farm Community, 1940–1970," Vol. 68, No. 2, *Agricultural History* (Spring 1994), p. 170.

4. Laura Baskes Litwin, *Fannie Lou Hamer: Fighting for the Right to Vote* (Berkeley Heights, NJ: Enslow, 2002), p. 13.

5. David Rubel, *Fannie Lou Hamer: From Sharecropping to Politics* (New York: Silver Burdett, 1990), p. 16.

6. *Ibid.*, p. 15.

7. Litwin, *Fannie Lou Hamer: Fighting for the Right to Vote*, p. 12.

8. Rubel, *Fannie Lou Hamer*, p. 16.

9. George Alexander Sewell, *Mississippi Black History Makers* (Jackson: University Press of Mississippi), p. 346. Black farmers and sharecroppers often eked out a living picking cotton, or doing other odd and laborious jobs for white plantation owners, for poverty wages.

10. Rubel, *Fannie Lou Hamer*, p. 16.

11. Litwin, *Fannie Lou Hamer: Fighting for the Right to Vote*, p. 12.

12. Sewell, *Mississippi Black History Makers*, p. 346.

13. John Egerton, *A Mind to Stay Here: Profiles from the South* (New York: MacMillan, 1970), p. 96.

14. James R. Grossman, "Black Labor Is the Best Labor: Southern White Reactions to the Great Migration," in Alferdteen Harrison (ed., *Black Exodus: The Great Migration from the American South* (Jackson: University Press of Mississippi, 1991), p. 51. Many black children in the Delta remained oblivious to the world outside of Mississippi.

15. Litwin, *Fannie Lou Hamer: Fighting for the Right to Vote*, p. 15.

16. Edward P. Jones, *The Known World* (New York: Harper Collins, 2003), pp. 1–2. According to Penny Colman, Hamer's mother "would also help people slaughter hogs and hope that they would give her the hog's intestines or the feet and head to take home and cook for her family." See Penny Colman. *Fannie Lou Hamer and the Fight for the Vote* (Brookfield, CT: Millbrook, 1993), p. 11.

17. Jack O'Dell, "Life in Mississippi: An Interview with Fannie Lou Hamer," *Freedomways*, 2nd Quarter (1965), p. 232.

18. Penny Colman, *Fannie Lou Hamer and the Fight for the Vote* (Brookfield, CT: Millbrook, 1993), p. 11.

19. Egerton, *A Mind to Stay Here*, p. 96. See also O'Dell, *Life in Mississippi*.

20. Coleman, *Fannie Lou Hamer and the Fight for the Vote*, p. 11.

Chapter 3

1. Margaret Mead, "Some Theoretical Considerations on the Problem of Mother-Child Separation," *American Journal of Orthopsychiatry*, Vol. 24, Issue 3 (1954), p. 481.

2. Laura Baskes Litwn, *Fannie Lou Hamer: Fighting for the Right to Vote* (Berkeley Heights, NJ: Enslow, 2002), p. 15.

3. John Egerton, *A Mind to Stay Here: Profiles from the South* (New York: MacMillan, 1970), p. 96.

4. George Alexander Sewell, *Mississippi Black History Makers* (Jackson: University Press of Mississippi, 1977), p. 347.

5. Litwin. *Fannie Lou Hamer: Fighting for the Right to Vote*, p. 15.

6. June Jordan. *Fannie Lou Hamer* (New York: Thomas Y. Crowell, 1972), p. 17.

7. *Ibid.*

8. *Ibid.*

9. Sewell, *Mississippi Black History Makers*, p. 348.

10. Julius E. Thompson, *Lynchings in Mississippi: A History, 1865–1965* (Jefferson, NC: McFarland, 2007), p. 80.

11. Sewell, *Mississippi Black History Makers*, p. 348.

12. *Ibid.*

13. Elton C. Fax, *Contemporary Black Leaders* (New York: Dodd, Mead, 1970), p. 116.

14. Annelise Orleck, *Storming Caesars Palace: How Black Mothers Fought Their Own War on Poverty* (Boston: Beacon, 2007), p. 17.

15. *Ibid.*

16. Jordan, *Fannie Lou Hamer*, p. 11.

Chapter 4

1. Theodore Rosengarten, *All God's Dangers: The Life of Nate Shaw* (New York: Vintage, 1989), p. xxv.

2. June Jordan. *Fannie Lou Hamer* (New York: Thomas Y. Crowell, 1972), p. 11.

3. *Ibid.*

4. Marilyn Elias, "Racism Hurts Kids' Mental Health," *USA Today* (May 6, 2009), p. 5D.

5. Elton C. Fax, *Contemporary Black Leaders* (New York: Dodd, Mead, 1970), p. 117. According to Fax, Fannie Lou's parents were able "to save a little in spite of the cheating (by white landowners) that had kept them so poor."

6. *Ibid.* According to George Alexander

Sewell, the Townsends were able to buy "three mules and two cows, wagons," and other items and implements needed for a large farm. See George Alexander Sewell. *Mississippi Black History Makers* (Jackson: University Press of Mississippi, 1977), p. 347.

7. George Alexander Sewell, *Mississippi Black History Makers* (Jackson: University Press of Mississippi, 1977), p. 347.

8. Fax, *Contemporary Black Leaders*, p. 117. Because of some actions of white plantation owners, blacks were doomed to a life of failure.

9. Jordan, *Fannie Lou Hamer*, p. 17.

10. David Rubel, *Fannie Lou Hamer: From Sharecropping to Politics* (New York: Silver Burdett, 1990), p. 25.

11. Sewell, *Mississippi Black History Makers*, p. 347. Telling everyone, especially the local whites, about their good fortune was a costly mistake.

12. Chana Kai Lee, *For Freedom's Sake: The Life of Fannie Lou Hamer* (Chicago: University of Illinois Press, 1999), p. 17. Fannie Lou was twenty-two years old when her father died. See Laura Baskes Litwin, *Fannie Lou Hamer: Fighting for the Right to Vote* (Berkeley Heights, NJ: Enslow, 2002), p. 15.

13. J.H. O'Dell, "Life in Mississippi: An Interview with Fannie Lou Hamer," *Freedomways* (Spring 1965), p. 231.

14. Fax, *Contemporary Black Leaders*, p. 117.

15. O'Dell, "Life in Mississippi: An Interview with Fannie Lou Hamer," p. 230.

16. Sewell, *Mississippi Black History Makers*, p. 348.

17. Penny Colman, *Fannie Lou Hamer and the Fight for the Vote* (Brookfield, CT: Millbrook, 1993), p. 12.

Chapter 5

1. Earnest N. Bracey, "The Racist American Eugenics Program: A Crime Against Humanity," *Forum on Public Policy: A Journal of the Oxford Round Table* (on-line edition, 2007), p. 10 (copyright, 2006).

2. Penny Colman, *Fannie Lou Hamer and the Fight for the Vote* (Brookfield, CT: Millbrook, 1993), p. 12. Fannie Lou never questioned her looks or attractiveness with Pap Hamer.

3. June Jordan, *Fannie Lou Hamer* (New York: Thomas Y. Crowell, 1972), p. 18. When Fannie Lou befriended Pap Hamer, she found someone she thought she could love and believe in. Pap always tried to be a regular guy, and there was a gentleness to him that was always appealing to Fannie Lou.

4. Colman, *Fannie Lou Hamer and the Fight for the Vote*, p. 12.

5. Chana Kai Lee, *For Freedom's Sake: The Life of Fannie Lou Hamer* (Chicago: University of Illinois Press, 1999), p. 18.

6. *Ibid.*

7. *Ibid.*

8. *Ibid.*

9. Jordan, *Fannie Lou Hamer*, pp. 20–21.

10. Lee, *For Freedom's Sake*, p. 19.

11. *Ibid.*

12. Kay Mills, *This Little Light of Mine: The Life of Fannie Lou Hamer* (New York: Dutton, 1993), p. 21.

13. *Ibid.*

14. Laura Baskes Litwin, *Fannie Lou Hamer: Fighting for the Right to Vote* (Berkeley Heights, NJ: Enslow, 2002), p. 19.

15. Harriet A. Washington, *Medical Apartheid: The Dark History of Medical Experimentation on Black Americans from Colonial Times to the Present* (New York: Doubleday, 2006), p. 204.

16. Washington, *Medical Apartheid*, p. 205.

17. Bracey, "The Racist American Eugenics Program," p. 2.

18. Litwin, *Fannie Lou Hamer: Fighting for the Right to Vote*, p. 19. Pap Hamer provided the needed shoulder for Fannie Lou to cry on after learning that she had been sterilized. It changed her life and ultimately led her to become an advocate for women's rights.

19. Susan Kling, *Fannie Lou Hamer: A Biography* (Chicago: Women for Racial and Economic Equality, 1979), p. 15.

20. *Ibid.* See also Rubel, *Fannie Lou Hamer: From Sharecropping to Politics*, p. 29.

21. Jerry DeMuth, "Tired of Being Sick and Tired," *The Nation* (June 1, 1964), p. 549.

22. *Ibid.*

Chapter 6

1. C. Vann Woodward, *The Strange Career of Jim Crow*, 3rd Revised Edition (New York: Oxford University Press, 1974), p. 69.

2. Narendra Jadhav, *Untouchables: My Family's Triumphant Journey Out of the Caste System in Modern India* (New York: Scribner, 2003), p. 4.

3. Phyl Garland, "Negro Heroines of Dixie Play Major Role in Challenging Racist Traditions," *Ebony Magazine* (August 1966), p. 29.

4. Mark Mathabane, *Kaffir Boy: The True Story of a Black Youth's Coming of Age in Apartheid South Africa* (New York: Plume, 1986), p. x.

5. Annelise Orleck, *Storming Caesars Palace: How Black Mothers Fought Their Own War on Poverty* (Boston: Beacon, 2005), p. 21.

6. Stephen J. Whitfield, *A Death in the Delta: The Story of Emmett Till* (Baltimore, MD: Johns Hopkins University Press, 1992), p. 91.

7. W.J. Cash, *The Mind of the South* (New York: Vintage, 1960), p. 131.

8. Woodward, *The Strange Career of Jim Crow*, p. 101.

9. James W. Silver, *Mississippi: The Closed Society* (New York: Harcourt, Brace & World, 1966), p. 25.

10. Roger Wilkins, "Preface," in Eric Etheridge,

Breach of Peace: Portraits of the 1969 Mississippi Freedom Riders (New York: Atlas, 2008), p. 15.

11. Richard Wright, "The Ethics of Living Jim Crow," in *Uncle Tom's Children* (New York: Harper & Row, 1940), p. 10.

12. Todd Zewan, "Times Changing for Multicultural Families," *Las Vegas Review-Journal* (June 15, 2008), p. 12A.

13. David L. Hudson, Jr., "Banning the Noose," *SPLC Intelligence Report* (Winter 2008), p. 61.

14. Julius E. Thompson,. *Lynchings in Mississippi: A History, 1865–1965* (Jefferson, NC: McFarland, 2007), pp. 115–175.

15. Orleck, *Storming Caesars Palace*, p. 19.

16. Scott Poulson-Bryant, *Hung: A Meditation on the Measure of Black Men in America* (New York: Doubleday, 2005), p. 28.

17. Whitfield, *A Death in the Delta*, p. 7.

18. Kate Tuttle, "Lynching" (3/29/01), pp. 2–3, African.com.wysiwyg://28/http://www.africana.com/tt_374.htm. Many thought that black men were frightening and a threat. Black men, of course, understood very well that they could be lynched for the slightest infraction.

19. *Ibid.*, p. 3. According to Tuttle, some "historians have proposed a new interpretation of lynching, seeing it as a political and economic tool." She also pointed out that had it not been for "racism to divide poor blacks and whites from each other, workers on both sides of the color line could [have] unite[d] against the capitalist oppressors."

20. Whitfield, *A Death in the Delta*, p. 3.

21. Tuttle, "Lynching," p. 1.

22. Heribert Adam and Kogila Moodley, *The Opening of the Apartheid Mind: Options for the New South Africa* (Los Angeles: University of California Press, 1981), p. 15.

Chapter 7

1. Kennell Jackson, *America Is Me: 170 Fresh Questions and Answers on Black American History* (New York: Harper Collins, 1996).

2. Kim Lacy Rogers, *Life and Death in the Delta: African American Narratives of Violence, Resilience, and Social Change* (New York: Palgrave Macmillan, 2006), p. 21.

3. James B. Stewart and Joyce E. Allen-Smith, *Blacks in Rural America* (New Brunswick, NJ: Transaction, 1995), p. 3.

4. *Ibid.* For some blacks living in the Delta, every day was just another story of hunger, another day of poverty. Even Christmas was just another work day.

5. Phyl Garland, "Negro Heroines of Dixie Play Major Role in Challenging Racist Tradition," *Ebony Magazine* (August 1966), p. 27.

6. James W. Silver, *Mississippi: The Closed Society* (New York: Harcourt, Brace & World, 1966), p. 90.

7. Susan Kling, *Fannie Lou Hamer: A Biog-*

raphy (Chicago, IL: Women for Racial and Economic Equality, 1979), p. 14.

8. Foster Davis, "Darkness on the Delta," *The Reporter* (September 21, 1967), p. 36.

9. June Jordan, *Fannie Lou Hamer* (New York: Thomas Y. Crowell, 1972), p. 21.

10. Silver, *Mississippi: The Closed Society*, p. 87.

11. Chris Myers Asch, *The Senator and the Sharecropper: The Freedom Struggles of James O. Eastland and Fannie Lou Hamer* (New York: New Press, 2008), p. 171.

12. Jordan, *Fannie Lou Hamer*, p. 21.

13. Jack O'Dell, "Life in Mississippi: An Interview with Fannie Lou Hamer," *Freedomways*, Volume 5, Issue 2 (Second Quarter 1965), p. 235.

14. Juan Williams, *Eyes on the Prize: America's Civil Rights Years, 1954–1965* (New York: Viking Penguin, 1988), p. 245.

15. Penny Colman, *Fannie Lou Hamer and the Fight for the Vote* (Brookfield, CT: Millbrook, 1993), p. 13.

16. Jordan, *Fannie Lou Hamer*, p. 21. It should be understood that black people are not going to forget what happened to their relatives and ancestors.

17. Laura Baskes Litwin, *Fannie Lou Hamer: Fighting for the Right to Vote* (Berkeley Heights, NJ: Enslow, 2002), p. 25.

18. George Alexander Sewell, *Mississippi Black History Makers* (Jackson: University Press of Mississippi, 1977), p. 348.

Chapter 8

1. John Oliver Killens, *'Sippi* (New York: Thunder's Mouth, 1967), p. 3.

2. David Rubel, *Fannie Lou Hamer: From Sharecropping to Politics* (New York: Silver Burdett, 1990), p. 44. Whites in Mississippi felt a repulsion towards blacks that was matched only by what was happening in South Africa at that time.

3. Richard Wright, *Black Boy: A Record of Childhood and Youth* (New York: Harper-Perennial, 1993), p. 196.

4. William H. Harris and Judith S. Levers (eds.), "Civil Rights," *The New Columbia Encyclopedia* (New York: Columbia University Press, 1975), p. 566.

5. Laura Baskes Litwin, *Fannie Lou Hamer: Fighting for the Right to Vote* (Berkeley Heights, NJ: Enslow, 2002), p. 25.

6. "Mississippi Movement: Interview with Ella Jo Baker & Fannie Lou Hamer, *Southern Exposure*, Vol. 9, Issue 1 (September 1981), p. 47.

7. Emily Stoper, "The Student Nonviolent Coordinating Committee: Rise and Fall of a Redemptive Organization," *Journal of Black Studies*, Vol. 8, No. 1 (September 1977), p. 18.

8. David Rubel, *Fannie Lou Hamer: From Sharecropping to Politics* (New York: Silver Burdett, 1990), p. 44.

9. Clayborne Carson, *In Struggle: SNCC and*

the Black Awakening of the 1960s (Cambridge, MA: Harvard University Press, 1981), p. 74.

10. Frank Lambert, *The Battle of Ole Miss: Civil Rights v. States' Rights* (New York: Oxford University Press, 2010), p. 5.

11. Chris Myers Asch, *The Senator and the Sharecropper: The Freedom Struggles of James O. Eastland and Fannie Lou Hamer* (New York: New Press, 2008), p. 178.

12. Harriet A. Washington, *Medical Apartheid: The Dark History of Medical Experimentation on Black Americans from Colonial Times to the Present* (New York: Doubleday, 2006), p. 189.

13. Litwin, *Fannie Lou Hamer: Fighting for the Right to Vote*, p. 25.

14. "Mississippi Movement Interview with Ella Jo Baker & Fannie Lou Hamer," p. 47.

15. *Ibid.*

16. George Alexander Sewell, *Mississippi Black History Makers* (Jackson: University Press of Mississippi, 1977), p. 349.

17. Phyl Garland, "Negro Heroines of Dixie Play Major Role in Challenging Racist Tradition," *Ebony Magazine* (August 1966), p. 27.

18. *Ibid.* Some have speculated that from the moment she sat at that local Ruleville church meeting, Hamer became an activist.

19. John Egerton, *A Mind to Stay Here: Profiles from the South* (New York: Macmillan, 1970), p. 98.

20. *Ibid.*

21. Jack O'Dell, "Life in Mississippi: An Interview with Fannie Lou Hamer," *Freedomways*, 2nd Quarter (1965), p. 235.

Chapter 9

1. Fannie Lou Hamer, Foreword to Tracy Sugarman, *Stranger at the Gates: A Summer in Mississippi* (New York: Hill and Wang, 1966), p. vii.

2. Charles McLaurin, "Voice of Calm," *Sojourners*, Vol. 11, No. 11 (December 1982), p. 12.

3. *Ibid.*

4. Anne Moody, *Coming of Age in Mississippi* (New York: Dell, 1968), p. 253.

5. McLaurin, "Voice of Calm," p. 13.

6. Molefi Kete Asante, *100 Greatest African Americans: A Biographical Encyclopedia* (New York: Prometheus, 2002), p. 148.

7. Dona Richards, "With Our Minds Set on Freedom," *Freedomways*, Vol. 5, Issue 2 (1965), p. 337.

8. Gene Roberts, "The Story of Snick: From 'Freedom High' to Black Power," *New York Times* (September 25, 1966), p. 30.

9. *Ibid.*

10. Louis E. Lomax, *The Negro Revolt* (New York: Harper & Brothers, 1962), p. 127.

11. Roberts, "The Story of Snick," p. 30.

12. Phyl Garland, "Negro Heroines of Dixie Play Major Role in Challenging Racist Traditions," *Ebony Magazine* (August 1966), p. 29.

13. Roberts, "The Story of Snick," p. 30.

14. June Jordan, *Fannie Lou Hamer* (New York: Thomas Y. Crowell, 1972), p. 21.

15. Roberts, "The Story of Snick," p. 30.

16. "Mississippi Movement: Interview with Ella Jo Baker & Fannie Hamer," *Southern Exposure*, Vol. 9, Issue 1 (September 1981), p. 48.

17. Laura Baskes Litwin, *Fannie Lou Hamer: Fighting for the Right to Vote* (Berkeley Heights, NJ: Enslow, 2002), p. 27.

18. Asante, *100 Greatest African Americans*, p. 148.

19. Sara Evans, *Personal Politics: The Roots of Women's Liberation in the Civil Rights Movement and the New Left* (New York: Vintage, 1979), p. 53.

20. Taylor Branch, *Parting the Waters: America in the King Years, 1954–63* (New York: Touchstone, 1988), p. 635.

21. Norm Fruchter, "Mississippi: Notes on SNCC," *Studies on the Left* (Winter 1965), p. 77.

22. *Ibid.*

23. Roberts, "The Story of Snick," p. 122.

24. Litwin, *Fannie Lou Hamer: Fighting for the Right to Vote*, p. 27.

25. Gayle Graham Yates, *Mississippi Mind: A Personal Cultural History of an American State* (Knoxville: University of Tennessee Press, 1990), p. 267.

26. *Ibid.* Hamer had a strong mind and willingness to do the right thing, especially for those who couldn't help themselves. But she never used high pressure tactics to get others to operate in accordance with her wishes.

27. Jessie Carney Smith and Linda T. Wynn (eds.). *Freedom Facts and Firsts: 400 Years of the African American Civil Rights Experience* (Canton, MI: Visible Ink, 2009), p. 270.

28. *Ibid.*

29. *Ibid.*

30. David L. Chappell, *A Stone of Hope: Prophetic Religion and the Death of Jim Crow* (Chapel Hill: University of North Carolina Press, 2004), p. 76.

31. Elton C. Fax, *Contemporary Black Leaders* (New York: Dodd, Mead, 1970), p. 119.

32. Richard Newman and Marcia Sawyer, *Everybody Say Freedom: Everything You Need to Know About African-American History* (New York: Plume, 1996), p. 264.

33. Darlene Clark Hine and Kathleen Thompson, *A Shining Thread of Hope: The History of Black Women in America* (New York: Broadway, 1998), p. 282.

34. *Ibid.*

35. *Ibid.*

Chapter 10

1. Nancy Woloch, *Women and the American Experience: A Concise History* (New York: McGraw-Hill, 1996), p. 345.

2. Thomas C. Jackson, Quoted in "William

Zantzinger 69, Subject of Bob Dyan Protest Song, Dies," *Las Vegas Review-Journal* (January 1, 2009), p. 7B.

3. Sara Evans, *Personal Politics: The Roots of Women's Liberation in the Civil Rights Movement and the New Left* (New York: Vintage, 1979), p. 54.

4. Susan Johnson, "Fannie Lou Hamer: Mississippi Grassroots Organizer," *The Black Law Journal*, Vol. 2 (Summer 1972), p. 155.

5. *Ibid.*

6. Penny Colman, *Fannie Lou Hamer and the Fight for the Vote* (Brookfield, CT: Millbrook, 1993), p. 14.

7. Robert F. Williams, "Can Negroes Afford to Be Pacifists?" *New Left Review*, Vol. 1 (January 1960), p. 44.

8. *Ibid.*

9. "Sharecropper's Daughter Has Seen Horizons Widen," *Clarion-Ledger* (September 12, 1980), p. 13A.

10. William Rotch, "Cotton, Cordiality and Conflict," *New South*, Vol. 12 (March 1957), p. 6.

11. Jessie Carney Smith and Linda T. Wynn (eds.). *Freedom Facts and Firsts: 400 Years of the African American Civil Rights Experience* (Canton, MI: Visible Ink, 2009), p. 222.

12. Penny Colman, *Fannie Lou Hamer and the Fight for the Vote*, p. 14.

13. Jerry DeMuth, "Tired of Being Sick and Tired," *The Nation* (June 1, 1964), p. 550.

14. *Ibid.*

15. *Ibid.*

16. Smith and Wynn, *Freedom Facts and Firsts*, p. 222.

17. Susan Kling, *Fannie Lou Hamer: A Biography* (Chicago: Women for Racial and Economic Equality, 1979), p. 19.

18. George Alexander Sewell, *Mississippi Black History Makers* (Jackson: University Press of Mississippi, 1977), p. 350.

19. John Egerton, *A Mind to Stay Here: Profiles from the South* (New York: Macmillan, 1970), p. 99.

20. L.C. Dorsey, "Fannie Lou Hamer," *Jackson Advocate* (February 26/March 6, 1981), Section C, p. 1. According to Dorsey, white thugs fired the sixteen rounds into "the home of Mr. and Mrs. Robert Coker," where she was staying.

21. *Ibid.*

22. June Jordan, *Fannie Lou Hamer* (New York: Thomas Y. Crowell, 1972), p. 23.

23. *Ibid.*

24. Susan Johnson, "Fannie Lou Hamer: Mississippi Grassroots Organizer," p. 162.

25. Smith and Wynn, *Freedom Facts and Firsts*, p. 222.

26. Fannie Lou Hamer, "Foreword" in Tracey Sugarman, *Stranger at the Gates: A Summer in Mississippi* (New York: Hill and Wang, 1966), p. vii.

27. *Ibid.*

28. David L. Chappell, *A Stone of Hope: Prophetic Religion and the Death of Jim Crow* (Chapel Hill: University of North Carolina Press, 2004), p. 71.

29. Sara Evans, "*Personal Politics*," pp. 53–54.

30. Fannie Lou Hamer, "Foreword," in *Stranger at the Gate*, p. vii.

31. *Ibid.*

32. Chappell, *A Stone of Hope*, p. 71.

33. *Ibid.*

34. Henry Hampton and Steve Fayer, *Voices of Freedom: An Oral History of the Civil Rights Movement from the 1950s Through the 1980s* (New York: Bantam, 1991), p. 177.

35. DeWayne Wickham, "Historic Freedom Riders Deserve a Degree of Respect," *USA Today* (April 15, 2008), p. 11A. Also see Raymond Arsenault, *Freedom Riders: 1961 and the Struggle for Racial Justice* (New York: Oxford University Press, 2006).

36. Andrew J. DeRoche, *Andrew Young: Civil Rights Ambassador* (Wilmington, DE: Scholarly Resources, 2003), p. 16.

37. *Ibid.*

38. *Ibid.*

Chapter 11

1. Thomas C. Jackson, quoted in "William Zantzinger 60, Subject of Bob Dyan Protest Song, Dies," *Las Vegas Review-Journal* (January 1, 2009), p. 7B.

2. Fannie Lou Hamer, "Foreword" in Tracy Sugarman, *Stranger at the Gates: A Summer in Mississippi* (New York: Hill and Wang, 1966), p. viii.

3. David Rubel, *Fannie Lou Hamer: From Sharecropping to Politics* (New York: Silver Burdett, 1990), p. 46.

4. John Herbers, "Communiqué from the Mississippi Front," *New York Times* (November 8, 1964), p. 34.

5. *Ibid.*

6. Marian A. Wright, "The Right to Protest," *New South*, Vol. 17, Issue 2 (February 1962), p. 6.

7. "Mississippi Movement: Interview with Ella Jo Baker and Fannie Lou Hamer," *Southern Exposure*, Vol. 9, Issue 1 (September 1981), p. 48.

8. Juan Williams. *Eyes on the Prize: America's Civil Rights Years, 1954–1965* (New York: Penguin, 1987), p. 247.

9. "Mississippi Movement," p. 48.

10. Jerry DeMuth, "Tired of Being Sick and Tired," *The Nation* (June 1, 1964), p. 550.

11. L.C. Dorsey, "Fannie Lou Hamer," *Jackson Advocate* (February 26/March 6, 1981), Section C, p. 1.

12. DeMuth, "Tired of Being Sick and Tired," p. 550.

13. Penny Colman, *Fannie Lou Hamer and the Fight for the Vote* (Brookfield, Connecticut: Millbrook, 1993), p. 19.

14. John Egerton, *A Mind to Stay Here: Profiles from the South* (New York: Macmillan, 1970), p. 97.

15. Colman, *Fannie Lou Hamer and the Fight for the Vote*, pp. 19–20.

16. Egerton, *A Mind to Stay Here*, p. 99.

17. Dorsey, "Fannie Lou Hamer."

18. *Ibid.*
19. *Ibid.*
20. Egerton, *A Mind to Stay Here*, p. 100.
21. Phyl Garland, "Negro Heroines of Dixie Play Major Role in Challenging Racist Tradition," *Ebony Magazine* (August 1966), p. 28.
22. *Ibid.*
23. Chana Kai Lee, *For Freedom's Sake: The Life of Fannie Lou Hamer* (Chicago: University of Illinois Press, 1999), p. 59.
24. Egerton, *A Mind to Stay Here*, p. 100.
25. Dorsey, "Fannie Lou Hamer," p. 1.
26. Mark Newman, *The Civil Rights Movement* (Westport, CT: Praeger, 2004), p. 103.
27. John Lewis, with Michael D'Orso, *Walk with the Wind: A Memoir of the Movement* (New York: Simon & Schuster, 1998), p. 238.

Chapter 12

1. Fannie Lou Hamer, "Foreword" to Tracy Sugarman, *Stranger at the Gates: A Summer in Mississippi* (New York: Hill and Wang, 1966), p. viii.
2. David Chalmers, *Backfire: How the Ku Klux Klan Helped the Civil Rights Movement* (Lanham, MD: Rowman & Littlefield, 2003), p. 47.
3. Jerry De Muth, "Tired of Being Sick and Tired," *The Nation* (June 1, 1964), p. 550. The Ku Klux Klan, along with officials, murdered Chaney, Schwerner and Goodman, then buried them "in an earthen dam in Neshoba County." See Jack Bass and Walter De Vries, *The Transformation of Southern Politics: Social Change and Political Consequence Since 1945* (New York: Basic, 1976), p. 204.
4. Molefi Kete Asante, *100 Greatest African Americans: A Biographical Encyclopedia* (New York: Prometheus, 2002), p. 148.
5. Chalmers, *Backfire*, p. 54.
6. Paulo Freire, *Pedagogy of the Oppressed* (New York: Continuum International, 2002), p. 94.
7. Frank Lambert, *The Battle of Old Miss: Civil Rights v. States' Rights* (New York: Oxford University Press, 2010), p. 7.
8. *Ibid.*
9. *Ibid.*, p. 105.
10. Samuel J. Surace and Melvin Seeman, "Some Correlates of Civil Rights Activism," *Social Forces*, Vol. 46, No. 2 (December 1967), p. 207.
11. Chris Myers Asch, *The Senator and the Sharecropper: The Freedom Struggles of James O. Eastland and Fannie Lou Hamer* (New York: New Press, 2008), p. 209.
12. Howell Raines, *My Soul Is Rested: Movement Days in the Deep South Remembered* (New York: G. Putnam's Sons, 1977), p. 253.
13. Laura Baskes Litwin, *Fannie Lou Hamer: Fighting for the Right to Vote* (Berkeley Heights, NJ: Enslow, 2002), p. 31.
14. David Rubel, *Fannie Lou Hamer: From Sharecropping to Politics* (New York: Silver Burdett, 1990), p. 74.
15. Penny Colman, *Fannie Lou Hamer and the Fight for the Vote* (Brookfield, CT: Millbrook, 1993), p. 20.
16. L.C. Dorsey, "Fannie Lou Hamer," p. 1. At that time and place, in the Winona jail, Fannie Lou Hamer was more scared than she had ever been in her life because she didn't know what the white law enforcement officials would ultimately do to her and the others. Some of the female workers had been stripped naked and beaten.
17. Litwin, *Fannie Lou Hamer: Fighting for the Right to Vote*, p. 27.
18. John Egerton, *A Mind to Stay Here: Profiles from the South* (New York: MacMillan, 1970), pp. 1000–101.
19. Chana Kai Lee, *For Freedom's Sake: The Life of Fannie Lou Hamer* (Chicago: University of Illinois Press, 1999), p. 59.
20. Litwin, *Fannie Lou Hamer: Fighting for the Right to Vote*, pp. 29–30.
21. Lee, *For Freedom's Sake*, p. 53.
22. *Ibid.*
23. *Ibid.*, p. 54.
24. Andrew Young, *An Easy Burden: The Civil Rights Movement and the Transformation of America* (New York: Harper-Collins, 1996), p. 257.
25. *Ibid.*, p. 253.
26. *Ibid.*, p. 256.
27. Litwin, *Fannie Lou Hamer: Fighting for the Right to Vote*, pp. 31.
28. *Ibid.*
29. *Ibid.*
30. Young, *An Easy Burden*, p. 257.
31. *Ibid.*
32. *Ibid.*
33. Rubel, *Fannie Lou Hamer: From Sharecropping to Politics*, p. 74.
34. Susan Kling, *Fannie Lou Hamer: A Biography* (Chicago: Women for Racial and Economic Equality, 1979), p. 23.
35. *Ibid.*
36. Raines, *My Soul Is Rested*, p. 254.
37. Rubel, *Fannie Lou Hamer: From Sharecropping to Politics*, p. 74.

Chapter 13

1. Robert A. Dahl, *On Political Equality* (New Haven & London: Yale University Press, 2006), p. 1.
2. Howell Raines, *My Soul Is Rested: Movement Days in the Deep South Remembered* (New York: G.P. Putnam's Sons, 1977), p. 254.
3. Andrew Young, *An Easy Burden: The Civil Rights Movement and Transformation of America* (New York: Harper Collins, 1996), p. 257.
4. Fannie Lou Hamer, "To Praise Our Bridge," reprinted in Manning Marable et al. (eds.), *Freedom On My Mind: The Columbia Documentary History of the African American Experience* (New York: Columbia University Press, 2003), p. 425.

5. Sally Belfrage, *Freedom Summer* (New York: Viking, 1965), p. 123.

6. *Ibid.*

7. Pat Watters and Reese Cleghorn, *Climbing Jacob's Ladder: The Arrival of Negroes in Southern Politics* (New York: Harcourt, Brace & World, 1967), p. 365.

8. *Ibid.*, pp. 365–366.

9. Laura Baskes Litwin. *Fannie Lou Hamer: Fighting for the Right to Vote* (Berkeley Heights, NJ: Enslow, 2002), p. 31.

10. Chris Myers Asch, *The Senator and the Sharecropper: The Freedom Struggles of James O. Eastland and Fannie Lou Hamer* (New York: New Press, 2008), p. 209. It should been noted that some radical blacks hated whites — perhaps even more intensely than white racists hated blacks.

11. Charles M. Payne, *I've Got the Light of Freedom: The Organizing Tradition and the Mississippi Freedom Struggle* (Los Angeles: University of California Press, 2007), p. 194.

12. *Ibid.*, p. 266.

13. Sande Smith, *Who's Who in African-American History* (New York: Smithmark, 1994), p. 66. See also Mamie E. Locke, "Is This America? Fannie Lou Hamer and the Mississippi Freedom Democratic Party," in Vicki L. Crawford, Jacqueline Anne Roose, and Barbara Woods (eds.), *Women in the Civil Rights Movement: Trailblazers & Torchbearers, 1941–1965* (Indianapolis: Indiana University Press, 1993), p. 30. Fannie Lou Hamer helped form the MFDP to make a political point about the marginalization and disenfranchisement of blacks in Mississippi. And she would burst with pride when discussing the many accomplishments of the MFDP.

14. Locke, "Is This America?" p. 29.

15. Darlene Clark Hine and Kathleen Thompson, *A Shining Thread of Hope: The History of Black Women in America* (New York: Broadway, 1998), p. 282.

16. Molefi Kete Asante, *100 Greatest African Americans: A Biographical Encyclopedia* (Amherst, NY: Prometheus, 2002), p. 148.

17. Susan Kling, *Fannie Lou Hamer: A Biography* (Chicago: Women for Racial and Economic Equality, 1979), p. 25.

18. Elton C. Fax, *Contemporary Black Leaders* (New York: Dodd, Mead, 1970), p. 125.

19. Asante, *100 Greatest African Americans*, p. 148.

20. Kling, *Fannie Lou Hamer: A Biography*, p. 25.

21. Asante, *100 Greatest African Americans*.

22. Jerry DeMuth, "Tired of Being Sick and Tired," *The Nation* (June 1, 1964), p. 551.

23. "Mississippi Movement: Interview with Ella Jo Baker and Fannie Lou Hamer," *Southern Exposure*, Vol. 9, Issue 1 (September 1981), p. 42.

24. *Ibid.* It was with the understanding that the MFDP would function as a sort of adjunct for black Democrats in Mississippi, as long as it existed.

25. John Dittmer, "The Politics of the Missis-sippi Movement, 1954–1964," in Charles W. Eagles (ed.), *The Civil Rights Movement in America* (Jackson: University Press of Mississippi, 1986), p. 83.

26. Jack Bass and Walter DeVries, *The Transformation of Southern Politics: Social Change and Political Consequence Since 1945* (New York: Basic, 1976), p. 204.

27. Juan Williams, *Eyes on the Prize: America's Civil Rights Years, 1954–1965* (New York: Penguin 1988), p. 234.

28. Dittmer, "The Politics of the Mississippi Movement, 1954–1964," p. 83.

29. Fax, *Contemporary Black Leaders*, p. 125.

30. *Ibid.*, pp. 125–126. Kling writes, "It opened its frontal attack on the status quo by sending representatives around the country, to give a picture of life in Mississippi, and how impossible it was to get blacks elected to the Democratic Party Convention." See Kling, *Fannie Lou Hamer: A Biography*, p. 25.

Chapter 14

1. Fannie Lou Hamer, "To Praise Our Bridges," in Manning Marable (ed.), *Freedom on My Mind: The Columbia Documentary History of the African American Experience* (New York: Columbia University Press, 2003), p. 426.

2. *Ibid.*

3. *Ibid.*

4. Joanne Grant, *Ella Baker: Freedom Bound* (New York: John Wiley and Sons, 1998), p. 173.

5. *Ibid.*

6. Bill Minor, "Hamer at '64 Dem Convention Fueled Miss. Party's Defection," *The Clarion-Ledger* (February 26, 2006), p. 3G.

7. Sara Evans, *Personal Politics: The Roots of Women's Liberation in the Civil Rights Movement and the New Left* (New York: Vintage, 1979), pp. 90–91.

8. Mamie E. Locke, "Is This America? Fannie Lou Hamer and the Mississippi Freedom Democratic Party," in Vicki L. Crawford, Jacqueline Anne Rouse, and Barbara Woods. *Women in the Civil Rights Movement: Trailblazers & Torchbearers, 1941–1965* (Indianapolis: Indiana University Press, 1993), p. 35.

9. Minor, "Hamer at '64 Dem Convention Fueled Miss. Party's Defection," p. 3G.

10. *Ibid.*

11. Dona Richards, "With Our Minds Set on Freedom," *Freedomways*, Vol. 5, Issue 2 (1965), p. 337.

12. Jack Minnis, "The Mississippi Freedom Democratic Party: A New Declaration of Independence," *Freedomways*, Vol. 5, Issue 3 (1965), p. 269.

13. Lawrence Guyot and Mike Thelwell, "The Politics of Necessity and Survival in Mississippi," *Freedomways*, Vol. 6, Issue 2 (1966), p. 120. There was a deepening concern on the part of blacks about the violence of white police officials.

14. Leslie Burl McLemore, "The Mississippi

Freedom Democratic Party: A Case Study of Grassroots Politics," *Ph.D. Dissertation*, University of Massachusetts, Amherst, 1971, pp. vii–viii.

15. Edwin King, "Go Tell It on the Mountain: A Prophet from the Delta," *Sojourners* (December 1982), p. 18.

16. Elton C. Fax, *Contemporary Black Leaders* (New York: Dodd, Mead, 1970), p. 126.

17. John Dittmer, "The Politics of the Mississippi Movement, 1954–1964," in Charles W. Eagles (ed.), *The Civil Rights Movement in America* (Jackson: University Press of Mississippi, 1986), p. 83.

18. John Lewis, with Michael D'Orso, *Walking with the Wind: A Memoir of the Movement* (New York: Simon & Schuster, 1998), p. 277.

19. *Ibid.*

20. Fannie Lou Hamer, "To Praise Our Bridges," p. 426.

21. Jerry DeMuth, "Tired of Being Sick and Tired," *The Nation* (June 1, 1964), p. 548.

22. Darlene Clark Hine and Kathleen Thompson, *A Shining Thread of Hope: The History of Black Women in America* (New York: Broadway, 1998), p. 282.

23. Susan Kling, *Fannie Lou Hamer: A Biography* (Chicago: Women for Racial and Economic Equality, 1979), p. 27.

24. Aaron Henry, with Constance Curry, *Aaron Henry: The Fire Ever Burning* (Jackson: University Press of Mississippi, 2000), p. 168.

25. Phyl Garland, "Builders of a New South: Negro Heroines of Dixie Play Major Role in Challenging Racist Traditions," *Ebony Magazine* (August 1966), p. 28.

26. Susan Johnson, "Fannie Lou Hamer: Mississippi Grassroots Organizer," *The Black Law Journal* (Summer 1972), p. 152.

27. Kling, *Fannie Lou Hamer: A Biography*, p. 26.

28. Jerry DeMuth, "Summer in Mississippi: Freedom Moves in to Stay," *The Nation* (September 14, 1942), p. 104.

29. *Ibid.*

30. Sande Smith, *Who's Who in African American History* (New York: Smithmark, 1994), pp. 66–67. According to Laura Baskes Litwin, Hamer had absolutely "no chance of beating James Whitten," because "he was a senior member of Congress with a lot of influence." Fannie Lou Hamer "entered the race to prove that anyone who wanted to could get involved in politics." See Laura Baskes Litwin, *Fannie Lou Hamer: Fighting for the Right to Vote* (Berkeley Heights, NJ: Enslow, 2002), p. 39.

31. Linda Reed, "Fannie Lou Hamer (1917–1977)," in Darlene Clark Hine, Elsa Barkley Brown and Rosalyn Terborg-Penn (eds.), *Black Women in America: A Historical Encyclopedia* (Indianapolis: Indiana University Press, 1993), p. 518.

32. DeMuth, "Tired of Being Sick and Tired," p. 551. According to DeMuth, black political candidate James Monroe Houston challenged Robert Bell Williams in the Third Congressional District,

the Rev. John E. Cameron faced William Meyers Colmer in the Fifth, and Mrs. Victoria Jackson Gray campaigned extremely hard for the Federal Senate seat held by John Stennis, but ultimately lost.

33. Hine and Thompson, *A Shining Thread of Hope*, p. 282.

Chapter 15

1. J.M. Coetzee, *Dusklands* (New York: Penguin, 1982), p. 2.

2. David Rubel, *Fannie Lou Hamer: From Sharecropping to Politics* (Englewood Cliffs, NJ: Silver Burdett, 1990), p. 105.

3. Elton C. Fax, *Contemporary Black Leaders* (New York: Dodd, Mead, 1970), p. 125. Unfortunately, the white Democratic Party in Mississippi was a group that saw things through the prism of racism. Therefore, they could never come to terms with the MFDP, especially in any constructive way.

4. L.C. Dorsey, "Fannie Lou Hamer," *Jackson Advocate* (February 26/March 6, 1981), Section C, p. 1.

5. Kenneth O'Reilly, *Racial Matters: The FBI's Secret File on Black America, 1960–1972* (New York: Free Press, 1989), p. 3.

6. Sara Evans, *Personal Politics: The Roots of Women's Liberation in the Civil Rights Movement and the New Left* (New York: Vintage, 1979), p. 71.

7. John Egerton, *A Mind to Stay Here: Profiles from the South* (New York: Macmillan, 1970), p. 101.

8. O'Reilly, *Racial Matters*, p. 3.

9. Andrew Young, *An Easy Burden: The Civil Rights Movement and the Transformation of America* (New York: Harper Collins, 1996), p. 257.

10. Egerton, *A Mind to Stay Here*, p. 101. According to Kenneth O'Reilly, "Hoover justified his reluctance to investigate the Winona brutality aggressively by reference to the constraints of existing federal statutes' rights principles." See O'Reilly, *Racial Matters*, p. 6. Hamer, of course, was dubious about any help from the FBI or other governmental agencies.

11. O'Reilly, *Racial Matters*, p. 4. Fannie Lou Hamer criticized the state government and the FBI for parochialism and unprofessionalism. And Hamer's doubts about the FBI never changed over time. She also believed that there wasn't really an investigation into what really happened to her and other civil rights workers.

12. George Alexander Sewell, *Mississippi Black History Makers* (Jackson: University Press of Mississippi, 1977), p. 353.

13. *Ibid.*

14. Susan Johnson, "Fannie Lou Hamer: Mississippi Grassroots Organizer," *The Black Law Journal* (Summer 1972), p. 159.

15. Richard Newman and Marcia Sawyer. *Everybody Say Freedom: Everything You Need to Know About African-American History* (New York: Plume, 1996), p. 262. Fortunately for Fannie Lou

Hamer, Ella Baker was there to guide her; she was her guardian angel, so to speak.

16. "Mississippi Movement: Interview with Ella Jo Baker and Fannie Lou Hamer," *Southern Exposure*, Vol. 9, Issue 1 (September 1981), p. 47.

17. Chana Kai Lee, *For Freedom's Sake: The Life of Fannie Lou Hamer* (Chicago: University of Illinois Press, 1999), p. 86. Some of the MFDP delegates also arrived by "train, dilapidated cars and even hitchhiking." See Sanford Wexler, *The Civil Rights Movement: An Eyewitness History* (New York: Facts on File, 1993), p. 202.

18. Susan Kling, *Fannie Lou Hamer: A Biography* (Chicago: Women for Racial and Economic Equality, 1979), p. 24.

19. Egerton, *A Mind to Stay Here*, p. 102.

20. Juan Williams, *Eyes on the Prize: America's Civil Rights Years, 1954–1965* (New York: Penguin, 1987), p. 234.

21. *Ibid.*

22. John Dittmer, *Local People: The Struggle for Civil Rights in Mississippi* (Chicago: University of Illinois Press, 1994), p. 273.

23. Jack Minnis, "The Mississippi Freedom Democratic Party: A New Declaration of Independence," *Freedomways*, Vol. 5, Issue 2 (1965), p. 269.

24. *Ibid.*

25. Williams, *Eyes on the Prize*, p. 234.

26. *Ibid.*

27. Newman and Sawyer, *Everybody Say Freedom*, p. 264.

28. Darlene Clark Hine and Kathleen Thompson, *A Shining Thread of Hope: The History of Black Women in America* (New York: Broadway, 1998), p. 282.

29. Vicki L. Ruiz, with Ellen Carol DuBois (eds.), *Unequal Sisters: An Inclusive Reader in U.S. Women's History, 4th Edition* (New York: Routledge, 2008), p. 7.

30. David J. Garrow, *Bearing the Cross: Martin Luther King, Jr., and the Southern Christian Leadership Conference* (New York: Harper Collins, 1986), p. 346.

31. Frances Fox Piven, Lorraine C. Minnite and Margaret Groarke, *Keeping Down the Black Vote: Race and the Demobilization of American Voters* (New York: New Press, 2009), p. 10.

32. Sanford Wexler, *The Civil Rights Movement: An Eyewitness History* (New York: Facts on File, 1993), Appendix B, p. 313.

33. Quintard Taylor, *From Timbuktu to Katrina: Readings in African American, Vol. II* (Boston: Thomson Wadsworth, 2008), p. 103.

34. *Ibid.*

35. Wexler, *The Civil Rights Movement*, p. 202.

36. *Ibid.*, Appendix B, p. 313.

Chapter 16

1. Ronald V. Dellums, *Lying Down with the Lions: A Public Life from the Streets of Oakland to the Halls of Power* (Boston: Beacon, 2000), p. 2.

2. Sandy Donovan, *Fannie Lou Hamer* (Chicago: Raintree, 2004), pp. 46–48.

3. Laura Baskes Litwin, *Fannie Lou Hamer: Fighting for the Right to Vote* (Berkeley Heights, NJ: Enslow, 2002), p. 39.

4. Juan Williams, *Eyes on the Prize: America's Civil Rights Years, 1954–1965* (New York: Penguin, 1988), p. 234.

5. Donovan, *Fannie Lou Hamer*, p. 48.

6. *Ibid.* It must be clearly understood that the all-white Mississippi Democratic Party delegation had traditionally been regarded as the sole political power in the state, but this would eventually change.

7. June Jordan, *Fannie Lou Hamer* (New York: Thomas Y. Crowell, 1972), p. 28. Hamer's statement before the 1964 Democratic Convention was a poignant, evocative scene in which Fannie Lou Hamer told the ugly truth. She certainly didn't act skittish about the matter. In this way, Hamer was able to capture the public's imagination. Moreover, she tried to make a positive impression. And it was the most important event of her life. That day became important to others in the civil rights movement as well. Fannie Lou Hamer would win praise from liberal groups throughout the United States. She would become a household name. Finally, Hamer's philosophical comments about the social and political issues of the day were always quotable. And she showed the nation how things truly were in Mississippi.

8. Nick Kotz, *Judgment Days: Lyndon Baines Johnson, Martin Luther King, Jr., and the Laws That Changed America* (New York: Houghton Mifflin, 2005), p. 203.

9. Donovan, *Fannie Lou Hamer*, p. 50. According to journalist Nick Kotz, 417 telegrams were sent to the White House recommending that the Mississippi Freedom Democrats be seated. But it was to no avail. See Nick Kotz, *Judgment Days*, p. 205.

10. David J. Garrow, *Bearing the Cross: Martin Luther King, Jr., and the Southern Christian Leadership Conference* (New York: Harper Collins, 1986), p. 346.

11. John Dittmer, *Local People: The Struggle for Civil Rights in Mississippi* (Chicago: University of Illinois Press, 1994), p. 285.

12. Kotz, *Judgment Days*, p. 194. According to Kotz, President Johnson and members of his staff had tried to find a specific way "to prevent the black Mississippi delegation from disrupting party unity," but they were unable to come up with anything substantive that would work.

13. "Mississippi Movement: Interview with Ella Jo Baker and Fannie Lou Hamer," *Southern Exposure*, Vol. 9, Issue 1 (September 1981), p. 47.

14. Frances Fox Piven, Lorraine C. Minnite and Margaret Groarke, *Keeping Down the Black Vote: Race and the Demobilization of American Voters* (New York: New Press, 2009), pp. 211–212.

15. Kotz, *Judgment Days*, p. 205.

16. Bill Minor, "Hamer at '64 Dem Convention Fueled Miss. Party's Defection," *The Clarion-Ledger* (February 26, 2006), p. 3G.

17. *Ibid.*

18. Litwin, *Fannie Lou Hamer: Fighting for the Right to Vote*, p. 55.

19. John Dittmer, "The Politics of the Mississippi Movement, 1954–1964," in Charles W. Eagles, *The Civil Rights Movement in America* (Jackson: University Press of Mississippi, 1986), p. 84.

20. Sara Evans, *Personal Politics: The Roots of Women's Liberation in the Civil Rights Movement and the New Left* (New York: Alfred A. Knopf, 1979), p. 91.

21. Elton C. Fax, *Contemporary Black Leaders* (New York: Dodd, Mead, 1970), p. 127.

22. Garrow, *Bearing the Cross*, p. 349.

23. David Rubel, *Fannie Lou Hamer: From Sharecropping to Politics* (Englewood Cliffs, NJ: Silver Burdett, 1990), p. 105.

24. *Ibid.*

25. "Mississippi Movement: Interview with Ella Jo Baker and Fannie Lou Hamer," p. 48.

26. Locke, *Is This America?* p. 33. White politicians began to realize that they would no longer retain absolute power and political control in Mississippi; nor would they wield total, unfettered authority over blacks.

27. Garrow, *Bearing the Cross*, p. 348.

28. Donovan, *Fannie Lou Hamer*, p. 51.

29. Susan Kling, *Fannie Lou Hamer: A Biography* (Chicago: Women for Racial and Economic Equality, 1979), p. 29.

30. Molefi Kete Asante, *100 Greatest African Americans: A Biographical Encyclopedia* (New York: Prometheus, 2002), p. 149.

31. *Ibid.*

32. Donovan, *Fannie Lou Hamer*, p. 51.

33. Gayle Graham Yates. *Mississippi Mind: A Personal Cultural History of an American State* (Knoxville: University of Tennessee Press, 1990), p. 267.

34. *Ibid.*, p. 268.

Chapter 17

1. V.O. Key, Jr., *Southern Politics in State and Nation* (Knoxville: University of Tennessee Press, 1984), p. 224.

2. Nick Kotz, *Judgment Days: Lyndon Baines Johnson, Martin Luther King, Jr., and the Laws That Changed America* (New York: Houghton Mifflin, 2005), p. 218.

3. Craig Robertson, "Civil Rights Activist: Fannie Lou Hamer Remembered," *Delta Democrat-Times* (March 16, 1977), p. 1.

4. Paul Krugman, "How Racial Polarization Benefited Reagan, GOP," *Las Vegas Sun* (November 20, 2007), p. 6.

5. Robertson, "Fannie Lou Hamer Remembered," p. 1.

6. "Mississippi Movement: Interview with Ella Jo Baker & Fannie Lou Hamer," *Southern Exposure*, Vol. 9, Issue 1 (September 1981), p. 48.

7. Kitz, "Judgment Days," p. 195. It should be noted that the MFDP met at the Union Temple Baptist Church on Tuesday and again on Saturday morning, "listening to the counsel of civil rights leaders and liberal leaders" about the "art of compromise." In the end, as mentioned, the MFDP leaders still voted against accepting *any* compromise. See Jack Minnis, "The Mississippi Freedom Democratic Party: A New Declaration of Independence," *Freedomways*, Vol. 5, Issue 2 (1965), p. 271.

8. Gayle Graham Yates, *Mississippi Mind: A Personal Cultural History of an American State* (Knoxville: University of Tennessee Press, 1990), p. 267.

9. Edwin King, "Go Tell It on the Mountain: A Prophet from the Delta," *Sojourners*, Vol. 11, No. 11 (December 1982), p. 18.

10. George Sewell, "Remembrance of Things Past: Fannie Lou Hamer's Light Still Shines," *Encore American & Worldwide News* (July 18, 1977), p. 3.

11. King, "Go Tell It on the Mountain," p. 18.

12. Lawrence Guyot and Mike Thelwell, "Toward Independent Political Power," *Freedomways*, Vol. 6, Issue 3 (1966), pp. 246–247.

13. Susan Kling, *Fannie Lou Hamer: A Biography* (Chicago: Women for Racial and Economic Equality, 1979), p. 31.

14. Bill Minor, "Hamer at '64 Dem Convention Fueled Miss. Party's Defection," *The Clarion-Ledger* (February 26, 2006), p. 3G.

15. *Ibid.* It was not at all a foregone conclusion that the MFDP delegates would be seated. It would take the 1968 Democratic Convention for this to finally happen.

16. Joanne Grant, "Mississippi and the Establishment," *Freedomways*, Vol. 5, Issue 2 (second quarter 1965), p. 300.

17. King, "Go Tell It on the Mountain," p. 18.

18. Joseph A. Sinsheimer, "The Freedom Vote of 1963: New Strategies of Racial Protest in Mississippi," *The Journal of Southern History*, Vol. LV, No. 2 (May 1989), p. 219.

19. Elliot Jaspin, *Buried in the Bitter Waters: The Hidden History of Racial Cleansing in America* (New York: Basic, 2007), p. 8.

20. King, "Fannie Lou Hamer," p. 31.

21. Mamie E. Locke, "Is This America? Fannie Lou Hamer and the Mississippi Freedom Democratic Party," in Vicki L. Crawford, Jacqueline Anne Rouse and Barbara Woods, *Women in the Civil Rights Movement: Trailblazers & Torchbearers, 1941–1965* (Indianapolis: Indiana University Press, 1993), p. 34.

22. Jeannine Herron, "Mississippi Underground Election," *The Nation* (December 7, 1963), p. 387.

23. John Egerton, *A Mind to Stay Here: Profiles from the South* (New York: Macmillan, 1970), p. 103.

24. Don Whitehead, *Attack on Terror: The FBI Against the Ku Klux Klan in Mississippi* (New York: Funk and Wagnalls, 1970), p. 101. Many whites acted impulsively when they attacked blacks, and many lacked any remorse. Such hateful activity

was the accepted paradigm regarding race in Mississippi and in the South.

25. Jerry DeMuth, "Tired of Being Sick and Tired," *The Nation* (June 1, 1964), p. 551.

26. Sue Kirchhoff, "Surplus U.S. Food Supplies Dry Up," *USA Today* (May 2, 2008), p. 1B.

27. Mark Newman, *The Civil Rights Movement* (Westport, CT: Praeger, 2004), p. 51.

28. Whitehead, *Attack on Terror*, p. 101. There was major (hateful and racist) grumblings among white segregationists, especially in their zeal to undermine and sabotage the civil rights movement. Their actions, however, were misguided and failed in the long run.

29. DeWayne Wickham, "Helms Subtly Carried Torch of White Supremacy," *USA Today* (July 8, 2008), p. 11A. Some white racists in Mississippi were hell-bent on driving Fannie Lou Hamer out of the state, just because they thought they could.

30. Fannie Lou Hamer, "Foreword" to Tracy Sugarman. *Stranger at the Gates: A Summer in Mississippi* (New York: Hill and Wang, 1966), p. ix. No one could have effectively argued that Mississippi was truly democratic, because it wasn't. Indeed, because of the state's racist policies, most blacks were denied their Constitutional rights.

31. Hodding Carter, III, "Citadel of the Citizens Council," *The New York Times* (November 12, 1961), p. SM125.

32. Hodding Carter, "A Wave of Terror Threatens the South," *Look Magazine* (March 22, 1955), p. 32.

33. Carter, "Citadel of the Citizens Council," p. 125.

34. Neil R. McMillan, *The Citizens' Council: Organized Resistance to the Second Reconstruction, 1954–1964* (Chicago: University of Illinois Press, 1971), p. 11.

35. *Ibid.*, p. 215.

36. Frank Lambert, *The Battle of Ole Miss: Civil Rights vs. States' Rights* (New York: Oxford University Press, 2010), p. 39.

37. *Ibid.* The White Citizens Council started in the Delta town of Indianola, Mississippi, in the 1950s, according to Lambert.

38. Phillip Abbott Luce, "The Mississippi White Citizens Council: 1954–1959," *Masters Thesis* (Ohio State University, 1960), p. 5. In 1954, the Supreme Court ruled in the famous Brown vs. Board of Education case (of Topeka) that racial segregation was unconstitutional and violated the 14th Amendment to the U.S. Constitution, which states that no State may deny equal protection of the law to its citizens.

39. Paul Krugman, "How Racial Polarization Benefited Reagan, GOP," *Las Vegas Sun* (November 20, 2007), p. 7.

40. Luce, "The Mississippi White Citizens Council: 1954–1959," p. 5.

41. Kenneth O'Reilly, *Racial Matters: The FBI's Secret File on Black America, 1960–1972* (New York: Free Press, 1989), p. 6.

42. *Ibid.*, p. 4.

Chapter 18

1. John H. Hallowell, *The Moral Foundation of Democracy* (Indianapolis: Amagi/Liberty Fund, 2007), p. 102.

2. Phyl Garland, "Negro Heroines of Dixie Play Major Role in Challenging Racist Traditions," *Ebony Magazine* (August 1966), p. 28.

3. *Ibid.*

4. *Ibid.*

5. Elliot Jaspin, *Buried in the Bitter Water: The Hidden History of Racial Cleansing in America* (New York: Basic, 2007), p. 8.

6. *Ibid.*

7. David Rubel, *Fannie Lou Hamer: From Sharecropping to Politics* (Englewood Cliffs, NJ: Silver Burdett, 1990), p. 107. Whites in political leadership positions talked down to blacks, as if they were interlopers or children. In this way, white politicians were dismissive and condescending.

8. *Ibid.*, p. 116. White Mississippians, in a last desperate effort to resist black equality and integration, devoted much time to terrorism and threats of violence. White racists and segregationists didn't want an inclusive state government. Nor did many want to come to terms with the reality regarding the brutal treatment of black people. Furthermore, instead of finding race-relation solutions, white politicians in Mississippi stalled, arguing that things like integration and inclusiveness should be done gradually.

9. Juan Williams, *Eyes on the Prize: America's Civil Rights Years, 1954–1965* (New York: Penguin, 1988), p. 244. White leaders were afraid of a large, uncontrolled black population, especially those who believed that blacks were entitled to freedom and equality.

10. Yasuhiro Katagiri, *The Mississippi State Sovereignty Commission: Civil Rights and States' Rights* (Jackson: University Press of Mississippi, 2001), p. xii. The pressure on whites and their control on politics would continue to grow with each passing day, especially with whites in the state still weilding all of the political power. In the early 1960s, whites swiftly and ruthlessly resisted the demands of blacks to share power.

11. *Ibid.*

12. *Ibid.*, p. xiv. Some white leaders even blamed outsiders for their state's racial woes. White politicians urged outsiders not to stick their noses in the politics of the state of Mississippi and stirring up their black folk. Communist accusations were injected into the debate.

13. *Ibid.*, p. xiii. Widely criticized for its segregationist stance, the Mississippi State Sovereignty Commission was known to spy on black activists, much like a totalitarian police state. The group shrugged off any social or political concerns blacks had in Mississippi; they did almost anything to keep blacks from gaining *any* political power.

14. Irving L. Janis, *Victims of Groupthink: A Psychological Study of Foreign-Policy Decision and Fiascoes* (Boston: Houghton Mifflin, 1972), p. 9.

15. Laura Baskes Litwin, *Fannie Lou Hamer: Fighting for the Right to Vote* (Berkeley Heights, NJ: Enslow, 2002), p. 61.
16. Rubel, *Fannie Lou Hamer: From Sharecropping to Politics*, p. 116.
17. Elton C. Fax. *Contemporary Black Leaders* (New York: Dodd, Mead, 1970), p. 128.
18. L.C. Dorsey, "Fannie Lou Hamer," *Jackson Advocate* (February/March 1981), Section C, p. 1.
19. Chana Kai Lee, *For Freedom's Sake: The Life of Fannie Lou Hamer* (Chicago: University of Illinois Press, 1999), p. 103.

Chapter 19

1. Quoted in Katie Kissinger, "Acting in and on the World," *Rethinking Schools*, Vol. 22, No. 2 (Winter 2007-08), p. 48.
2. Jack Minnis, "The Mississippi Freedom Democratic Party: A New Declaration of Independence," *Freedomways*, Vol. 5, Issue 2 (1965), p. 264.
3. Charles McLaurin, "Voice of Calm," Vol. 11, No. 11, *Sojourners* (December 1982), p. 13.
4. Penny Colman, *Fannie Lou Hamer and the Fight for the Vote* (Brookfield, CT: Millbrook, 1993), p. 21.
5. Susan Altman, *Extraordinary Black Americans: From Colonial to Contemporary Times* (Chicago: Children's Press, 1989), p. 194.
6. Colman, *Fannie Lou Hamer and the Fight for the Vote*, p. 21.
7. Billie Jean Young, *Fear Not the Fall, Poems, and Fannie Lou Hamer: This Little Light... A Two-Act Drama* (Montgomery, AL: New South, 2004), p. 134. It was not in Hamer's nature to harbor any ill will or resentment by hating white people. But the mood in the state of Mississippi at that time was one of ambivalent optimism for black people. Whites were extremely afraid of blacks, and the white privileged classes lashed out.
8. Laura Baskes Litwin, *Fannie Lou Hamer: Fighting for the Right to Vote* (Berkeley Heights, NJ: Enslow, 2002), p. 98.
9. Maya Angelou, *Letter to My Daughter* (New York: Random House, 2008), p. 85.
10. Elton C. Fax, *Contemporary Black Leaders* (New York: Dodd, Mead, 1970), p. 115.
11. *Ibid.*, p. 194. Whites seemed not to care about the racial issues unless they held some personal meaning for them. There wasn't any mutual respect per se, as many believed that blacks could not be taken seriously. Beyond the rhetoric, the central issue was whether blacks were equal to whites. This should have weighed heavily on the mind of some whites in Mississippi, but it did not. Many whites in the state were terribly afraid of change. Some were mentally shackled by prejudice. White Southerners also failed to realize that their abhorrence of black people was easy for them because they dominated. It all came down to a power struggle over who would be in control of Mississippi politics.

12. Joseph Crespino, *In Search of Another Country: Mississippi and the Conservative Counterrevolution* (Princeton, NJ: Princeton University Press, 2007), p. 11.
13. Tom Hayden, "The Politics of the Movement," *Dissent*, Vol. XIII, Issue 1 (January 1966), p. 75.
14. Edwin King, "Go Tell It on the Mountain: A Prophet from the Delta," *Sojourners*, Vol. 11, No. 11 (December 1982), p. 19.
15. *Ibid.*
16. *Ibid.*, p. 20.
17. L.C. Dorsey, "A Prophet Who Believed," *Sojourners*, Vol. 11, No. 11 (December 1982), p. 21.
18. Phyl Garland, "Negro Heroines of Dixie Play Major Role in Challenging Racist Traditions," *Ebony Magazine* (August 1966), p. 27.
19. George Alexander Sewell, *Mississippi Black History Makers* (Jackson: University of Mississippi Press, 1977), p. 353. It would have been easy for her to become frustrated with people, but this was not a characteristic of Fannie Lou Hamer. Perhaps her ability to connect with people was the most valuable thing she had to offer.
20. Litwin, *Fannie Lou Hamer: Fighting for the Right to Vote*, p. 81.
21. Susan Kling, *Fannie Lou Hamer: A Biography* (Chicago: Women for Racial and Economic Equality, 1979), p. 32.
22. Litwin, *Fannie Lou Hamer: Fighting for the Right to Vote*, p. 81.
23. Joyce A. Ladner, "Fannie Lou Hamer: In Memoriam," *Black Enterprise* (May 1977), p. 56.
24. *Ibid.*
25. Sandy Donovan, *Fannie Lou Hamer* (Chicago: Raintree, 2004), p. 54.
26. Ladner, "Fannie Lou Hmaer: In Memoriam," p. 56.
27. William E. Leuchtenburg, *A Troubled Feast: American Society Since 1945* (Boston: Little, Brown, 1973), p. 200.
28. A. John Adams and Joan Martin Burke, *Civil Rights: A Current Guide to the People, Organizations, and Events* (New York: R.R. Bowker, 1970), p. 49.
29. David Rubel, *Fannie Lou Hamer: From Sharecropping to Politics* (Englewood Cliffs, NJ: Silver Burdett, 1990), p. 117.
30. Adams and Burke, *Civil Rights*, p. 49.
31. William Simpson, "The Birth of the Mississippi Loyalist Democrats (1965–1968)," *The Journal of Mississippi History*, Vol. 44, No. 1 (February 1982), p. 44.
32. Litwin, *Fannie Lou Hamer: Fighting for the Right to Vote*, p. 87.
33. Simpson, *Birth of the Mississippi Loyalist Democrats*, p. 44.
34. Litwin, *Fannie Lou Hamer: Fighting for the Right to Vote*, p. 86.
35. Colman, *Fannie Lou Hamer and the Fight for the Vote*, p. 26.
36. John Egerton, *A Mind to Stay Here: Profiles from the South* (New York: Macmillan, 1970), p. 103.

Chapter 20

1. Grace Elizabeth Hale, *Making Whiteness: The Culture of Segregation in the South, 1890–1940* (New York: Vintage, 1998), p. 295.

2. Floyd W. Hayes III (ed.), *A Turbulent Voyage: Readings in African American Studies*, Third Edition (San Diego: Collegiate, 2000), p. 540.

3. *Ibid.*

4. *Ibid.*

5. Edwin King, "Go Tell It on the Mountain: A Prophet from the Delta," *Sojourners*, Vol. 11, No. 11 (December 1982), p. 20.

6. *Ibid.*

7. *Ibid.*

8. *Ibid.*

9. Laura Baskes Litwin, *Fannie Lou Hamer: Fighting for the Right to Vote* (Berkeley Heights, NJ: Enslow, 2002), p. 103.

10. Linda Reed, "Fannie Lou Hamer (1917–1977)," in Darlene Clark Hine, Elsa Barkley Brown and Rosalyn Terborg-Penn, (eds.), *Black Women in America: An Historical Encyclopedia* (Indianapolis: Indiana University Press, 1993), p. 519.

11. *Ibid.*

12. Jane Rhodes, "Black Radicalism in 1960s California: Women in the Black Panther Party," in Quintard Taylor and Shirley Ann Wilson Moore, *African American Women Confront the West, 1600–2000* (Norman: University of Oklahoma Press, 2003), p. 348.

13. Reed, "Fannie Lou Hamer (1917–1977)," p. 519.

14. Rhodes, "Black Radicalism in California," pp. 348–349.

15. Reed, "Fannie Lou Hamer (1917–1977)," p. 519.

16. George Sewell, "Fannie Lou Hamer," *The Black Collegian* (May/June 1978), p. 20.

17. Neil R. McMillen, "Black Enfranchisement in Mississippi: Federal Enforcement and Black Protest in the 1960s," *The Journal of Southern History*, Vol. 43, No. 3 (August 1977), p. 354.

18. *Ibid.*, p. 371. McMillen writes that the percent of blacks eligible to vote was probably an "overly optimistic estimate."

19. "Civil Rights Leader Fannie Hamer Dies," *McComb Enterprise Journal* (March 16, 1977), p. 13.

20. Hayes, *A Turbulent Voyage*, p. 540.

21. Pat Waters and Reese Cleghorn, *Climbing Jacob's Ladder: The Arrival of Negroes in Southern Politics* (New York: Harcourt, Brace, 1967), p. 285.

22. *Ibid.*

23. Joyce Ladner, "What 'Black Power' Means to Negroes in Mississippi," *Trans-action*, Vol. 5 (November 1967), p. 12.

24. *Ibid.*

25. *Ibid.*, p. 8. According to Ladner, "The black-power concept was ... successfully communicated to Mississippi Negroes because of the failure of integration."

26. *Ibid.*, p. 7.

27. June Jordan, *Fannie Lou Hamer* (New York: Thomas Y. Crowell, 1972), p. 30.

28. Ladner, "What 'Black Power' Means to Negroes in Mississippi," p. 14.

29. *Ibid.*

30. Aaron Henry with Constance Curry, *Aaron Henry: The Fire Ever Burning* (Jackson: University Press of Mississippi, 2000), p. 197.

31. Ladner, "What 'Black Power' Means to Negroes in Mississippi," p. 14.

Chapter 21

1. Koigi Wa Wamwere, *Negative Ethnicity: From Bias to Genocide* (New York: Seven Stories, 2003), p. 193.

2. Pat Watters and Reese Cleghorn, *Climbing Jacob's Ladder: The Arrival of Negroes in Southern Politics* (New York: Harcourt, Brace, 1967), p. 295.

3. Penny Colman, *Fannie Lou Hamer and the Fight for the Vote* (Brookfield, CT: Millbrook, 1993), p. 26.

4. Marjorie Vernell, *Leaders of Black Civil Rights* (San Diego: Lucent, 2000), p. 85.

5. Raymond Arsenault, *Freedom Riders: 1961 and the Struggle for Racial Justice* (New York: Oxford University Press, 2006), p. 278.

6. *Ibid.*

7. Walter Rugaber, "In the Delta, Poverty Is a Way of Life," *The New York Times* (July 31, 1967), p. 16, Column 3.

8. *Ibid.*

9. *Ibid.*

10. Floyd W. Hayes III, *A Turbulent Voyage* (San Diego: Collegiate, 2000), p. 537.

11. Colman, *Fannie Lou Hamer and the Fight for the Vote*, p. 28.

12. David Rubel, *Fannie Lou Hamer: From Sharecropping to Politics* (Englewood Cliffs, NJ: Silver Burdett, 1990), p. 119.

13. Laura Baskes Litwin, *Fannie Lou Hamer: Fighting for the Right to Vote* (Berkeley Heights, NJ: Enslow, 2002), p. 104. According to Mark Newman, the "SNCC's rapidly dwindling finances were a product not only of white opposition to Black Power but also of its white financial supporters focusing instead on opposing the Vietnam War." See Mark Newman. *The Civil Rights Movement* (Westport, CT: Praeger, 2004), p. 125.

14. Newman, *The Civil Rights Movement*, p. 125.

15. *Ibid.*, p. 119.

16. Molefi Kete Asante, *100 Greatest African Americans: A Biographical Encyclopedia* (New York: Prometheus, 2002), p. 149.

17. Peter B. Levy, *The Civil Rights Movement* (Westport, CT: Greenwood, 1998), p. 133.

18. Sandy Donovan, *Fannie Lou Hamer* (Chicago: Raintree, 2004), p. 54.

19. Sande Smith (ed.), *Who's Who in African-American History* (New York: Smithmark, 1994),

p. 67. Hamer also expected to produce her own milk from farm-raised cows on Freedom Farm. Members planted fruit trees and all kinds of vegetables. They also raised chickens and pigs for slaughter.

20. Linda Reed, "Fannie Lou Hamer (1917–1977)," in Darlene Clark Hine, Elsa Barkley Brown and Rosalyn Terborg-Penn (eds.), *Black Women in America: A Historical Encyclopedia* (Indianapolis: Indiana University Press, 1993), p. 519.

21. Hayes, *A Turbulent Voyage*, p. 540.

22. Smith, *Who's Who in African-American History*, p. 67.

23. Rubel, *Fannie Lou Hamer: From Sharecropping to Politics*, p. 120. According to Donovan, "The food grown on Freedom Farm helped feed 1,500 people." But that's a conservative estimate. Clearly there were more people helped by her Freedom Farm. See Sandy Donovan, *Fannie Lou Hamer* (Chicago: Raintree, 2004), p. 54.

24. Vernell, "Leaders of Black Civil Rights," p. 88. Fannie Lou Hamer wanted a sort of consecrated land where everyone would be useful and welcomed. In this way, she made a difference for a lot of black people living in the Mississippi Delta.

25. Elton C. Fax, *Contemporary Black Leaders* (New York: Dodd, Mead, 1970), p. 129.

26. Rubel, *Fannie Lou Hamer: From Sharecropping to Politics*, p. 120.

27. Litwin, *Fannie Lou Hamer: Fighting for the Right to Vote*, p. 104.

Chapter 22

1. Gayle Graham Yates, *Mississippi Mind: A Personal Cultural History of an American State* (Knoxville: University of Tennessee Press, 1990), p. 268.

2. June Jordan, *Fannie Lou Hamer* (New York: Thomas Y. Crowell, 1972), p. 35.

3. Molefi Kete Asante, *100 Greatest African Americans: A Biographical Encyclopedia* (New York: Prometheus, 2002), p. 149.

4. George Alexander Sewell, *Mississippi Black History Makers* (Jackson: University Press of Mississippi, 1977), p. 354.

5. *Ibid.* It should be remembered that Fannie Lou Hamer had not forgotten what it was like to be hungry and scared. Friends thought it would have been easier for Hamer to just step back and smell the roses. But she was never able to take such advice.

6. *Ibid.*

7. John Egerton, *A Mind to Stay Here: Profiles from the South* (New York: Macmillan, 1970), p. 105.

8. Chana Kai Lee, *For Freedom's Sake: The Life of Fannie Lou Hamer* (Chicago: University of Illinois Press, 1999), p. 161.

9. *Ibid.*, p. 159.

10. Jordan, *Fannie Lou Hamer*, p. 39.

11. L.C. Dorsey, "Fannie Lou Hamer," *Jackson*

Advocate (February 26/March 6, 1981), section C, p. 1.

12. Sanford Wexler, *The Civil Rights: An Eyewitness History* (New York: Facts on File, 1993), p. 197. See also: Aaron Henry, with Constance Curry, *Aaron Henry: The Fire Ever Burning* (Jackson: University Press of Mississippi, 2000).

13. *Ibid.* It should be noted that in 1962, Aaron Henry was also head of the NAACP in Mississippi.

14. Mary King, *Freedom Song: A Personal Story of the 1960s Civil Rights Movement* (New York: William Morrow, 1987), p. 526.

15. Dorsey, "Fannie Lou Hamer," section C, p. 1.

16. Sandy Donovan, *Fannie Lou Hamer* (Chicago: Raintree, 2004), pp. 55–56.

17. Bernice Johnson Reagon, "Women as Culture Carriers in the Civil Rights Movement: Fannie Lou Hamer," in Vicki L. Crawford, Jacqueline Anne Rouse, and Barbara Woods (eds.), *Women in the Civil Rights Movement: Trailblazers and Torchbearers, 1941–1965* (Indianapolis: Indiana University Press, 1993), p. 213.

18. Michael Weber, *Causes and Consequences of the African American Civil Rights Movement* (Austin, TX: Steck-Vaughn, 1998), p. 57.

19. *Ibid.*

20. Susan Kling, *Fannie Lou Hamer: A Biography* (Chicago: Women for Racial and Economic Equality, 1979), p. 35.

21. Florence Howe, "Mississippi's Freedom Schools: The Politics of Education," Vol. 35, Issue 2, *Harvard Educational Review* (Spring 1965), p. 159. See also "Mississippi Movement: Interview with Ella Jo Baker & Fannie Lou Hamer," *Southern Exposure*, Vol. 9, Issue 1 (September 1981), p. 42.

22. Eleanor Homes Norton, "The Woman Who Changed the South: A Memory of Fannie Lou Hamer," *Ms. Magazine*, Vol. 6 (July 1977), p. 98.

23. Howell Raines, *My Soul Is Rested: Movement Days in the Deep South Remembered* (New York: G.P. Putnam's Sons, 1977), p. 253.

24. Laura Baskes Litwin, *Fannie Lou Hamer: Fighting for the Right to Vote* (Berkeley Heights, NJ: Enslow, 2002), p. 104.

25. Raines, *My Soul Is Rested*, p. 254.

26. Lee, *For Freedom's Sake*, p. 176.

27. *Ibid.*

28. Mark Newman, *The Civil Rights Movement* (Westport, CT: Praeger, 2004), p. 145. Fannie Lou Hamer was dubious about whether blacks would attain economic equality even if they achieved political equality. She was also upset that many white racists had not received their comeuppance.

29. *Ibid.* Hamer openly admitted that sometimes she was not so optimistic about the future of blacks. Furthermore, Hamer never quite reconciled herself to the negative behavior of some whites, which she which she observed over a lifetime of confrontations.

30. L.C. Dorsey, "A Prophet Who Believed," *Sojourners*, Vol. II, No. 11 (December 1982), p. 21.

31. *Ibid.*

Conclusions

1. Maya Angelou, *Letter to My Daughter* (New York: Random House, 2008), p. 85.

2. Howell Raines, *My Soul Is Rested: Movement Days in the Deep South Remembered* (New York: G.P. Putnam's Sons, 1977), p. 255.

3. Margaret Burroughs and Eugene Feldman Book review of Susan Kling, *Fannie Lou Hamer: A Biography* (Evanston, IL: 1979), in *Freedomways*, Vol. 20, Issue 1 (1980), p. 51.

4. L.C. Dorsey, "Fannie Lou Hamer," *Jackson Advocate* (February 26/March 6, 1981), section C, p. 1.

5. Graig Robertson, "Civil Rights Activist: Fannie Lou Hamer Remembered," *Delta Democrat-Times* (March 16, 1977), p. 1.

6. Joyce A. Ladner, "Fannie Lou Hamer: In Memoriam," *Black Enterprise* (May 1977), p. 56.

7. "Mississippi Movement: Interview with Ella Jo Baker and Fannie Lou Hamer," *Southern Exposure*, Vol. 9, Issue 1, (September 1981), p. 47.

8. Jack Bass and Walter deVries, *The Transformation of Southern Politics: Social Change and Political Consequence Since 1945* (New York: Basic, 1976), p. 206.

9. National Women's Hall of Fame — Women of the Hall. http://www.greatwomen.org/women.php?action=viewone&id=72 (4/23/2008), p. 1.

10. *Ibid.*

11. Susan Johnson, "Fannie Lou Hamer: Mississippi Grassroots Organizer," *The Black Law Journal*, Vol. 2 (Summer 1972), p. 161.

12. *Ibid.*

13. Rachel Davis DuBois and Mew-Soong Li, *Reducing Social Tension and Conflict: Through the Group Conversation Method* (New York: Association Press, 1971), p. 143.

14. Melba J. Duncan, *African American History* (Indianapolis: Alpha, 2003), pp. 187–188.

15. Johnson, "Fannie Lou Hamer: Mississippi Grassroots Organizer," pp. 160–161.

16. Joanne Grant, "Way of Life in Mississippi," *National Guardian*, Vol. 16, No. 19 (February 13, 1964), p. 12.

17. *Ibid.*

18. Sandy Donovan, *Fannie Lou Hamer* (Chicago: Raintree, 2004), p. 57.

19. *Ibid.*

20. Chana Kai Lee, *For Freedom's Sake: The Life of Fannie Lou Hamer* (Chicago: University of Illinois Press, 1999), p. 175.

21. *Ibid.*

22. Sharon Bramlett-Solomon, "Civil Rights Vanguard in the Deep South: Newspaper Portrayal of Fannie Lou Hamer, 1964–1977," *Journalism Quarterly* (Fall 1991), p. 515.

23. *Ibid.*

24. E.C. Foster, "A Time of Challenge: Afro-Mississippi Political Developments Since 1965," *The Journal of Negro History*, Vol. 68, No. 2 (Spring 1983), p. 186.

25. *Ibid.*

26. Kay Mills, *This Little Light of Mine: The Life of Fannie Lou Hamer* (New York: Dutton, 1993), p. 310.

27. George Sewell, "Fannie Lou Hamer," *The Black Collegian* (May/June 1978), p. 20.

28. Ladner, "Fannie Lou Hamer," p. 56.

29. Charles M. Payne, *I've Got the Light of Freedom: The Organizing Tradition and the Mississippi Freedom Struggle* (Berkeley and Los Angeles: University of California Press, 1995), p. 408.

Epilogue

1. Patricia Hill Collins, "The Social Construction of Black Feminist Thought," *Signs*, Vol. 14, Issue 4 (Summer 1989), p. 745.

2. Paul Rogat Loeb, "Ordinary People Produce Extraordinary Results," *Los Angeles Times* (January 14, 2000), page unknown.

3. Charles M. Payne, *I've Got the Light of Freedom: The Organizing Tradition and the Mississippi Freedom Struggle* (Berkeley and Los Angeles: University of California Press, 2007), p. 425.

4. L.C. Dorsey, "Fannie Lou Hamer," *Jackson Advocate* (February 26/March 6, 1981), section C, p. 1.

5. Sandy Donovan, *Fannie Lou Hamer* (Chicago: Raintree, 2004), p. 57.

6. "Fannie Lou Hamer Flame Keepers," http://www.fannielouhamer.info/flamekeepers.html (11/2/2009), p. 1.

7. "Fannie Lou Hamer Statue Drive," http://www.fannielouhamer.info/hamerstatue.html (11/2/2009), p. 1.

8. Michelle D. Deardorff, R.M. Mvusi, Leslie Burl McLemore and Jeffrey Kolnick, "The Fannie Lou Hamer National Institute on Citizenship and Democracy: Engaging Curriculum and Pedagogy," *The History Teacher*, Vol. 38, No. 4 (August 2005), pp. 441–442. It should be noted that Dr. Leslie Burl McLemore is the current director of the Fannie Lou Hamer Institute.

9. Michelle D. Deardorff and Leslie Burl McLemore, *The Fannie Lou Hamer National Institute on Citizenship and Democracy, 2005-2006*, Annual Report (April 17, 2006), p. 3.

10. *Fannie Lou Hamer National Institute on Citizenship and Democracy: The Hamer Institute* brochure (Jackson, MS: Jackson State University), p. 2.

11. "Fannie Lou Hamer Flame Keepers," p. 3.

12. *A Long Road to Freedom (a play): Fannie Lou Hamer* (Scholastic.com). http://www2.scholastic.com/browse/article.jsp?idz.4788 & print=1 (11/2/2009), p. 5.

13. *Ibid.*

Bibliography

Adam, Heribert, and Kogila Moodley. *The Opening of the Apartheid Mind: Options for the New South Africa.* Berkeley: University of California Press, 1981.

Adams, A. John, and Joan Martin Burke. *Civil Rights: A Current Guide to the People, Organizations, and Events.* New York: R. R. Bowker, 1970.

Altman, Susan. *Extraordinary Black Americans: From Colonial to Contemporary Times.* Chicago: Children's Press, 1989.

Angelou, Maya. *Letter to My Daughter.* New York: Random House, 2008.

Arsenault, Raymond. *Freedom Riders: 1961 and the Struggle for Racial Justice.* New York: Oxford University Press, 2006.

Asante, Molefi Kete. "Fannie Lou Hamer, 1917–1977." *100 Greatest African Americans: A Biographical Encyclopedia.* New York: Prometheus Books, 2002.

Asch, Chris Myers. *The Senator and the Sharecropper: The Freedom Struggles of James O. Eastland and Fannie Lou Hamer.* New York: The New Press, 2008.

Asim, Jabari. *The N Word: Who Can Say It, Who Shouldn't, and Why.* New York: Houghton Mifflin, 2007.

Bass, Jack, and Walter DeVries. *The Transformation of Southern Politics: Social Change and Political Consequence Since 1945.* New York: Basic Books, 1976.

Belfrage, Sally. *Freedom Summer.* New York: Viking Press, 1965.

Bracey, Earnest N. "The Racist American Eugenics Program: A Crime Against Humanity," *Forum on Public Policy: A Journal of the Oxford Round Table.* On-line edition, 2007.

Bramlett-Solomon, Sharon. "Civil Rights Vanguard in the Deep South: Newspaper Portrayal of Fannie Lou Hamer, 1964–1977." *Journalism Quarterly*, Fall 1991.

Branch, Taylor. *Parting the Waters: America in the King Years, 1954–63.* New York: A Touchstone Book, 1988.

_____. *Pillar of Fire: America in the King Years, 1963–64.* New York: Simon & Schuster, 1998.

Burroughs, Margaret, and Eugene Feldman. Book review of Susan Kling, *Fannie Lou Hamer: A Biography.* Evanston, IL, 1979. In *Freedomways*, Vol. 20, Issue 1, 1980.

Carson, Clayborne. *In Struggle: SNCC and the Black Awakening of the 1960s.* Cambridge, MA: Harvard University Press, 1981.

Carter, Hodding. "Citadel of the Citizens Council." *The New York Times.* November 12, 1961.

_____. "A Wave of Terror Threatens the South." *Look Magazine*, March 22, 1955.

Cash, W. J. *The Mind of the South.* New York: Vintage Books, 1960.

Chalmers, David. *Backfire: How the Ku Klux Klan Helped the Civil Rights Movement.* Lanham, MD: Rowman & Littlefield, 2003.

Chappell, David L. *A Stone of Hope: Prophetic Religion and the Death of Jim Crow.* Chapel Hill: University of North Carolina Press, 2004.

"Civil Rights Leader Fannie Hamer Dies." *McComb Enterprise Journal*, March 16, 1977.

Coetzee, J. M. *Dusklands.* New York: Penguin Books, 1982.

Collins, Patricia Hill. "The Social Construction of Black Feminist Thought." *Signs*, Vol. 14, Issue 4, Summer 1989.

Colman, Penny. *Fannie Lou Hamer and the Fight for the Vote*. Brookfield, CT: Millbrook Press, 1993.

Crespino, Joseph. *In Search of Another Country: Mississippi and the Conservative Counterrevolution*. Princeton, NJ: Princeton University Press, 2007.

Dahl, Robert A. *On Political Equality*. New Haven: Yale University Press, 2006.

Davis, Foster. "Darkness on the Delta." *The Reporter*, September 21, 1967.

Deardorff, Michelle D., and Leslie Burl McLemore. *The Fannie Lou Hamer National Institute on Citizenship and Democracy, 2005-2006*. Annual Report April 17, 2006.

Deardorff, Michelle, D. Thandekile, R. M. Mvusi, Leslie Burl McLemore, and Jeffrey Kolnick. "The Fannie Lou Hamer National Institute on Citizenship and Democracy: Engaging Curriculum and Pedagogy." *The History Teacher*, Vol. 38, No. 4, August 2005.

Dellums, Ronald V. *Lying Down with the Lions: A Public Life from the Streets of Oakland to the Halls of Power*. Boston: Beacon Press, 2000.

DeMuth, Jerry. "Summer in Mississippi: Freedom Moves in to Stay." *The Nation*, September 14, 1942.

_____. "Tired of Being Sick and Tired." *The Nation*, June 1, 1964.

DeRoche, Andrew J. *Andrew Young: Civil Rights Ambassador*. Wilmington, DE: Scholarly Resources, 2003.

Dittmer, John. "The Politics of the Mississippi Movement, 1954–1964." In Charles W. Eagles (ed.), *The Civil Rights Movement in America*. Jackson: University Press of Mississippi, 1986.

_____. *Local People: The Struggle for Civil Rights in Mississippi*. Chicago: University of Illinois Press, 1994.

Donovan, Sandy. *Fannie Lou Hamer*. Chicago: Raintree, 2004.

Dorsey, L. C. "Fannie Lou Hamer." *Jackson Advocate*, February 26/March 6, 1981.

_____. "A Prophet Who Believed." *Sojourners*, Vol. 11, No. 11, December 1982.

DuBois, Rachel Davis, and Mew-Soong Li. *Reducing Social Tension and Conflict: Through the Group Conversation Method*. New York: Association Press, 1971.

Duncan, Melba J. *African American History*. Indianapolis: Alpha Books, 2003.

Egerton, John. *A Mind to Stay Here: Profiles from the South*. New York: Macmillan, 1970.

Elias, Marilyn. "Racism Hurts Kids' Mental Health." *USA Today*, May 6, 2009.

Erikson, Erik H. *Gandhi's Truth: On the Origins of Militant Nonviolence*. New York: Norton, 1969.

Evans, Sara. *Personal Politics: The Roots of Women's Liberation in the Civil Rights Movement and the New Left*. New York: Vintage Books, 1979.

Fannie Lou Hamer Flame Keepers. http://www.fannielouhamer.info/flamekeepers.html 11/2/2009.

Fannie Lou Hamer National Institute on Citizenship and Democracy. *The Hamer Institute*. Brochure. Jackson State University, Jackson, MS.

Fannie Lou Hamer Statue Drive. http://www.fannielouhamer.info/hamerstatue.html 11/2/2009.

Fax, Elton C. *Contemporary Black Leaders*. New York: Dodd, Mead, 1970.

Foster, E. C. "A Time of Challenge: Afro-Mississippi Political Developments Since 1965." *The Journal of Negro History*, Vol. 68, No. 2, Spring 1983.

Freire, Paulo. *Pedagogy of the Oppressed*. New York: Continuum, 2002.

Fruchter, Norm. "Mississippi: Notes on SNCC." *Studies on the Left*, Winter 1965.

Garland, Phyl. "Builders of a New South: Negro Heroines of Dixie Play Major Role in Challenging Racist Traditions." *Ebony Magazine*, August 1966.

Garrow, David J. *Bearing the Cross: Martin Luther King, Jr., and the Southern Christian Leadership Conference*. New York: Harper Collins, 1986.

Grant, Joanne. *Ella Baker: Freedom Bound*. New York: John Wiley, 1998.

_____ "Mississippi and the Establishment." *Freedomways*, Vol. 5, Issue 2, second quarter 1965.

_____. "Way of Life in Mississippi." No. 19, Vol. 16, *National Guardian* February 13, 1964.

Grim, Valerie. "The Impact of Mechanized Farming on Black Farm Families in the

Rural South: A Study of Farm Life in the Brooks Farm Community, 1940–1970." *Agricultural History,* Vol. 68, No. 2, Spring 1994.

Grossman, James R. "Black Labor Is the Best Labor: Southern White Reactions to the Great Migration." In Alferdteen Harrison (ed.), *Black Exodus: The Great Migration from the American South.* Jackson: University Press of Mississippi, 1991.

Guyot, Lawrence, and Mike Thelwell. "The Politics of Necessity and Survival in Mississippi." *Freedomways,* Vol. 6, Issue 2, 1966.

_____. "Toward Independent Political Power." *Freedomways,* Vol. 6, Issue 3, 1966.

Hale, Grace Elizabeth. *Making Whiteness: The Culture of Segregation in the South, 1890–1940.* New York: Vintage Books, 1998.

Hallowell, John H. *The Moral Foundation of Democracy.* Indianapolis: Amagi/Liberty Fund, 2007.

Hamer, Fannie Lou. "Foreword." In Tracy Sugarman, *Stranger at the Gates: A Summer in Mississippi.* New York: Hill and Wang, 1966.

Hamer, Fannie Lou. "To Praise Our Bridge." Reprinted in Manning Marable, et al. (eds.), *Freedom on My Mind: The Columbia Documentary History of the African American Experience.* New York: Columbia University Press, 2003.

Hampton, Henry, and Steve Fayer. *Voices of Freedom: An Oral History of the Civil Rights Movement from the 1950s Through the 1980s.* New York: Bantam Books, 1991.

Harris, William H., and Judith S. Levers (eds.), "Civil Rights." *The New Columbia Encyclopedia.* New York: Columbia University Press, 1975.

Hayden, Tom. "The Politics of the Movement." *Dissent,* Vol. XIII, Issue 1, January 1966.

Hayes, Floyd W., III (ed.). *A Turbulent Voyage: Readings in African American Studies,* 3rd ed. San Diego: Collegiate Press, 2000.

Henry, Aaron, with Constance Curry. *Aaron Henry: The Fire Ever Burning.* Jackson: University Press of Mississippi, 2000.

Herbers, John. "Communiqué from the Mississippi Front." *New York Times,* November 8, 1964.

Herron, Jeannine. "Mississippi Underground Election." *The Nation,* December 7, 1963.

Hine, Darlene Clark, and Kathleen Thompson. *A Shining Thread of Hope: The History of Black Women in America.* New York: Broadway Books, 1998.

Howe, Florence. "Mississippi's Freedom Schools: The Politics of Education." Vol. 35, Issue 2, *Harvard Educational Review,* Spring 1965.

Hudson, David L. Jr. "Banning the Noose." *SPLC Intelligence Report,* Winter 2008.

Jackson, Kennell. *America Is Me: 170 Fresh Questions and Answers on Black American History.* New York: Harper Collins, 1996.

Jackson, Thomas C. Quoted in "William Zantzinger 69, subject of Bob Dylan Protest Song, Dies." *Las Vegas Review-Journal,* January 1, 2009.

Jadhav, Narendra. *Untouchables: My Family's Triumphant Journey Out of the Caste System in Modern India.* New York: Scribner, 2003.

Janis, Irving L. *Victims of Groupthink: A Psychological Study of Foreign-Policy Decision and Fiascoes.* Boston: Houghton Mifflin, 1972.

Jaspin, Elliot. *Buried in the Bitter Waters: The Hidden History of Racial Cleansing in America.* New York: Basic Books, 2007.

Johnson, Susan. "Fannie Lou Hamer: Mississippi Grassroots Organizer." *The Black Law Journal,* Vol. 2, Summer 1972.

Jones, Edward P. *The Known World.* New York: Harper Collins, 2003.

Jordan, June. *Fannie Lou Hamer.* New York: Thomas Y. Crowell, 1972.

Katagiri, Yasuhiro. *The Mississippi State Sovereignty Commission: Civil Rights and States' Rights.* Jackson: University Press of Mississippi, 2001.

Key, V. O., Jr. *Southern Politics in State and Nation.* Knoxville: University of Tennessee Press, 1984.

Killens, John Oliver. *'Sippi.* New York: Thunder's Mouth Press, 1967.

King, Edwin. "Go Tell It on the Mountain: A Prophet from the Delta." *Sojourners,* December 1982.

King, Mary. *Freedom Song: A Personal Story of the 1960s Civil Rights Movement.* New York: William Morrow, 1987.

Kirchhoff, Sue. "Surplus U.S. Food Supplies Dry Up." *USA Today,* May 2, 2008.

Kissinger, Katie. "Acting in and on the World." *Rethinking Schools,* Vol. 22, No. 2, Winter 2007-08.

Klarman, Michael J. *Unfinished Business: Racial Equality in American History.* New York: Oxford University Press, 2007.

Kling, Susan. *Fannie Lou Hamer: A Biography.* Chicago: Women for Racial and Economic Equality, 1979.

Kotz, Nick. *Judgment Days: Lyndon Baines Johnson, Martin Luther King, Jr., and the Laws That Changed America.* New York: Houghton Mifflin, 2005.

Krugman, Paul. "How Racial Polarization Venefited Reagan, GOP." *Las Vegas Sun,* November 20, 2007.

Ladner, Joyce. "Fannie Lou Hamer: In Memoriam." *Black Enterprise,* May 1977.

_____. "What 'Black Power' Means to Negroes in Mississippi." *Trans-Action,* Vol. 5, November 1967.

Lambert, Frank. *The Battle of Ole Miss: Civil Rights v. States' Rights.* New York: Oxford University Press, 2010.

Lee, Chana Kai. *For Freedom's Sake: The Life of Fannie Lou Hamer.* Chicago: University of Illinois Press, 1999.

Leuchtenburg, William E. *A Troubled Feast: American Society Since 1945.* Boston: Little, Brown, 1973.

Levy, Peter B. *The Civil Rights Movement.* Westport, CT: Greenwood Press, 1998.

Lewis, John, with Michael D'Orso. *Walk with the Wind: A Memoir of the Movement.* New York: Simon & Schuster, 1998.

Litwin, Laura Baskes. *Fannie Lou Hamer: Fighting for the Right to Vote.* Berkeley Heights, NJ: Enslow, 2002.

Locke, Mamie E. "Is This America? Fannie Lou Hamer and the Mississippi Freedom Democratic Party." In Vicki L. Crawford, Jacqueline Anne Roose, and Barbara Woods (eds.), *Women in the Civil Rights Movement: Trailblazers & Torchbearers, 1941–1965.* Indianapolis: Indiana University Press, 1993.

Loeb, Paul Rogat. "Ordinary People Produce Extraordinary Results." *Los Angeles Times,* January 14, 2000.

Lomax, Louis E. *The Negro Revolt.* New York: Harper & Brothers, 1962.

A Long Road to Freedom (a Play): Fannie Lou Hamer (Scholastic.com). http://www2.scholastic.com/browse/article.jsp? idz.4788 & print=1 11/2/2009.

Luce, Phillip Abbott. "The Mississippi White Citizens Council: 1954–1959." Master's thesis. Ohio State University, 1960.

Mathabane, Mark. *Kaffir Boy: The True Story of a Black Youth's Coming of Age in Apartheid South Africa.* New York: A Plume Book, 1986.

McLaurin, Charles. "Voice of Calm." *Sojourners,* Vol. 11, No. 11, December 1982.

McLemore, Leslie Burl. "The Mississippi Freedom Democratic Party: A Case Study of Grassroots Politics." Ph.D. Dissertation, University of Massachusetts, Amherst, 1971.

McMillan, Neil R. "Black Enfranchisement in Mississippi: Federal Enforcement and Black Protest in the 1960s." *The Journal of Southern History,* Vol. 43, No. 3, August 1977.

_____. *The Citizens' Council: Organized Resistance to the Second Reconstruction, 1954–1964.* Chicago: University of Illinois Press, 1971.

Mead, Margaret. "Some Theoretical Considerations on the Problem of Mother-Child Separation." *American Journal of Orthopsychiatry,* Vol. 24, Issue 3, 1954.

Mills, Kay. *This Little Light of Mine: The Life of Fannie Lou Hamer.* New York: A Dutton Book, 1993.

Minnis, Jack. "The Mississippi Freedom Democratic Party: A New Declaration of Independence." *Freedomways,* Vol. 5, Issue 3, 1965.

Minor, Bill. "Hamer at '64 Dem Convention Fueled Miss. Party's Defection." *The Clarion-Ledger,* February 26, 2006.

"Mississippi Movement: Interview with Ella Jo Baker & Fannie Lou Hamer." *Southern Exposure,* Vol. 9, Issue 1 September 1981.

Moody, Anne. *Coming of Age in Mississippi.* New York: Dell, 1968.

National Women's Hall of Fame — Women of the Hall. http://www.great women.org/

women.php?action=viewone&id=72 4/23/2008.

Newman, Mark. *The Civil Rights Movement.* Westport, CT: Praeger, 2004.

Newman, Richard, and Marcia Sawyer. *Everybody Say Freedom: Everything You Need to Know About African-American History.* New York: A Plume Book, 1996.

Norton, Eleanor Homes. "The Woman Who Changed the South: A Memory of Fannie Lou Hamer." *Ms. Magazine,* Vol. 6, July 1977.

O'Dell, Jack. H. "Life in Mississippi: An Interview with Fannie Lou Hamer." *Freedomways,* 2nd quarter, Spring 1965.

O'Reilly, Kenneth. *Racial Matters: The FBI's Secret File on Black America, 1960–1972.* New York: Free Press, 1989.

Orleck, Annelise. *Storming Caesars Palace: How Black Mothers Fought Their Own War on Poverty.* Boston: Beacon Press, 2007.

Payne, Charles M. *I've Got the Light of Freedom: The Organizing Tradition and the Mississippi Freedom Struggle.* Berkeley: University of California Press, 2007.

Percy, Walker. "Mississippi: The Fallen Paradise." *Harper's Magazine,* April 1965.

Piven, Frances Fox, Lorraine C. Minnite, and Margaret Groarke. *Keeping Down the Black Vote: Race and the Demobilization of American Voters.* New York: New Press, 2009.

Poulson-Bryant, Scott. *Hung: A Meditation on the Measure of Black Men in America.* New York: Doubleday, 2005.

Raines, Howell. *My Soul Is Rested: Movement Days in the Deep South Remembered.* New York: G. P. Putnam's Sons, 1977.

Reagon, Bernice Johnson. "Women as Culture Carriers in the Civil Rights Movement: Fannie Lou Hamer." In Vicki L. Crawford, Jacqueline Anne Rouse, and Barbara Woods (eds.), *Women in the Civil Rights Movement: Trailblazers and Torchbearers, 1941–1965.* Indianapolis: Indiana University Press, 1993.

Reed, Linda. "Hamer, Fannie Lou." In Darlene Clark Hine, Elsa Barkley Brown, and Rosalyn Terborg-Penn, *Black Women in America: A Historical Encyclopedia.* Indianapolis: Indiana University Press, 1993.

Rhodes, Jane. "Black Radicalism in 1960s California: Women in the Black Panther Party." In Quintard Taylor and Shirley Ann Wilson Moore, *African American Women Confront the West, 1600–2000.* Norman: University of Oklahoma Press, 2003.

Richards, Dona. "With Our Minds Set on Freedom." *Freedomways,* Vol. 5, Issue 2, 1965.

Roberts, Gene. "The Story of Snick: From 'Freedom High' to Black Power." *New York Times,* September 25, 1966.

Robertson, Craig. "Civil Rights Activist: Fannie Lou Hamer Remembered." *Delta Democrat-Times,* March 16, 1977.

Rogers, Kim Lacy. *Life and Death in the Delta: African American Narratives of Violence, Resilience, and Social Change.* New York: Palgrave Macmillan, 2006.

Rogers, Mary Beth, and Barbara Jordan. *American Hero.* New York: Bantam Books, 2000.

Rosengarten, Theodore. *All God's Dangers: The Life of Nate Shaw.* New York: Vintage, 1989.

Rotch, William. "Cotton, Cordiality and Conflict." *New South,* Vol. 12, March 1957.

Rubel, David. *Fannie Lou Hamer: From Sharecropping to Politics.* Englewood Cliffs, NJ: Silver Burdett Press, 1990.

Rugaber, Walter. "In the Delta, Poverty Is a Way of Life." *The New York Times,* July 31, 1967.

Ruiz, Vicki L., with Ellen Carol DuBois (eds.). *Unequal Sisters: An Inclusive Reader in U.S. Women's History,* 4th ed. New York: Routledge, 2008.

Sewell, George. "Fannie Lou Hamer." *The Black Collegian* May/June 1978.

_____. *Mississippi Black History Makers.* Jackson: University Press of Mississippi, 1977.

_____. "Remembrance of Things Past: Fannie Lou Hamer's Light Still Shines." *Encore American & Worldwide News,* July 18, 1977.

"Sharecropper's Daughter Has Seen Horizons Widen." *Clarion-Ledger,* September 12, 1980.

Sharpe, Rochelle. "More Money, More Kids." *USA Weekend,* April 4–6, 2008.

Silver, James W. *Mississippi: The Closed Society*. New York: Harcourt, Brace & World, 1966.

Simpson, William. "The Birth of the Mississippi Loyalist Democrats (1965–1968)." *The Journal of Mississippi History*, Vol. 44, No. 1, February 1982.

Sinsheimer, Joseph A. "The Freedom Vote of 1963: New Strategies of Racial Protest in Mississippi." *The Journal of Southern History*, Vol. LV, No. 2, May 1989.

Smith, Jessie Carney, and Linda T. Wynn (eds.). *Freedom Facts and Firsts: 400 Years of the African American Civil Rights Experience*. Canton, MI: Visible Ink Press, 2009.

Smith, Sande. *Who's Who in African-American History*. New York: Smithmark, 1994.

Stewart, James B., and Joyce E. Allen-Smith. *Blacks in Rural America*. New Brunswick, NJ: Transaction, 1995.

Stoper, Emily. "The Student Nonviolent Coordinating Committee: Rise and Fall of a Redemptive Organization." *Journal of Black Studies*, Vol. 8, No. 1, September 1977.

Surace, Samuel J., and Melvin Seeman. "Some Correlates of Civil Rights Activism." *Social Forces*, Vol. 46, No. 2, December 1967.

Taylor, Quintard. *From Timbuktu to Katrina: Readings in African-American History*, Volume II. Boston: Thomson Wadsworth, 2008.

Thompson, Julius E. *Lynchings in Mississippi: A History, 1865–1965*. Jefferson, NC: McFarland, 2007.

Tuttle, Kate. "Lynching." African.com.wysiwyg://28/http://www.africana.com//tt_374.htm 3/29/01.

Vernell, Marjorie. *Leaders of Black Civil Rights*. San Diego: Lucent Books, 2000.

Walker, Alice. Review of June Jordan, *Fannie Lou Hamer* (New York: Thomas Y. Crowell, 1972), in *The New York Times*, April 29, 1973.

Wamwere, Koigi Wa. *Negative Ethnicity: From Bias to Genocide*. New York: Seven Stories Press, 2003.

Washington, Harriet A. *Medical Apartheid: The Dark History of Medical Experimentation on Black Americans from Colonial Times to the Present*. New York: Doubleday, 2006.

Waters, Pat, and Reese Ceghorn. *Climbing Jacob's Ladder: The Arrival of Negroes in Southern Politics*. New York: Harcourt, Brace & World, 1967.

Weber, Michael. *Causes and Consequences of the African American Civil Rights Movement*. Austin, TX: Steck-Vaughn, 1998.

Wexler, Sanford. *The Civil Rights Movement: An Eyewitness History*. New York: Facts on File, 1993.

Whitehead, Don. *Attack on Terror: The FBI Against the Ku Klux Klan in Mississippi*. New York: Funk and Wagnalls, 1970.

Whitfield, Stephen J. *A Death in the Delta: The Story of Emmett Till*. Baltimore: Johns Hopkins University Press, 1992.

Wickham, DeWayne. "Helms Subtly Carried Torch of White Supremacy." *USA Today*, July 8, 2008.

Wickham, DeWayne. "Historic Freedom Riders Deserve a Degree of Respect." *USA Today*, April 15, 2008.

Wilkins, Roger. "Preface." In Eric Etheridge, *Breach of Peace: Portraits of the 1969 Mississippi Freedom Riders*. New York: Atlas, 2008.

Williams, Juan. *Eyes on the Prize: America's Civil Rights Years, 1954–1965*. New York: Penguin Books, 1987.

Williams, Robert F. "Can Negroes Afford to Be Pacifists?" *New Left Review*, Vol. 1, January 1960.

Woloch, Nancy. *Women and the American Experience: A Concise History*. New York: McGraw-Hill, 1996.

Woodward, C. Vann. *The Strange Career of Jim Crow*, 3rd rev. ed. New York: Oxford University Press, 1974.

Wright, Marian A. "The Right to Protest." *New South*. Volume 17, Issue 2, February 1962.

Wright, Richard. *Black Boy: A Record of Childhood and Youth*. New York: Harper Perennial, 1993.

_____. "The Ethics of Living Jim Crow," in *Uncle Tom's Children*. New York: Harper & Row, 1940.

Yafa, Stephen. *Big Cotton: How a Humble Fiber Created Fortunes, Wrecked Civiliza-*

tion, *and Put America on the Map.* New York: Viking, 2005.

Yates, Gayle Graham. *Mississippi Mind: A Personal Cultural History of an American State.* Knoxville: University of Tennessee Press, 1990.

Young, Andrew. *An Easy Burden.* New York: Harper Collins, 1996.

Young, Billie Jean. *Fear Not the Fall, Poems, and Fannie Lou Hamer: This Little Light … A Two-Act Drama.* Montgomery, AL: New South Books, 2004.

Young, Whitney M., Jr. "A Vanishing Era." *Harper's Magazine* April 1965.

Zewan, Todd. "Times Changing for Multi-Cultural Families." *Las Vegas Review-Journal,* June 15, 2008.

Index